Patristic Essentials

Christianity in the First and Second Centuries, Kevin D. Hill, ed.
Irenaeus, Ched Spellman, ed.

IRENAEUS

Irenaeus

Essential Readings

Edited and Introduced by
Ched Spellman

Fontes

Irenaeus: Essential Readings

Copyright © 2023 by Ched Spellman

ISBN-13: 978-1-948048-93-4 (paperback)
ISBN-13: 978-1-948048-94-1 (epub)

All rights reserved. No part of this publication may be reproduced, stored in a retrieval system, or transmitted in any form or by any means—electronic, mechanical, photocopy, recording, or any other—except for brief quotations in printed reviews, without the prior permission of the publisher.

Typeset by Monolateral in Brill and Modesto Text

FONTES PRESS
DALLAS, TX
www.fontespress.com

Contents

SERIES PREFACE xiii

1. AN ORIENTATION TO IRENAEUS OF LYONS............................1
   Biography: Who Was Irenaeus of Lyons?..........................1
   Bibliography: What Did Irenaeus Write?......................... 4
   Theology: What Did Irenaeus Believe?........................... 7
      God as Creator and Revealer................................. 7
      Christ and the Divine Economy............................... 8
      Humanity and the End of All Things 10
   Reception: Who Cares about Irenaeus?..........................12
      For the Study of Early Christianity 12
      For Biblical and Theological Studies........................14
      For Ministry among the Churches.............................17
   Plan for This Volume: How Should You Read Irenaeus?...........17

2. REFUTING FALSEHOOD WITH THE RULE OF FAITH:
   BOOKS 1–2 OF *AGAINST HERESIES* 19
   Overview..19
   Summary and Selected Quotations...............................19
      Challenge: The Danger and Diversity of False Teaching......19
         They Used the Same Words but with Different Meanings....20
         They Told a Different Story about How the World Began .. 22
         Their System Separated God from Humanity and
            the Material World................................... 25
         Their Saving Knowledge Was Secret and Selective 26
         Their Teachers Were Deceptive and Destructive........... 27
      Response: The Safety and Stability of the Rule of Faith... 28
         The Order and Connection of the Scriptures is Discernible
            and Able to Guide Readers 28
         The Rule of Faith Secures the Unity of the Testaments and
            the Unity of the Churches 33
         The Coherence of the Rule of Faith Exposes the Incoherence
            of False Teaching 36
      Detail and Development in the Flow of Books 1–2 38

3. PREACHING THE GOSPEL WITH THE RULE OF FAITH:
   DEMONSTRATION OF THE APOSTOLIC PREACHING 45
   Overview.. 45
   Part One: The Storyline of Scripture and the Preaching of the Apostles ... 45
   Part Two: The Gospel according to the Scriptures............. 62

4. **THE GOSPEL ACCORDING TO THE SCRIPTURES:**
   SELECTIONS FROM BOOK 3 OF *AGAINST HERESIES* 85
   - Overview 85
   - The Purpose of Book 3 85
   - The Soundness of the Apostolic Preaching and the Apostolic Writings ... 86
   - The Connection of the Churches to the Apostolic Preaching 87
   - The Truth of the Apostolic Preaching about God's Being 91
   - The Truth of the Apostolic Preaching about God the Son 93
   - The Gospels Proclaim the Same God Revealed by the Prophets 96
   - The Shape and Theological Function of the Fourfold Gospel 106
   - The Unified Preaching of the Apostles among the Early Churches 109
   - The God of the Jews is the God of the Gentiles 110
   - Paul Preaches the Same Message as the Apostles 112
   - What Was Lost in Adam is Gained in Christ 114
   - The Reality of the Son's Incarnation 116
   - The Weakness of False Teaching and the Gift of Sound Doctrine 118
   - The Sovereign God is Both Good and Just 119
   - Praying with Hope for the Heretic 120

5. **THE TESTIMONY OF CHRIST AND HIS APOSTLES:**
   SELECTIONS FROM BOOKS 4–5 OF *AGAINST HERESIES* 123
   - Overview 123
   - The Purpose of Book 4 123
   - There Is No Other God than the One Proclaimed by the Scriptures 125
   - God is Above All and Will Endure Forever 128
   - The Old Covenant and Its Institution Are Fulfilled in the
     New Covenant 129
   - The God Who Promises Is the Same as the God Who Fulfills 130
   - The One Creator is the God and Father of Jesus Christ 132
   - The Unknown God Is Revealed in and by the Son 134
   - The Revelation of the Son is From the Beginning 136
   - The Same God Establishes Both the Old and New Covenants 137
   - Christ's Advent Foretold by Moses 140
   - Humans Are Granted Knowledge of God by God Alone 141
   - The Author of the Law and the Gospel Is the Same 143
   - The One God Is above All Created Things 146
   - God Was Never Without His Word and His Wisdom 148
   - The Incomprehensible God Is Made Known through
     Christ's Incarnation 152
   - Christ Is the Treasure of the Scriptures 154
   - Both Testaments Are from One and the Same God 155

Summary of Book 4 and the Purpose of Book 5	157
The Reality and Revelation of the Incarnation	158
The Resurrection of the Body and the Nature of Resurrected Life	160
Reasons Why the Word Became Flesh	163
The Summing Up of All Things in Christ	165
The Reality of Future Incorruption and Resurrection Life	168
The Salvation Accomplished by the Mission of the Son	170

FURTHER READING 171

WORKS CONSULTED 173
    Translations Used in This Volume 173
    Translations and Critical Editions Consulted 173

SCRIPTURE INDEX 175

For Luke. May you be mighty in the Scriptures and a man of peace.

Series Preface

Since the middle of the twentieth century, English readers have seen a resurgence in English translations and editions of early Christian texts, including writings from the Patristic era.[1] New translations and critical editions have been produced for both popular and lesser-known texts. Compilations dedicated to specific themes have also emerged, such as a series on Patristic interpretations of Scripture. In light of this resurgence, readers may ask, quite understandably, do we need another series?

This series was borne out of the conviction that, despite this welcome resurgence in Patristic resources, certain gaps remain. With the increasing number of Patristic works available, students and non-experts face greater difficulties determining which texts to focus on. Should one begin with the classics, such as those by Athanasius and Augustine, and then move out from there? Or is it best to work through early Christian literature chronologically? Regardless of one's chosen path, readers must still determine the specific works and editions to read. Older translations of many works are available online, but these translations are often in archaic English, and they do not benefit from the latest scholarship and critical editions. Modern translations and editions benefit from improved accuracy and readability, but at times they are difficult to access due to cost and availability.

The present series aims to partially solve these problems by providing expertly curated readings in accessible translations at an affordable cost. Each volume includes a helpful introduction written by a leading or emerging scholar. To reduce cost, existing translations have been revised to reflect contemporary English and improve accuracy in consultation with the original

---

1 Loosely defined as the period from about the end of the first century AD to the Second Council of Nicaea (AD 787).

languages (using critical editions where possible). The editors and curators have also consulted newer translations of difficult passages (indicated in the footnotes). To make references and further research more accessible to a broad English audience, references have been generally restricted to a limited number of useful secondary sources available in English, and the names of Patristic texts and other ancient works have been given in English rather than Latin.

The specific writers and texts included in each volume have been carefully considered to provide selections that will represent the broader body of Patristic literature and will also be useful to readers as diverse as students, theologians, and church leaders. To facilitate this goal, selections focus on the following five categories, listed alphabetically.

1. **Biblical Interpretation.** Material that represents significant early Christian hermeneutics and exegesis, including early Christian uses of Scripture, interpretations of key Scriptures, and contributions to the formation of the canon of Scripture.
2. **Christian Spirituality and Practice.** Material that represents significant early Christian ethics, spiritual practices, and other perspectives on living in the world as followers of Christ.
3. **Church History and Context.** Material that represents historical contexts, including significant early Christian events, experiences, or practices.
4. **Reception History.** Material that is of considerable influence or significance in Christian thought or in the reception of ancient Christian literature.
5. **Theology.** Material that is representative of significant early Christian theological beliefs, perspectives, debates, or questions.

In sum, Patristic Essentials is designed to provide a curated collection of essential readings from early Christian literature for a broad audience, in an accessible and attractive format, with new introductions written by experts familiar with the latest scholarship.

Jacob N. Cerone
Michael A.G. Haykin
Kevin Douglas Hill
Todd A. Scacewater

1

An Orientation to Irenaeus of Lyons

IRENAEUS OF LYONS WAS a memorable and historically significant theologian in the second century AD. His life and writing ministry have had an enduring influence on theological discussion ranging from the nature of the gospel, the shape of the Scriptures, and the structure of the church. He did not establish the foundational tenets of Christianity, but he articulated its full scope in a way that had not been done before. Many leaders of the church in subsequent generations built upon the groundwork he so diligently developed. Though not much is known about Irenaeus's life, there are enough comments from the early church historian Eusebius and within Irenaeus's own works to sketch a relatively stable outline of his life and ministry.[1]

Biography: Who Was Irenaeus of Lyons?

Irenaeus was born in the mid-second century and raised in Asia Minor, probably around Smyrna. As a young man, he heard the preaching and teaching of Polycarp, an important leader among the earliest churches in this area. Hearing Polycarp's testimony about the gospel message and theological reflections on various topics made a lasting impression, and Irenaeus notes these memories and draws upon this teaching at several places in his works.[2]

---

1 Recent studies of Irenaeus's biography and bibliography include John Behr, *Irenaeus of Lyons: Identifying Christianity* (Oxford University Press, 2013); Sara Parvis and Paul Foster, eds., *Irenaeus: Life, Scripture, and Legacy* (Fortress, 2012); Denis Minns, *Irenaeus: An Introduction* (T&T Clark, 2010); and Robert M. Grant, *Irenaeus of Lyons* (Routledge, 2006).

2 For example, see *Haer.* 2.3.4. Eusebius notes this connection in *Hist. eccl.* 5.5.8–9: "Pothinus having died with the other martyrs in Gaul at ninety years of age, Irenaeus succeeded him in the episcopate of the church at Lyons. We have learned that, in his youth, he was a hearer of Polycarp."

In a letter from later in his life, Irenaeus remembers this formative experience:

> I remember the events of that time more clearly than those of recent years. For what boys learn, growing with their mind, becomes joined with it; so that I am able to describe the very place in which the blessed Polycarp sat as he discoursed, and his goings out and his comings in, and the manner of his life, and his physical appearance, and his discourses to the people, and the accounts which he gave of his interactions with John and with the others who had seen the Lord. And as he remembered their words, and what he heard from them concerning the Lord, and concerning his miracles and his teaching, having received them from eyewitness of the "Word of Life," Polycarp related all things in harmony with the Scriptures. These things being told to me by the mercy of God, I listened attentively, noting them down, not on paper, but in my heart. And continually, through God's grace, I recall them faithfully.[3]

At some point, Irenaeus traveled west and began to serve the churches in the region of Gaul as a presbyter. During this time, the threat of Montanism arose and the leaders of the churches in Lyons sent Irenaeus as a representative to deliver a letter of response to the current bishop of Rome, Eleutherius.[4] In this letter, the leaders of Lyons commended Irenaeus and also noted his established position in the Christian community. "We have requested our brother and comrade Irenaeus," they wrote, "to carry this letter to you, and we ask you to hold him in esteem as zealous for the covenant of Christ."[5]

Meanwhile, during Irenaeus's trip to Rome, there was an outbreak of persecution against Christians in the region of Gaul and Lyons.[6] As part of this regional program of persecution, Pothinus, the bishop of Lyons was killed.[7]

---

3 Eusebius, *Hist. eccl.* 5.20.5–7. Translation from NPNF.

4 Montanism refers to the teaching of a leader named Montanus in the mid-second century who emphasized asceticism and the priority of ongoing prophetic revelation. Irenaeus was likely sent to Eleutherius with both theological and social concerns (e.g., either the ongoing or impending persecution of the churches in the area).

5 Eusebius, *Hist. eccl.* 5.4.1–2. They also add that if they "thought that office should confer righteousness upon anyone," they would commend Irenaeus "among the first as a presbyter of the church, which is his position" (5.4.2).

6 Eusebius recounts this outbreak of persecution along with a representative catalog of the surviving "confessors" in *Hist. eccl.* 5.1–2. On the persecution of Christians during this era and the wider social and religious context of Lyons and Rome, see Behr, *Irenaeus of Lyons*, 13–21; and James G. Bushur, *Irenaeus of Lyons and the Mosaic of Christ: Preaching Scripture in the Era of Martyrdom* (Routledge, 2017), 1–18.

7 A partial account of this persecution in Vienne and Lyons (perhaps written by Irenaeus himself) is recounted in Eusebius, *Hist. eccl.* 5.1–3.

An Orientation to Irenaeus of Lyons

Around 177, then, Irenaeus was installed as the bishop of the churches in Lyons. The city of Lyons was west of Rome in the southern part of modern-day France. From this location, Irenaeus served his people but also addressed some of the most pressing challenges that arose in this era. Perhaps during his visit to Rome, Irenaeus encountered several strands of heterodox teaching. Influential figures like Marcion and Valentinus spread teaching that Irenaeus felt compelled to engage and refute. In contrast to those who isolated themselves from the "great church" through novel teaching, Irenaeus sought to connect his approach to the Scriptures and his theological reflection directly to the preaching of the apostles. To this end, he drew upon earlier Christian theologians and also corresponded with other churches and individual friends about these theological matters.[8]

Later in his life, Irenaeus served as a representative of a group of churches during a conflict about the proper way to celebrate and commemorate the resurrection of Christ.[9] Some held that Easter should always coincide with the traditional date of Passover, while others believed that the commemoration of the resurrection should always be on the first day of the week in order to mark the day Jesus rose from the grave. This conflict known as the "Quartodeciman controversy" became an urgent matter when some churches in the West moved to excommunicate the churches in Asia Minor that observed Easter on a different date. Irenaeus appealed to Victor, the bishop of Rome at that time (Pope Victor I), and argued for an ecumenical rapprochement among the churches on this particular point of contention.

Irenaeus sought to communicate the importance of this issue but also prioritized reconciliation between the churches of the East and the churches near Rome. Noting a disagreement between Polycarp and another leader, he observed that even though "matters were in this shape, they communed together . . . and they parted from each other in peace, both those who observed, and those who did not, maintaining the peace of the whole church."[10] Eusebius notes on this point that "Irenaeus, who was truly well-named, became a peacemaker in this matter, exhorting and negotiating in this way in behalf of the peace of the churches."[11]

---

8 See the works listed and described in the next section. Theologians that Irenaeus drew upon include Justin Martyr and Theophilus of Antioch. For essential readings from these two figures, see Kevin Douglas Hill, ed., *Christianity in the First and Second Centuries: Essential Readings*, Patristic Essentials (Fontes, 2022), 189–265, 293–305.

9 This conflict occurred perhaps in the late 190s.

10 Eusebius, *Hist. eccl.* 5.24.16–18. One of Irenaeus's key points was that "disagreement in regard to the fast confirms the agreement in the faith" (5.24.13).

11 Eusebius, *Hist. eccl.* 5.24.18. Eusebius draws the connection between Irenaeus's name and the Greek word εἰρήνη (*eirēnē*), which means "peace."

While he was gentle and tolerant with others about the intramural debate over the Easter celebration, he was critical and pointed toward those who espoused what he considered to be dangerous heresy. Irenaeus was thus one who sought to establish peace among the churches but also one who was willing to confront false teaching. Irenaeus continued his ministry in this vein until his death sometime in the early third century.[12]

Bibliography: What Did Irenaeus Write?

As an extension of his ministry among the churches, Irenaeus also wrote broadly both in private correspondence and in publicly circulated works. Among the surviving manuscripts of these texts are two of his most well-known writings. In *Demonstration of the Apostolic Preaching*, he articulates the message of the apostles and relates it to the flow of redemptive history as portrayed in the Old Testament. In *Against Heresies*, Irenaeus seeks to refute the theological assertions and biblical interpretation of the groups in second-century Rome that he views as heretical. A brief consideration of the composition and message of these books serves as an instructive window into Irenaeus's ministry and his personal theological development.[13]

The first major project that Irenaeus publishes is the opening two sections of *Against Heresies* (Books 1–2). One of Irenaeus's friends had sent him several questions about gnostic teaching in his region. Irenaeus pens and sends these first two books in order to explain the content of these false teachings, and also to provide a pathway for Christians to respond to this alternate system of theology.[14]

The next phase of Irenaeus's writing project includes a smaller work titled *On the Demonstration of the Apostolic Preaching*. Whereas in Books 1–2 of *Against Heresies* Irenaeus surveys alternate systems and distorted claims about biblical texts, in this work his aim is to produce a positive articulation

---

12 The claim that Irenaeus was martyred during a time of persecution is possibly accurate but also historically late and isolated to a passing reference in Jerome's commentary on Isaiah in the early fifth century. In this scenario, Irenaeus would have been killed as part of a regional persecution during the reign of Roman Emperor Septimius Severus who ruled from AD 193–211. See the relevant details listed by Minns, *Irenaeus*, 3n11; and Behr, *Irenaeus of Lyons*, 14n4.

13 That Irenaeus took care in the formulation and reception of his written works can be seen in a note that comes at the end of one of his smaller texts: "I adjure you, who shall transcribe this book, by our Lord Jesus Christ, and by his glorious appearing, when he comes to judge the living and the dead, that you compare what you have transcribed and be careful to set it right according to this copy from which you have transcribed; also, that you likewise copy down this adjuration and insert it in the transcript" (quoted in Eusebius, *Hist. eccl.* 5.20.2–3).

14 Chapter two of this volume gives an overview and analysis of this opening section of *Against Heresies*.

of the message of the gospel in relation to the Scriptures as a whole. *Demonstration* was written as a freestanding work but also with a clear relation to Irenaeus's broader project in *Against Heresies*. At the conclusion of Book 2 of *Against Heresies*, Irenaeus mentions that he plans to "devote a special book to the Scriptures" that might be seen to prefigure and anticipate the person and work of Jesus in his incarnation. He says further that he aims to "plainly set forth from these divine Scriptures proofs to satisfy all the lovers of truth" (*Haer.* 2.34.5). Though this description fits some of the content of Book 3 of *Against Heresies*, it also resonates particularly well with the shape and development of *Demonstration*. In his closing comments of this work, Irenaeus returns to the warning against those who deny that God the Father is the creator of the natural order. Those who make this theological disconnect "are impious and blasphemers against their creator and against the Father, as we have shown in the *Exposure and Overthrow of Knowledge falsely so-called.*"[15] While it is possible that Irenaeus refers here to *Against Heresies* as a completed work, it is also possible that he has in mind the opening section of Books 1–2, the place where he most directly addresses the content of this teaching.[16] With regard to conceptual development if not compositional history, then, Irenaeus's reflection in *Demonstration* is strategically connected to his broader theological project.

As *Demonstration* unfolds, Irenaeus summarizes key moments of redemptive history drawn from the biblical storyline. He also traces the events of Jesus's incarnate life through Old Testament prophetic passages. Because of its brief size yet comprehensive scope, *Demonstration* functions as a constructive expression of the core features of the rule of faith that guided the reading of the Scriptures in many early Christian textual communities.

As a follow-up to both the polemical development of Books 1–2 of *Against Heresies* and the positive articulation of *Demonstration*, Irenaeus takes up the challenge of false teaching through a targeted exposition of the fourfold Gospel and the apostolic writings of the New Testament. In Book 3 of *Against Heresies*,

---

15 *Epid.* is the abbreviation of the first word of the Greek title of *Demonstration*, which in transliteration is *Epideixis tou apostolikou kērygmatos*.

16 For this way of understanding the historical development of these works and Irenaeus's comments about his own writing, see Behr, *Irenaeus of Lyons*, 66–71. Most scholars note that Irenaeus composes the five books of *Against Heresies* sequentially and over an extended period of time (with each book being sent as it is written). It's also possible that the final paragraphs of *Demonstration* are composed at a later date. However, because of the paucity of external evidence for this reconstruction, most acknowledge the tentative nature of any proposed chronology. Recognizing this historical scenario, Behr nonetheless suggests that "between the second and third books of *Against the Heresies* would be a natural context for sketching out the apostolic preaching from the Scriptures, such as we see in the *Demonstration*" (*Irenaeus of Lyons*, 68–69).

Irenaeus examines the teaching of Jesus in the Gospels with a special focus on the parables. In Book 4, he discusses some of Jesus's speeches and teaching in addition to the parables. He also begins a discussion of key passages in the letters of Paul. In the final Book 5, Irenaeus engages some of the other New Testament texts with a focus on the apostolic vision of eschatological realities.

The opening comments of Book 4 are an apt summary of Irenaeus's apologetic and evangelistic purpose in *Against Heresies* as a whole. He writes,

> My very dear friend, by transmitting to you this fourth book of the work which is entitled *The Detection and Refutation of False Knowledge*, as I have promised, I shall add weight to what I have already advanced by means of the words of the Lord; so that you also, as you have requested, may obtain from me the means of refuting all the heretics everywhere, and not permit them, beaten back at all points, to launch out further into the depths of error nor to be drowned in the sea of ignorance; but that by turning them into the haven of the truth you may cause them to attain their salvation. (*Haer.* 4.0.1)

Alongside these major works, Irenaeus writes to congregations and individuals throughout his ministry.[17] Because of his local leadership position, it is also possible that Irenaeus was the primary author of the pastoral letter that provides an account of the persecution of Christians in Vienne and Lyons.[18] Accordingly, most of Irenaeus's pastoral and intellectual ministry is pursued in the context of a community that was experiencing social tension and physical suffering.

He also engages false teaching on a smaller scale in correspondence with a friend named Florinus. Florinus was a former acquaintance of Irenaeus who was removed from being an elder in Rome because of his heretical views (likely influenced by the teachings of Valentinus). Irenaeus appeals to apostolic tradition and also their shared experience of Polycarp's guidance in order to exhort Florinus to reject his heretical positions. He urges, "These doctrines, O Florinus, to speak mildly, are not of sound judgment." These doctrines disagree with the church, encourage impiety, are not even spoken by most heretics, and were not delivered by "the presbyters who were before us and who were companions of the apostles" (*Hist. eccl.* 5.20.6).

---

17 Among others, Irenaeus writes letters to Blastus (*On Schism*) and Florinus (*On the Monarchy*, or *That God is not the Author of Evil*; and *On the Ogdoad*). For these titles, see Eusebius, *Hist. eccl.* 5.20.1–8; 5.26.1. Further, regarding the Easter celebration controversy, Eusebius notes that Irenaeus "conferred by letter about this mooted question, not only with Victor, but also with most of the other rulers of the churches" (*Hist. eccl.* 5.24.18).

18 See Eusebius, *Hist. eccl.* 5.1–3.

Eusebius also mentions that Irenaeus published a collection of "various dissertations" that included quotations and discussions of texts like the letter to the Hebrews and the "so-called Wisdom of Solomon" (*Hist. eccl.* 5.26.1).

Theology: What Did Irenaeus Believe?

In the course of his extensive responses to false teaching in *Against Heresies* and *Demonstration*, Irenaeus describes and develops a variety of theological themes. Though there are several significant doctrinal areas that are worth noting, the following section briefly surveys some of the central emphases across Irenaeus's corpus.[19]

God as Creator and Revealer

One of the most important theological resources that Irenaeus employs in his defense of Christianity is the clear and absolute distinction between God as creator and all other created beings. The world did not come into being through the struggle and corruption of multiple deities, demigods, or intermediaries. Rather, the one God who acts throughout redemptive history is the maker of the heavens and the earth. For Irenaeus, this foundational starting point marks the comprehensive difference between Christianity and other religious systems. As he directly states, "In this respect God differs from man, that God indeed makes, but man is made" (*Haer.* 4.11.2). Further, "he who makes is always the same; but that which is made must receive both beginning, and middle, addition, and increase" (*Haer.* 4.11.2). God creates "after a skillful manner" while humanity always remains skillfully created. This creator/creature distinction is the hinge upon which much of his argument against gnostic teaching is secured.

This theology of creation is embedded within Irenaeus's broader theology proper. God the Father creates but never apart from the Word and the Spirit. In a paradigmatic articulation, Irenaeus argues that "God did not stand in need of [any other beings] in order to accomplish what he had himself determined with himself beforehand should be done, as if he did not possess his

---

19 For recent extensive studies of some of the theological themes noted here, see *inter alia* Anthony Briggman, *God and Christ in Irenaeus* (Oxford University Press, 2019); Anthony Briggman, *Irenaeus of Lyons and the Theology of the Holy Spirit* (Oxford University Press, 2012); John Behr, *Asceticism and Anthropology in Irenaeus and Clement* (Oxford University Press, 2017); Behr, *Irenaeus of Lyons*, 121–203; Stephen Presley, *The Intertextual Reception of Genesis 1–3 in Irenaeus of Lyons* (Brill, 2015); M. C Steenberg, *Of God and Man: Theology as Anthropology from Irenaeus to Athanasius* (T&T Clark, 2009); and Thomas Holsinger-Friesen, *Irenaeus and Genesis: A Study of Competition in Early Christian Hermeneutics* (Eisenbrauns, 2009).

own hands. For with him were always present the Word and Wisdom, the Son and the Spirit, by whom and in whom, freely and spontaneously, he made all things" (*Haer.* 4.20.1).

When Irenaeus articulates the contours of the rule of faith, this Trinitarian framework is woven into his assertions about creation.[20] As he says toward the beginning of *Demonstration*, "There is therefore one God, the Father, not made, invisible, creator of all things; above whom there is no other God, and after whom there is no other God. Since God is rational, therefore by the Word he created the things that were made. And God is Spirit, and by the Spirit he adorned all things" (*Epid.* 5).[21] In the sections that follow these statements, Irenaeus connects creation to both the meaning of God's revelation and the nature of God's redemption.[22]

For Irenaeus, a clear corollary of this theology of creation relates to the nature and necessity of God's special revelation. Because God is the transcendent creator and humanity depends upon God for all things, knowledge of God and his ways unavoidably requires divine initiative. Irenaeus states strongly that "the Lord taught us that no man is capable of knowing God, unless he be taught of God; that is, that God cannot be known without God" (*Haer.* 4.6.4). Irenaeus clarifies further that knowledge of God is in fact "the express will of the Father" and is secured by the revelation of the Son and the testimony of the Spirt" (*Haer.* 4.6.4–6). For Irenaeus, then, both the incomprehensibility and knowability of God are rooted in a robust theology of creation.

Christ and the Divine Economy

Another clear distinctive of Irenaeus's theological discourse is his relentless focus on Jesus as the center of the apostolic preaching. The preaching of the apostles, in turn, is inextricably linked to the testimony of the Old Testament

---

20 While he does not have a formal discussion of God's triunity in his work, Irenaeus articulates God's person and work (especially in the creation of mankind in the image of God) in a way that anticipates some of the Trinitarian discussions of the third and fourth centuries leading up to the councils of Nicaea (AD 325) and Constantinople (AD 381). For recent scholarship that notes the nature and extent of Irenaeus's Trinitarian theology, see Michel Barnes, "Irenaeus's Trinitarian Theology," *Nova et Vetera* 7.1 (2009): 67–106; Jackson Lashier, *Irenaeus on the Trinity* (Brill, 2014); and chapter two of Michael Haykin, *Giving Glory to the Consubstantial Trinity: An Essay on the Quintessence of the Christian Faith* (Free Grace, 2018).

21 Irenaeus specifies further that "since the Word establishes, that is to say, gives body and grants the reality of being, and the Spirit gives order and form to the diversity of the powers; rightly and fittingly is the Word called the Son and the Spirit called the Wisdom of God." For Irenaeus, the Father is "over all," the Son is the one through whom "all things were made by the Father," and the Spirit is the one who "fashions man into the likeness of God."

22 See the sequence of topics addressed in *Epid.* 5–7.

Scriptures. Drawing on the shape of a two-testament witness to Christ, Irenaeus insists that what Jesus reveals is what the prophets foretold and the apostles proclaimed. This theological unity across redemptive history is due to the unity of God's being and the coherence of his action in the world.

In particular, Irenaeus argues that in the incarnation, Jesus "recapitulates" (or "sums up") the entire history of humanity in order to make salvation possible and heal the corruption of sin. The advent of God the Son in the flesh is the culmination of God's well-ordered plan of redemption (his "divine economy") and an integral part of God's revelation of himself. For Irenaeus, then, the Old Testament provides not only a historical background for but also a prefigural articulation of the life, ministry, death, and resurrection of Jesus as the Christ. Accordingly, the apex and epitome of the divine economy is the incarnation where God the Son takes on a human nature and sums up in himself the history of Israel and all of mankind. For Irenaeus, salvation comes "not by the many words of the law, but by the brevity of faith and love" displayed in the incarnation (*Epid.* 87). The incarnation, then, is God's "concise word" that redeems humanity.[23]

After discussing the nature of sin and the need for salvation, Irenaeus articulates this concept directly in the final sections of *Against Heresies*. "In his work of recapitulation," Irenaeus argues, Christ "summed up all things" and crushed "him who had at the beginning led us away as captives in Adam, and trampled upon his head" (*Haer.* 5.21.1). Reflecting on the implications of the promise that the "seed of the woman" would "crush the head of the serpent" (Gen 3:15), Irenaeus characterizes Christ as the new and better Adam who reverses the curse that came about because of disobedience.[24]

It is fitting, also, that redemption would come through a human. Jesus professes himself to be "the Son of Man, comprising in himself that original man out of whom the woman was fashioned, in order that, as our species went down to death through a vanquished man, so we may ascend to life again through a victorious one" (*Haer.* 5.21.2).[25] As Irenaeus also says in

---

23 Behr summarizes Irenaeus's central point in *The Way to Nicaea* (SVS Press, 2001), 128: "Recapitulating in himself the exposition of the economy, Jesus Christ furnishes us with salvation through a resume, an epitome, which condenses or concentrates, and so makes visible and comprehensible, what had previously been invisible and incomprehensible." Cf. Stephen Presley, "The *Demonstration* of Intertextuality in Irenaeus of Lyons," in *Intertextuality in the Second Century*, ed. D. Jeffrey Bingham and Clayton Jefford (Brill, 2016), 195–213.

24 In this section, Irenaeus draws also upon Paul's discussion in texts like Gal 3:19 ("until the seed should come to whom the promise was made") and Gal 4:4 ("when the fullness of time was come, God sent forth his Son, born of a woman").

25 Cf. *Haer.* 5.1.2 ("For he would not have been one truly possessing flesh and blood by which he redeemed us, unless he had summed up in himself the ancient formation of Adam") and *Haer.* 5.14.2 ("Now this blood could not be required unless it also had the capability of

Demonstration, "It was necessary that Adam should be summed up in Christ, that mortality might be swallowed up and overwhelmed by immortality" (*Epid.* 33).[26] In fact, one of the marks of heretical teachers is that they reject the "advent of the Son of God and the economy of his incarnation, which is the summing up of mankind" (*Epid.* 33).[27] This way of understanding the nature of Christ's work of redemption is woven throughout Irenaeus's written works.

Humanity and the End of All Things

A final theological emphasis to note briefly is how Irenaeus brings his entire project to bear on the nature and purpose of humanity. For Irenaeus, the origin and destiny of mankind is directly related to God's overarching purpose in the world. Especially because he was engaging arguments that devalued and diminished the significance of the material order and the physical part of what it means to be human, Irenaeus addresses issues of theological anthropology from the beginning to the end of his major works.

As noted above, Irenaeus strongly affirms the distinction between God as creator on the one hand and all created things including humanity on the other. Further, humans are created in the image and likeness of God. God "formed man with his own hands," Irenaeus reflects, "taking from the earth that which was purest and finest, and mingling in measure his own power with the earth. For he traced his own form on the formation, that that which should be seen should be of divine form. For man was formed as the image of God and set on the earth" (*Epid.* 11).[28]

For Irenaeus, this biblical truth is organically connected to the meaning of Christ's incarnation. After tracing the narratives of Genesis through the account of the flood (Genesis 1–9), Irenaeus takes note of the creation imagery in God's words to Noah and connects this notion to Christology: "For he made man the image of God; and the image of God is the Son, after whose image man was made. And for this reason, he appeared in the end of times

---

being saved; nor would the Lord have summed up these things in himself unless he had himself been made flesh and blood after the way of the original formation of man, saving in his own person at the end that which had in the beginning perished in Adam").

26 Both 1 Corinthians 15 and Romans 5 are important for Irenaeus's notion of recapitulation and Jesus as the second Adam.

27 Irenaeus adds, "As we have shown you briefly, this is what the apostles delivered and the prophets foretold."

28 Irenaeus also connects the image of God to the breath of life that man receives: "And that he might become living, he breathed on his face the breath of life; that both for the breath and for the formation man should be similar to God" (*Epid.* 11).

that he might show the image to be in his likeness" (*Epid.* 22). Accordingly, for Irenaeus, the creation of mankind *in the beginning* prefigures the advent of the incarnation *in the last days* when the Son of God took on a human nature.[29]

Because the purpose of humanity is fulfilled by Christ in the incarnation, human beings reflect the image of God and find their reason for being in communion with this same God. As Irenaeus reflects, "the glory of God is a living man; and the life of man consists in beholding God. For if the manifestation of God which is made by means of the creation affords life to all living in the earth, much more does that revelation of the Father which comes through the Word give life to those who see God" (*Haer.* 4.20.7).

In relation to eschatology, the creation of humanity and the incarnation are the proper end of the divine economy. As he closes Book 5 of *Against Heresies*, Irenaeus reflects upon humanity in the context of the future resurrection of the body. Because Christ truly took on a human nature, human beings have a sure hope of bodily resurrection. Believers will one day have life with God in resurrection bodies by the power of the Spirit. "If in the present time fleshly hearts are made partakers of the Spirit," Irenaeus reasons, "what is there astonishing if, in the resurrection, they receive that life which is granted by the Spirit?" (*Haer.* 5.13.4).

In the final words of *Against Heresies*, Irenaeus draws together these themes and connects them to the fundamental theological distinctives of Christianity. This brief statement also serves as a concise synthesis of his constructive theological argument as a whole. Irenaeus writes,

> For there is the one Son, who accomplished his Father's will; and one human race also in which the mysteries of God are brought about, "which the angels desire to look into" (1 Pet 1:12). And they are not able to search out the wisdom of God, by means of which his handiwork, confirmed and incorporated with his Son, is brought to perfection; that his offspring, the first begotten Word, should descend to the creature, that is, to what had been molded, and that it should be contained by him; and, on the other hand, the creature should contain the Word, and ascend to him, passing beyond the angels, and be made after the image and likeness of God. (*Haer.* 5.36.3)

---

29 Cf. Genesis 1–3 and Hebrews 1. This connection between creation, Christology, anthropology, and eschatology can help explain the pervasive allusions to the Genesis creation accounts in Irenaeus's works even as he moves through a wide variety of theological topics. Interestingly, the possible allusions to the letter to the Hebrews in Irenaeus are usually from the opening section of Heb 1:1–14 (e.g., *Haer.* 2.28.2–7; 2.30.1–9). The move the writer makes quickly in Heb 1:1–4 is one that Irenaeus makes repeatedly ("in these last days" God has spoken to us "in his Son").

Reception: Who Cares about Irenaeus?

For the Study of Early Christianity

Irenaeus is uniquely important for the study of early Christianity in the second century. He is a representative figure that had a sizeable impact on the development of Christian thought in this era. As Bingham has noted, during his lifetime, "Irenaeus was well-traveled, well-mentored, and well-thought of."[30] On multiple occasions, he helped leaders and congregations from different contexts to reconcile and rally around the core gospel message and the theological witness of the church. In this sense, Irenaeus was a unifying figure in an early Christian community that spanned the eastern and western parts of the Mediterranean world.[31] The person and work of Irenaeus, then, provides evidence against the notion that the earliest churches were isolated from one another or that there was an uncrossable boundary between the East and the West.

Irenaeus's theological writing is also significant for our current understanding of the state of Christian theology in the second century as well as the religious discourse with which it interacted. For many leaders in early Christianity, Irenaeus's lengthy discussion of teaching and movements considered false or heretical was an orienting primary source and common starting point.[32] With the discovery of the texts from the Nag Hammadi collection, the basic outline of Irenaeus's interaction with "the Gnostics" has proven relatively reliable.[33]

---

30 D. Jeffrey Bingham, "Irenaeus of Lyons," in *The Routledge Companion to Early Christian Thought*, ed. D. Jeffrey Bingham (Routledge, 2009), 139.

31 Cf. Jeffrey Bingham, "Irenaeus," 138: "What we have in Irenaeus is one man, one bishop, in whom resided the expression and faith of Christianity from a breadth of geographical and cultural locations." Bingham continues by noting in particular that "his life demonstrates a connection between Gaul, the Roman region, which among other parts of modern-day western Europe, included France, in which Lyons is located, and the eastern part of the empire."

32 For example, see Eusebius, *Hist. eccl.* 2.13.3–4. Eusebius comments that "it is possible for those who wish to know the origin and the lives and the false doctrines of each of the heresiarchs that have followed [Simon Magus], as well as the customs practiced by them all, to find them treated at length in the above-mentioned work of Irenaeus." Cf. *Hist. eccl.* 3.26.3: "These facts can be easily learned from the works of Irenaeus."

33 Cf. also Bingham, "Irenaeus of Lyons," 139: "Although some of his descriptions show stereotyping, polemical exaggeration, and faithfulness to rhetorical strategy, and although we may allow for some misunderstanding of his sources, Irenaeus's representations have been judged quite accurate and largely substantiated by our access to the Nag Hammadi library, discovered in the mid-twentieth century." Bingham notes the similar historical conclusion (along with the expected caveats) by Pheme Perkins in "Irenaeus and the Gnostics: Rhetoric and Composition in *Adversus Haereses* Book One," *Vigiliae Christianae* 30 (1976): 193–200. So too Mary Ann Donovan, *One Right Reading? A Guide to Irenaeus* (Liturgical Press, 1997), 175: "If

Of course, a full historical account of "Gnosticism" would require a much broader focus that situates Irenaeus's descriptions, characterizations, assertions, and rhetorical critiques within the literary and historical context of second and third century Christianity.[34] In order to address this challenge in a manageable way, Irenaeus often finds ways of associating divergent strands of teaching with one another. This has the pastoral benefit of helping readers make sense of a labyrinth of loose ends but is also not strictly a dispassionate historiography of the self-understanding of these various communities.[35] However, the basic system of teaching that Irenaeus engages in *Against Heresies* is discernible in Nag Hammadi texts like *The Gospel of Truth* and *The Gospel of Thomas*. This basic continuity makes Irenaeus an enduring resource for the study of early Christianity in the second century.

Additionally, Irenaeus's work demonstrates an early concern for boundaries of authoritative writings within the Christian community along with clear notions of truth and falsehood.[36] The burden of much of Irenaeus's writing involves delineating the "rule of truth" that enables one to recognize and reject teaching that is "false" and outside the bounds of Christian confession. Because Irenaeus is so direct on these points and also such an early figure in early Christianity, his literary and theological legacy has been variously championed or challenged. A theory that is still popular and widely held in scholarly contexts is the notion that there was no early consensus about the core teaching of Christianity. Rather, there was a wide and unwieldy diversity within early Christianity that was only subsequently consolidated and reinterpreted to be understood as an ancient continuity. In popular expression, this approach holds that the various "heresies" came first, and the notion of a normative "orthodoxy" came some time afterwards.[37] Consequently, Irenae-

---

read with attention to his goal and methodology the work of Irenaeus can yield a fair appreciation of the Valentinians. Study of the Nag Hamadi material has not thus far raised substantial challenges to this opinion."

34 Notable recent examples in this constantly growing field include David Brakke, *The Gnostics: Myth, Ritual, and Diversity in Early Christianity* (Harvard University Press, 2012); Einar Thomassen, *The Coherence of "Gnosticism"* (De Gruyter, 2020); and Einar Thomassen and Christoph Markschies, eds., *Valentinianism: New Studies* (Brill, 2019).

35 For example, Irenaeus characterizes a host of different teachings as the organic outgrowth of the influence of Simon Magus (see Acts 8:9–24; *Haer.* 1.23).

36 Cf. D. Jeffrey Bingham, "Senses of Scripture in the Second Century: Irenaeus, Scripture, and Noncanonical Christian Texts," *The Journal of Religion* 97, no. 1 (January 2017): 26–55; and Behr, *Way to Nicaea*, 11–48; 111–133.

37 For the range of scholarly opinion on this question see Bart D. Ehrman, *Lost Christianities: The Battles for Scripture and the Faiths We Never Knew* (Oxford University Press, 2005); and Andreas J. Köstenberger and Michael J. Kruger, *The Heresy of Orthodoxy: How Contemporary Culture's Fascination with Diversity has Reshaped our Understanding of Early Christianity* (Crossway, 2010).

us's work in the second century must be addressed in some way because it represents a challenge to this contemporary historiography.[38]

For Biblical and Theological Studies

Irenaeus's work is also relevant for the task of biblical and theological studies. In one respect, because of historical distance and the differing intellectual contexts of contemporary scholarship and the early church era, Irenaeus's work may seem completely foreign to the study of biblical texts today. This starting point is part of what led James Barr to assert that "what was thought about the Bible by Irenaeus or by Calvin is thus something quite other than biblical theology as here understood."[39] For Barr, biblical theology is done by scholars trained in the historical-critical disciplines, and so figures from earlier eras of interpretation should not be characterized as biblical theologians. Though these theologians "may at times have tried to use methods and levels belonging to biblical theology, such attempts have been very partial and on the whole received rather little serious attention."[40]

Conversely, if one of the central tasks of the discipline of biblical theology is to reflect upon the relationship between the two testaments of the Christian biblical canon and to consider individual texts in light of the larger theological and literary context of the Scriptures, then Irenaeus can be seen as an important precursor to this kind of study in early Christianity. For Brevard Childs, theologians like Irenaeus share a "family resemblance" to the task of biblical theology.[41] On these terms, Childs concludes that "it seems hard to question that Irenaeus was indeed a biblical theologian" and that "he has raised a variety of critical hermeneutical problems which are fully relevant to the modern debate." Childs especially highlights Irenaeus's relentless focus on the unity of the Scripture's witness to Christ: "Because of the unity of God's salvation, it was absolutely essential to the faith that the two testaments of

---

38 Cf. Charles E. Hill, *Who Chose the Gospels? Probing the Great Gospel Conspiracy* (Oxford, 2010), 34–68. Hill notes that in order to relativize Irenaeus's significance for this historiography, scholars either seek to isolate Irenaeus's influence (the "lonely Irenaeus") or call his character into question (the "ugly Irenaeus").

39 James Barr, *The Concept of Biblical Theology: An Old Testament Perspective* (SCM Press, 1999), 4. This conclusion also follows from Barr's essential definition of biblical theology: "The term 'biblical theology' has clarity only when it is understood to mean theology as it existed or was thought or believed within the time, languages, and cultures of the Bible itself" (4). For Barr, this strict definition is the only way that biblical theology's "difference from doctrinal theology, from later interpretation, and from later views about the Bible" can be maintained (4).

40 Barr, *Concept of Biblical Theology*, 2–3. Accordingly, Barr strongly critiques Brevard Childs's characterization of John Calvin and Karl Barth as "doing biblical theology."

41 Childs explains what he means by "family resemblance" in the history of interpretation in *The Struggle to Understand Isaiah as Christian Scripture* (Eerdmans, 2004), 299–321.

the Christian Bible be seen as a harmonious witness to the one redemptive purpose in history."[42]

This characterization of Irenaeus also follows from Childs's core understanding of the discipline of biblical theology. For Childs, "Biblical Theology is by definition theological reflection on both the Old Testament and the New Testament. It assumes that the Christian Bible consists of a theological unity formed by the canonical union of the two testaments."[43] Accordingly, Childs broadens "the scope of the inquiry" to recognize that "some of the greatest theologians of the church struggled to find models for dealing theologically with both testaments of scripture as a revelation of Jesus Christ."[44]

In his work, Irenaeus engages the interpretation of specific biblical texts (exegesis), considers the way the Scriptures as a whole fit together (biblical theology), and also reckons with the implications this study has for God's person and work (systematic theology). He also bases much of his argumentation on textual patterns that span Old and New Testaments and theological connections that require divine providence throughout the history of redemption. Those engaged in contemporary biblical theology along these lines will likely recognize a family resemblance with certain aspects of Irenaeus's approach to the biblical-theological task.[45]

Two features of Irenaeus's approach are worth noting in this regard. First, Irenaeus works with a concept of the canonical context that is flexible but clearly discernable. Though he is engaging highly speculative and technical discussions in his work, Irenaeus also draws on the broad shape of the biblical collection regularly. For instance, he argues that "the entire Scriptures, the prophets, and the Gospels, can be clearly, unambiguously, and harmoniously understood by all, although all do not believe them" (*Haer.* 2.27.2). Irenaeus concludes Book 2 of *Against Heresies* by summarizing, "Now, that the preaching of the apostles, the authoritative teaching of the Lord, the announcements of the prophets, the dictated utterances of the apostles, and the ministrations of the law ... are all in harmony with our statements" and show that "there is but one God, the Maker of all things" (*Haer.* 2.35.4). In the middle of this sentence, Irenaeus includes summary affirmations that these

---

42 Childs, *Biblical Theology of the Old and New Testaments*, 31.
43 Childs, *Biblical Theology of the Old and New Testaments*, 55.
44 Childs, *Biblical Theology of the Old and New Testaments*, 30.
45 See also Stephen Presley, "Biblical Theology and the Unity of Scripture in Irenaeus of Lyons," *CTR* 16.2 (Spring 2019): 3–24. For a brief discussion of Irenaeus as an exemplar of biblical theology before the modern period, see Ched Spellman, "The History of Biblical Theology as a Discipline," in *Invitation to Biblical Theology: Exploring the Shape, Storyline, and Themes of Scripture*, ed. Jeremy Kimble and Ched Spellman (Kregel, 2020), 21–34. Portions of the following two paragraphs draw from this source. Cf. also the older take on this characterization in John Lawson, *The Biblical Theology of Saint Irenaeus* (Epworth Press, 1948).

diverse sections of Scripture all "praise one and the same Being, the God and Father of all." When Irenaeus characterizes the Scriptures as a whole ("the entire Scriptures"), he shows remarkable sensitivity to the shape of the biblical canon, the notion of theological unity/diversity, the organic relationship between economic development in redemptive history (the prophets, the Lord, and the apostles) and ontological identification (the God of Israel is the Father of Jesus Christ), and the urgency of carefully specifying the proper object of worship across the entire collection of biblical texts.[46]

Second, this orientation to Scripture's broad scope informs Irenaeus's articulation of the church's "rule of faith." In Irenaeus's project, the rule of faith is a strategic summary of the message of the biblical writings that functions as a kind of hermeneutical guide for understanding the Scriptures as a whole.[47] Rather than a static deposit of doctrinal formulation, the rule of faith is "an expression, which can vary depending on context, of the coherence of Scripture as a mosaic of Christ."[48] In this guiding summary, it is clearly understood that the God of Abraham, Isaac, and Jacob is the God and Father of the Lord Jesus Christ. As a summary of the Scriptures, the rule of faith provides an interpretive lens that highlights the interconnections appearing across the Scriptures and the theological relationship between the Father, the Son, and the Holy Spirit.[49] Irenaeus insists throughout his writings that the two-testament portrait of God and redemption in Christ, found in the proclamation of the prophets and apostles, is textually consistent and theologically coherent. According to the presentation of the Scriptures, redemptive history begins with God's creative work and climaxes in Christ's redemptive death on the cross.[50] For Irenaeus, because there is a unity in God's plan of redemp-

---

46 Note also the connection of Irenaeus's phrasing to Peter's comment in 2 Pet 3:1–2. There Peter combats false teaching by reminding his readers of "the predictions of the holy prophets and the commandment of the Lord and Savior through your apostles" (3:2).

47 The scholarly discussion on Irenaeus's rule of faith is vast. Two major perspectives on the rule of faith are: (1) that it provides a summary of Scripture's overarching narrative as a whole; and (2) that it functions as an interpretive summary of Scripture's theological message. On the former, see Paul M. Blowers, "The *Regula Fidei* and the Narrative Character of Early Christian Faith," *Pro Ecclesia* 6 (1997): 199–228. On the latter, see Nathan MacDonald, "Israel and the Old Testament Story in Irenaeus's Presentation of the Rule of Faith," *Journal of Theological Interpretation* 3.2 (2009): 281–98.

48 Behr, *Irenaeus of Lyons*, 11.

49 For examples from *Against Heresies*, see the selections in chapter two below.

50 Cf. MacDonald, "Israel and the Old Testament Story," 293–94: "With his attention to the shape of the canon, we can justly speak of Irenaeus as the first canonical interpreter. There is a genuine diversity to Scripture in the different parts of the canon [for Irenaeus], but the Rule of Faith points to the Scripture's unity in the story of Jesus Christ." Emphasizing the *hermeneutical* function of the rule of faith for Irenaeus, Christopher Seitz argues that the rule is "the scripturally grounded articulation, based upon a proper perception of the hypothesis of Scripture, that Jesus Christ is one with the God who sent him and who is active in the Scriptures

tion, there is a unity in God's character and being. These features of Irenaeus's work remain a valuable resource for those who understand the task of biblical theology to be the study of the whole Bible on its own terms.

For Ministry among the Churches

Finally, Irenaeus can serve as a resource and a model for ministry among the churches. As Irenaeus himself states, his motivation in most of his work is to help other believers and church leaders as they navigate a highly complex form of teaching that differed in central ways from the apostolic message. Though most church leaders will not face the challenge of a fully-formed "Gnosticism," they will encounter issues and teachings that challenge the core message of the gospel in ways that are unexpected and difficult to discern.

The model that Irenaeus provides in this scenario is instructive: directly describe and engage the details of the issue, and then bring this analysis into dialogue with a constructive articulation of the central message of the Scriptures. In this way, the "rule of faith" can help rule out deviations from the core claims of the gospel regardless of the specific details. This particular mindset and theological method have been influential in the history of the church and can still provide a suggestive example of theological reflection, apologetic engagement, and pastoral ministry.

Plan for This Volume: How Should You Read Irenaeus?

There are several reasons why the major works of Irenaeus are sometimes neglected.

First, Irenaeus's most well-known work *Against Heresies* is a long, complex, and difficult book to work through as a whole. Only the most dedicated students will read this work from start to finish. A central reason for this difficulty is the complicated nature of Books 1–2 where Irenaeus delves into various gnostic systems at a granular level. As one editor has noted, in these first two books especially, "the patience of the reader is sorely tried, in following our author through those mazes of absurdity which he treads, in explaining and refuting these Gnostic speculations."[51]

Second, Irenaeus is usually associated with his strongly worded critiques and wide-ranging polemical arguments against the various heretical teachers.

---

inherited, the Holy Spirit being the means of testifying to his active, if hidden, life in the 'Old Testament' and our apprehension of that" (*The Character of Christian Scripture: The Significance of a Two-Testament Bible* [Baker, 2011], 198).

51 See the introductory note for *Against Heresies* in *Ante-Nicene Fathers*.

This has led many scholars and casual readers to view Irenaeus with varying levels of suspicion. These two factors (the difficulty of Books 1–2 and the notorious reputation of an unflinching "heresiologist") sometimes discourage people from considering Irenaeus's body of writing in its entirety and on its own terms. Finally, the available English translations of *Against Heresies* are generally antiquated and usually only available through larger collections in the public domain like the *Ante-Nicene Fathers* series.

This volume seeks to help readers of Irenaeus's works navigate each of these difficulties. Accordingly, the introduction above briefly situates Irenaeus in his historical context and notes the theological contributions he makes to the developing doctrine of second-century Christianity.[52] When viewed within his social and ecclesial context, Irenaeus can be appreciated for much more than his catalogue and critique of heretical views. The first chapter also provides a summary and synthesis of Books 1–2 of *Against Heresies* that helps explain the most critical issues addressed here and also recovers some of the hermeneutical gems that are embedded in this larger discourse. The remaining chapters include notable selections from across *Against Heresies* and *Demonstration of the Apostolic Preaching*. The goal in these selections has also been to preserve the shape of these works so that a reader might get a sense of the internal logic of Irenaeus's theological writings. To this end, each chapter begins with a brief overview that provides the literary setting of the following selections. New headings are likewise included at strategic locations to guide readers and track the flow of Irenaeus's larger argument. Each selection also begins with the book, chapter, and section number so that a reader can cite any included quotation with the original location in a given work.

In terms of structure, Irenaeus's constructive work *Demonstration of the Apostolic Preaching* is situated in the logical development of Irenaeus's project. Accordingly, the *Demonstration* serves as a concise articulation of the rule of faith that governs both his engagement with heretical writings (in *Against Heresies*, Books 1–2) and also his constructive analysis of biblical texts (in *Against Heresies*, Books 3–5). Finally, the English translations here have been updated to aid contemporary readers as they make their way through these texts. In line with the general aim of the Patristic Essentials series, the endgame of this volume is to introduce Irenaeus and his comprehensive vision of the one God's work of redemption to a new generation of readers.[53]

---

52 On the basic reliability of Irenaeus's writing in light of recent historical discoveries, see footnotes 32–37 above.

53 Special thanks to those who provided feedback on portions of this volume including Hope Spellman, JR Gilhooly, Brandon Smith, Jonathan Watson, Cody Barnhart, and several students from my biblical theology courses.

2

Refuting Falsehood with the Rule of Faith

Books 1-2 of *Against Heresies*

Overview

In Books 1–2, Irenaeus has a two-fold purpose: to explain and then refute the false teaching that was influential among some Christian communities in the mid-second century. First, he provides an overview of the provocative theological claims that certain "gnostic" teachers were making about who God is, how the world came to be, and how humankind can experience salvation. Second, he details and critically engages the specific doctrinal claims made by these heretical teachers and also their interpretation of a host of biblical texts. Irenaeus concludes that the exegesis and theological systems of these teachers is absurd and incoherent even on their own terms. The ultimate standard by which Irenaeus measures and evaluates these teachings is the testimony of the Scriptures and the guidance of the "rule of faith."

Summary and Selected Quotations

Challenge: The Danger and Diversity of False Teaching

Irenaeus explains his purpose in writing by first observing that "certain men have set the truth aside" and have used "vain genealogies" and "craftily constructed" arguments in order to "draw away the minds of the inexperienced and take them captive" (*Haer.* 1.0.1). By echoing Paul's language in 1 Tim 1:14, Irenaeus begins his characterization of this false teaching with a sense of theological urgency: "I have felt constrained, my dear friend, to compose the following treatise in order to expose and counteract their schemes" (*Haer.* 1.0.1).

The first summary of this teaching anticipates the major themes that Irenaeus will address in Books 1–2 of his work:

> These men falsify the oracles of God and prove themselves evil interpreters of the good word of revelation. They also overthrow the faith of many, by drawing them away, under a pretense of superior knowledge, from him who founded and adorned the universe; as if, indeed, they had something more excellent and sublime to reveal than that God who created the heavens and the earth and all things that are found within this world. By means of deceptive and plausible words, they cunningly allure the simple-minded to inquire into their systems; but they nevertheless clumsily destroy them, while they initiate them into their blasphemous and impious opinions respecting the Demiurge; and these simple ones are unable, even in such a matter, to distinguish falsehood from truth. (*Haer.* 1.0.1)

His goal in this apologetic endeavor is to equip his readers with a working knowledge of these false teachings so that they may in turn explain them to others and "exhort them to avoid such an abyss of madness and of blasphemy against Christ" (*Haer.* 1.0.2). Through his extended analysis he aims "to furnish the means of overthrowing them by showing how absurd and inconsistent with the truth their statements are" (*Haer.* 1.0.2). Acknowledging his lack of formal eloquence, he nevertheless expresses his goal of making known "those doctrines which have been kept in concealment until now, but which are at last, through the goodness of God, brought to light" (*Haer.* 1.0.2).

As he explains the challenge of this false teaching, Irenaeus identifies several strands of thinking that are problematic. He notes that he has read the commentaries of some of the followers of Valentinus and has spoken to some of these men in person.[1] The opening of *Against Heresies* describes and outlines some of the claims that seemed most relevant to address from these interactions. Throughout Books 1–2, Irenaeus articulates the nature of these various principles and shows how these methods and commitments compromise the teaching of the prophets and apostles.

They Used the Same Words but with Different Meanings

One urgent problem that Irenaeus notes early and often is that the gnostic teachers utilize some of the same words and phrases from biblical texts but

---

[1] Irenaeus further specifies that he is referring in his first section "especially to the disciples of Ptolemaeus, whose school may be described as a bud from that of Valentinus" (*Haer.* 1.0.2).

they fill them with different meanings. For Irenaeus, this feature of their teaching was one of the most dangerous and difficult to confront. "Error," he insists, "is never set forth in its naked deformity, lest by being thus exposed it should at once be detected. But it is craftily decked out in an attractive dress, so as, by its outward form, to make it appear to the inexperienced more true than truth itself (ridiculous as the expression may seem)" (*Haer.* 1.0.2). A piece of glass crafted to look like an expensive jewel might deceive an inexperienced person unless it were to be examined by "one able to test and expose the counterfeit" (*Haer.* 1.0.2).[2] He cautions his readers that "their language resembles ours, while their sentiments are very different" (*Haer.* 1.0.2).

A common example of this practice is the way these teachers allegorize narrative scenes in the Gospels and search for numbered patterns to signify elements of their own system of beliefs. The name "Aeon" was given to the invisible divine beings that multiplied and eventually generated the natural world. Some argued that Paul affirmed and referred to these beings when he uses the expression "forever and ever" or "age upon age."[3] Some versions of this teaching set the number of Aeons at thirty and supported this total from specific narrative details.

For example, Irenaeus notes that "they maintain also that these thirty Aeons are most plainly indicated in the parable of the laborers sent into the vineyard. For some are sent about the first hour, others about the third hour, others about the sixth hour, others about the ninth hour, and others about the eleventh hour." These hours of the day add up to a total of thirty ($1 + 3 + 6 + 9 + 11 = 30$). In a feat of theological arithmetic, the gnostic teachers then assert that this parable refers to the thirty divine beings that makeup the "pleroma" of divine beings. Irenaeus observes that they "maintain that these are great and wonderful mysteries" which were previously unknown but that it is now "their special function to develop." They employ this technique any time they are able to "find anything in the multitude of things contained in the Scriptures which they can adopt and accommodate to their baseless speculations" (*Haer.* 1.1.3).[4]

---

2 Irenaeus also gives the example of brass mixed with silver and a wolf in sheep's clothing.

3 See *Haer.* 1.3.1. Irenaeus mentions the use of this phrase in Eph 3:21 ("to him be glory in the church and in Christ Jesus throughout all generations, forever and ever," ESV).

4 These associations could come from a variety of angles: one group of Aeons was 12 in number, so this was supported by the fact that Jesus was 12 years old when he interacted with the Jewish leaders at the temple and then later chose 12 disciples. The "twelfth apostle" was Judas, which typifies the fact that Sophia came from this group of 12 Aeons and caused suffering. The woman who reached for the hem of Jesus's garment and was healed of a blood issue that she had for 12 years also supports this part of the gnostic creation account (for these examples, see *Haer.* 1.3.1–6). Irenaeus deals at length with numbers and symbolic extrapolation in other places (e.g., see his discussion of the claim that the letters of Jesus's name revealed elements of

Irenaeus usually responds to these types of readings by asserting that this approach runs against the grain of the textual context of the Scriptures and the theological commitments of the rule of faith. These teachers strive "to adapt the good words of revelation to their own wicked inventions. And it is not only from the writings of the evangelists and the apostles that they endeavor to derive proofs for their opinions by means of perverse interpretations and deceitful expositions. They deal in the same way with the Law and the Prophets, which contain many parables and allegories that can frequently be drawn into various senses, according to the kind of exegesis to which they are subjected." With this "great craftiness," these teachers adapt "such parts of Scripture to their own figments" and "lead away captive from the truth those who do not retain a steadfast faith in one God, the Father almighty, and in one Lord Jesus Christ, the Son of God" (*Haer.* 1.3.6).

They Told a Different Story about How the World Began

One core component of the gnostic system that Irenaeus describes in great detail is their account of how the world began. For Irenaeus, the creation of the world becomes one of the clearest points of divergence with these teachers. The material world comes about as a result of conflict and disorder within the complex hierarchy of divine beings.

"In the invisible and ineffable heights above," their story begins, "there exists a certain perfect, pre-existent Aeon" who is "invisible and incomprehensible" (*Haer.* 1.1.1). This divine being is known as "Propator" or "Bythus," and a variety of other names that imply first or beginning.[5] As an "eternal and unbegotten" being, "he remained throughout innumerable cycles of ages in profound serenity and quiescence" (*Haer.* 1.1.1). In this context, their story of creation begins: "At last this Bythus determined to send forth from himself the beginning of all things, and deposited this production (which he had resolved to bring forth) in his contemporary Sige [a projection of himself], even as seed is deposited in the womb." Once this conception happens, this Sige gives birth to a being named Nous "who was both similar and equal to him who had produced him, and was alone capable of comprehending his father's greatness." This Nous ("intelligence") is also known as Monogenes ("only begotten") and "the beginning of all things." It is Monogenes, then, who takes

---

the gnostic system in *Haer.* 1.15.1–6; and his charge that this interest in numbers derives from "the Pythagoreans," *Haer.* 2.14.6–7).

5 There are several names given to this initial being: Bythus ("profundity"), Proarche ("first beginning"), Propator ("first-Father"). For a list of these names and translational glosses (along with the main titles discussed in Books 1–2), see the editorial footnote in *Haer.* 1.1.2n6.

the initiative to generate the rest of the celestial beings. This one becomes known as "the father of all those who were to come after him, and the beginning and fashioning of the entire Pleroma" (*Haer.* 1.1.1).

From this juncture, those generated by Monogenes begin to join together to produce more beings who in turn do the same to generate a proliferation of celestial beings that make up the network of divine beings (often referred to as the Pleroma). Finally arriving at the number thirty, this "invisible and spiritual Pleroma" is divided in a three-part hierarchy with a grouping of 8 ("an ogdoad"), 10 ("a decad"), and 12 ("a duodecad").[6] A key part of this tiered structure is that the initial divine being (Propator, the Father) is incomprehensible by any of the other Aeons except Monogenes. The other beings longed to know the Propator, but they were restrained.[7] The result of this restraint was that "the rest of the Aeons also, in a kind of quiet way, had a wish to behold the author of their being, and to contemplate that first cause which had no beginning" (*Haer.* 1.2.1).

Within this complex system and cosmic setting, one of the youngest beings named "Sophia" ends up generating the material order through a corrupt desire to ascend the hierarchy of being and come to know the Father.[8] As Irenaeus notes, "this passion, they say, consisted in a desire to search into the nature of the Father; for she wished, according to them, to comprehend his greatness" (*Haer.* 1.2.2). According to some accounts, because of Sophia's failed attempt and the agony and grief it produced, she brought forth a substance that was inferior and corrupt. This substance formed the material world and was summarily rejected by the Aeons in the Pleroma. Accordingly, "they declare material substance had its beginning from ignorance and grief, and fear and bewilderment" (*Haer.* 1.2.3).[9] Order was only restored when the

---

6 See *Haer.* 1.1.3. On their motivation for this proliferation, Irenaeus notes that "these Aeons having been produced for the glory of the Father, and wishing, by their own efforts, to effect this object, sent forth emanations by means of conjunction" (*Haer.* 1.1.2).

7 Irenaeus notes that Monogenes "alone took pleasure in contemplating the Father, and exulting in considering his immeasurable greatness; while he also meditated on how he might communicate to the rest of the Aeons the greatness of the Father, revealing to them how vast and mighty he was, and how he was without beginning—beyond comprehension and altogether incapable of being seen." However, he was restrained (by Sige) because though this was impossible, Monogenes still intended "to lead them all to an acquaintance with the aforesaid Propator and to create within them a desire of investigating his nature" (*Haer.* 1.2.1).

8 Irenaeus summarizes: "But there rushed forth in advance of the rest that Aeon who was much the latest of them... namely Sophia, and suffered passion apart from the embrace of her consort Theletos. This passion, indeed, first arose among those who were connected with Nous and Aletheia, but passed by contagion to this degenerate Aeon, who acted under a pretense of love, but was in reality influenced by temerity, because she had not, like Nous, enjoyed communion with the perfect Father" (*Haer.* 1.2.2).

9 Irenaeus expands on this notion in 1.4.2: "This collection of passions they declare was

material world was placed outside the Pleroma and Sophia put away her desire to know the Father.

Once this restoration occurred, Monogenes then generated a pair of Aeons named Christ and the Holy Spirit. Their roles were to prevent any other divine beings from making the corrupted mistake that Sophia did. Christ's role was to teach and mediate to the other Aeons knowledge about the Father: "that he cannot be understood or comprehended, nor so much as be seen or heard, except insofar as he is known by Monogenes only" (*Haer.* 1.2.5). The Spirit then "taught them to be thankful that they had all been rendered equal among themselves. The Spirit thus led them to a state of true repose" (*Haer.* 1.2.6). The group of beings in the Pleroma were then in a state of order and satisfaction (among themselves and in relation to the incomprehensible Father).

This version of the creation account ends with the origin story of Jesus. Because Christ and the Spirit had led the entire Pleroma to a stable place, they were able to sing "praises with great joy to the Propator." Accordingly, "out of gratitude for the great benefit which had been conferred on them, the whole Pleroma of Aeons, with one design and desire, and with the concurrence of Christ and the Holy Spirit, their Father also setting the seal of his approval on their conduct, brought together whatever each one had in himself of the greatest beauty and preciousness." They united all of these contributions in order to "skillfully blend the whole" and produce "to the honor and glory of Bythus, a being of most perfect beauty, the very star of the Pleroma, and the perfect fruit of it, namely, Jesus" (*Haer.* 1.2.6). Irenaeus notes that they also refer to Jesus as "savior," "Christ," and "logos, and Everything, because he was formed from the contributions of all" (*Haer.* 1.2.6).[10]

Thus, as Irenaeus recounts, the gnostic system envisions the creation of the world as a byproduct of conflict and corrupt desire and views the generation of Jesus as a composition of many parts drawn from a complex hierarchy of beings.[11]

---

the substance of the matter from which this world was formed. For from here desire of returning to him who gave her life, every soul belonging to this world and that of the Demiurge himself, derived its origin. All other things owed their beginning to her terror and sorrow. For from her tears all that is of a liquid nature was formed; from her smile all that is lucent; and from her grief and perplexity all the corporeal elements of the world." Cf. *Haer.* 1.5.4–5.

10 The final part of this account describes how angels with a similar substance as Jesus were also produced in order to function as his bodyguards.

11 In this particular account, Jesus's nature as a composite confluence of celestial components provides a clear foil for Irenaeus's discussion of divine simplicity. See *Haer.* 2.13.3. There, in the midst of a broader discussion, Irenaeus affirms that God "is a simple, uncompounded being, without diverse members and altogether like and equal to himself, since he is wholly understanding, and wholly spirit, and wholly thought, and wholly intelligence, and wholly

Their System Separated God from Humanity and the Material World

One direct implication of this account of the creation of the world is that God (here the "Father" or Propator) is not able to have contact or interact with the material world. For humans and the material world, any contact with the divine required the imperfect mediation of divine and semi-divine beings. Humanity and the natural world are located outside of the Pleroma and remain completely inaccessible from the ultimate and incomprehensible deity. One iteration of this creational myth told that Sophia (or Achamoth) brought about a semi-divine being called the Demiurge who became the creator of everything outside of the Pleroma (i.e., the material world). Sophia herself, though, kept herself hidden from the Demiurge, leaving the Demiurge *to think* that he was the creator of everything in existence and the most powerful of beings in the world.[12]

Regarding this scenario, Irenaeus notes that they say that the Demiurge "imagined that he created all these things of himself, while in reality he made them in conjunction with the productive power of Achamoth." Accordingly, "He formed the heavens, yet was ignorant of the heavens; he fashioned man, yet did not know man; he brought light to the earth, yet had no acquaintance with the earth." They thus declared that "he was ignorant of the forms of all that he made, and did not even know of the existence of his own mother, but imagined that he himself was all things" (*Haer.* 1.5.3). On this account, too, he was "incapable of recognizing any spiritual essences" and therefore "imagined himself to be God alone and declared through the prophets, 'I Am God, and beside me there is no one else'" (*Haer.* 1.5.4).

As the "framer" of all things, the Demiurge created seven heavens and then made his dwelling place above these heavens.[13] From this position below, being ignorant of the higher Pleroma and separated from the earth by a series of heavens, the Demiurge also created "the earthy part of man, not taking him from this dry earth, but from an invisible substance ... and then afterwards breathed into him the animal part of his nature." This component of mankind is what was created "after his image and likeness." "After all this," Irenaeus continues, they say that man was "enveloped all around with a covering

---

reason, and wholly hearing, and wholly seeing, and wholly light, and the whole source of all that is good—even as the religious and pious tend to speak concerning God."

12 See this account in *Haer.* 1.5.1–6. "They affirm, therefore, that [the Demiurge] was made to be the Father and God of everything outside of the Pleroma, being the creator of all animal and material substances" (1.5.2).

13 Some also considered these heavens as "heavenly beings" that were a kind of angelic being (1.5.2).

of skin; by which they mean the outward sensitive flesh" (*Haer.* 1.5.6). The Demiurge only created the physical or "fleshly" part of humanity. Without his knowledge, Sophia is actually the one who implanted the "spiritual" part of mankind into the Demiurge's creation. It came to pass, therefore, that "without any knowledge of the part of the Demiurge, the man formed by his inspiration was at the same time, through an unspeakable providence, rendered a spiritual man by the simultaneous inspiration received from Sophia" (*Haer.* 1.5.6).[14]

Salvation for humankind, then, means something like redemption from the material substance with which they were formed. The "consummation of all things" will take place when "all that is spiritual has been formed and perfected by Gnosis (knowledge)." By this, Irenaeus notes, "they mean spiritual men who have attained to the perfect knowledge of God" and have been "initiated into these mysteries by Achamoth" (*Haer.* 1.6.1). Those who have not attained this higher plane of human existence are those of "animal substance" who are "established by their works" and by "a mere faith, while they do not have perfect knowledge." Those in the Christian church are those persons, and for these people "good works are necessary" for salvation. Conversely, those who have received the gnostic knowledge will be "entirely and undoubtedly saved, not by means of conduct, but because they are spiritual by nature" (*Haer.* 1.6.2). The division present between creator and creation thus also creates a division between different groups of created human beings.

Their Saving Knowledge Was Secret and Selective

From the perspective of these teachers, this secret knowledge was the path to freedom from this evil material world and also something known only to a select group of spiritual people. They described the revelation of the 30 Aeons, for example, "as being wrapped up, so to speak, in silence and known to none except these professing teachers" (*Haer.* 1.1.3). More directly, Irenaeus comments, "they tell us ... that this knowledge has not been openly divulged, because all are not capable of receiving it, but has been mystically revealed by the savior through means of parables to those qualified for understanding it" (*Haer.* 1.3.1). Truly restored human beings are those who possess the "gnosis" from Sophia herself, and as Irenaeus observes, "they represent themselves to be these persons" (*Haer.* 1.6.1). By strong contrast, Irenaeus will frequently

---

14 Irenaeus summarizes this mythological account of the creation of mankind: "This, then, is the kind of man whom they conceive of: he has his animal soul from the Demiurge, his body from the earth, his fleshy part from matter, and his spiritual man from the mother Achamoth" (1.5.6).

underline throughout all five books of *Against Heresies* that "the doctrine of the apostles is open and steadfast, holding nothing in reserve; nor did they teach one set of doctrines in private and another in public" (*Haer.* 3.15.1).

Their Teachers Were Deceptive and Destructive

Part of the allure of these teachers was their secrecy. This secrecy in turn convinced some to pay for access to this new knowledge. As Irenaeus comments, "they have good reason, as seems to me, why they should not feel inclined to teach these things to all in public, but only to those who are able to pay a high price for an acquaintance with such profound mysteries. For these doctrines are not at all similar to those of which our Lord said, 'Freely have you received, freely give.' On the contrary, they are costly and profound mysteries to be obtained only with great labor by those who are in love with falsehood" (*Haer.* 1.4.3).[15]

Irenaeus also notes that the gnostic vision of salvation shaped their ethical orientation. While most people needed to have faith and do good works, those with spiritual substance capable of receiving the elevated knowledge were free from these ethical constraints: "For, just as it is impossible that material substance should partake of salvation (since, indeed, they maintain that it is incapable of receiving it), so again it is impossible that spiritual substance (by which they mean themselves) should ever come under the power of corruption, whatever the sort of actions in which they indulged" (*Haer.* 1.6.2).[16] As a result of this stance, Irenaeus observes that "the most perfect" among them "addict themselves without fear to all those kinds of forbidden deeds of which the Scriptures assure us that 'they who do such things shall not inherit the kingdom of God'" (*Haer.* 1.6.3).[17] While engaged in this behavior, they also

---

15 With sarcasm, Irenaeus continues, "For who would not expend all that he possessed, if only he might learn in return that from the tears of the enthymesis of the Aeon involved in passion, seas, and fountains, and rivers, and every liquid substance derived its origin; that light burst forth from her smile; and that from her perplexity and consternation the corporeal elements of the world had their formation?" (1.4.4). This comment sets up an instance of *reductio ad absurdum* in the subsequent section.

16 Cf. *Haer.* 1.6.2: "For even as gold, when submersed in filth, loses not on that account its beauty, but retains its own native qualities, the filth having no power to injure the gold, so they affirm that they cannot in any measure suffer hurt, or lose their spiritual substance, whatever the material actions in which they may be involved."

17 The examples Irenaeus gives here are eating food offered to idols, participation in festivals dedicated to idols, attendance at gladiatorial games, general sexual promiscuity, and specifically the seduction of those whom they are teaching. He describes and argues against similar practices throughout Books 1–2 (e.g., see his extended discussion of the "deceptive arts" and "nefarious practices" of Marcus in *Haer.* 1.13.1–7).

mock those in the Christian communities "as utterly contemptible and ignorant persons" for abstaining from these types of practices (*Haer.* 1.6.4).

Other teachings of a similar kind involve active angelic influence on every corrupt action. As Irenaeus notes, some maintain that an angel "attends them in every one of their sinful and abominable actions and urges them to venture on audacity and incur pollution. Whatever the action, they declare that they do it in the name of the angel, saying 'O angel, I use your work; O power, I accomplish your operation!' And they maintain that this is 'perfect knowledge' without shrinking to rush into such actions as it is not lawful even to name" (*Haer.* 1.31.2).[18]

Response: The Safety and Stability of the Rule of Faith

After outlining and describing some versions of the false teaching he was facing, Irenaeus provides several ways of responding to these theological and textual challenges. Just as chapters 1–7 of Book 1 introduce the nature of the false teaching and show its danger and diversity, chapters 8–11 introduce the main types of counter-arguments Irenaeus will pursue in the remainder of his larger work.

The Order and Connection of the Scriptures is Discernible and Able to Guide Readers

One of the most significant ways Irenaeus pushes back against the false teaching he faces is to argue that there is an *order* and *connection* in the words and larger context of biblical texts that is discernable and sufficiently clear to guide readers. By drawing on the textual shape and broader scope of the scriptural collections, Irenaeus is able to respond roundly to the many different forms of false teaching and the theological systems that undergird them. He notes:

> Such, then, is their system, which neither the prophets announced, nor the Lord taught, nor the apostles delivered, but of which they boast that beyond all others they have a perfect knowledge. They gather their views from sources other than the Scriptures; and, to use a common proverb, they strive to weave ropes of sand while they endeavor to adapt with an air of probability to their own peculiar assertions the parables

---

18 Irenaeus notes here that this angelology was a feature of assertions about "Hystera" and was similar to the teachings of Carpocrates.

of the Lord, the sayings of the prophets, and the words of the apostles, in order that their scheme may not seem altogether without support. In doing so, however, they disregard the order and the connection of the Scriptures, and so far as in them lies, dismember and destroy the truth. By transferring passages and dressing them up anew and making one thing out of another, they succeed in deluding many through their wicked art in adapting the oracles of the Lord to their opinions. Their manner of acting is just as if one, when a beautiful image of a king has been constructed by some skillful artist out of precious jewels, should then take this likeness of the man all to pieces, should rearrange the gems and so fit them together as to make them into the form of a dog or of a fox, and even that but poorly executed; and should then maintain and declare that this was the beautiful image of the king which the skillful artist constructed, pointing to the jewels which had been admirably fitted together by the first artist to form the image of the king, but have been with bad effect transferred by the latter one to the shape of a dog; and by thus exhibiting the jewels, should deceive the ignorant who had no conception of what a king's form was like and persuade them that this miserable likeness of the fox was in fact the beautiful image of the king. In like manner do these persons patch together old wives' fables and then endeavor to adapt the oracles of God to their baseless fictions by violently drawing away words, expressions, and parables wherever they might be found from their proper connection. We have already stated how far they proceed in this way with respect to the interior of the Pleroma.

After this reflection on the shape and guidance of biblical texts and the broader context of the Scriptures, Irenaeus gives an extended exegetical example to illustrate the weakness of the false teachers' interpretive framework. In the earliest churches, the opening passage of John's Gospel played an important role (John 1:1–18). The gnostic theologians argued that these words supported their understanding of how the universe began by the multiplication of celestial beings (the Aeons).

Irenaeus recounts their claim that "John, the disciple of the Lord, wishing to set forth the origin of all things, so as to explain how the Father produced the whole, lays down a certain principle—that which was first-begotten by God, which being he has termed both the only-begotten Son and God, in whom the Father, after a seminal manner, brought forth all things. By him the Word was produced, and in him the whole substance of the Aeons, to which the Word himself afterwards imparted form" (*Haer.* 1.8.5). As they continue in this passage, the gnostic interpreter argues that each new key word in the passage is the production of a new celestial Aeon (e.g., God, "the beginning," Word, "life," "man," "church," etc.). Irenaeus summarizes this exegetical method (which he ascribes to a teacher named Ptolemaeus): John here "distinctly set forth the first Tetrad, when he speaks of the Father, and Charis, and Monogenes, and Aletheia. In this way, too, John tells of the first Ogdoad, and that which is the mother of all the Aeons. For he mentions the Father, and Charis, and Monogenes, and Aletheia, and Logos, and Zoe, and Anthropos, and Ecclesia" (*Haer.* 1.8.5).

Irenaeus responds to this way of reading John's prologue by appealing to the wording of the text and intention of the author. He writes, "You see, my friend, the method which these men use to deceive themselves, while they abuse the Scripture by endeavoring to support their own system out of them. For this reason, I have brought forward their modes of expressing themselves so that you might understand the deceitfulness of their procedure and the wickedness of their error" (*Haer.* 1.9.1). He first clarifies the wording of the pivotal text ("But what John really does say is this") and then corrects the exegetical errors in turn.

He states directly that "in the first place, if it had been John's intention to set forth that Ogdoad above, he would surely have preserved the order of its production and would doubtless have placed the primary Tetrad first, as being according to them, the most venerable. He would then have annexed the second so that by the sequence of the names, the order of the Ogdoad might be exhibited." In the next place, Irenaeus continues, "If he had meant to indicate their conjunctions, he certainly would not have omitted the name of Ecclesia . . . or if he enumerated the conjunctions of the rest, he would also have announced the spouse of Anthropos and would not have left us to find out her name by divination" (*Haer.* 1.9.1).

After addressing the surface-level incoherence of this reading, Irenaeus then provides a constructive interaction with this passage:

> The fallacy of this exposition is therefore made plain. For when John, proclaiming one God, the almighty, and one Jesus Christ, the only-begotten, by whom all things were made, declares that this was the Son of God, this the only-begotten, this the former of all things, this the true Light who enlightens every man, this the creator of the world, this he that came to his own, this he that became flesh and dwelt among us—these men, by a plausible kind of exposition, perverting these statements, maintain that there was another Monogenes, according to production, whom they

also style Arche. They also maintain that there was another savior and another logos, the son of Monogenes, and another Christ produced for the re-establishment of the Pleroma. Thus it is that by wresting from the truth every one of the expressions which have been cited and taking a bad advantage of the names, they have transferred them to their own system; so that, according to them, in all these terms John makes no mention of the Lord Jesus Christ. For if he has named the Father, and Charis, and Monogenes, and Aletheia, and Logos, and Zoe, and Anthropos, and Ecclesia, according to their hypothesis, he has by thus speaking referred to the primary ogdoad, in which there was as yet no Jesus and no Christ the teacher of John.

But that the apostle did not speak concerning their conjunctions but concerning our Lord Jesus Christ whom he also acknowledges as the Word of God, he himself has made evident. For, summing up his statements respecting the Word previously mentioned by him, he further declares, "And the Word was made flesh, and dwelt among us." But, according to their hypothesis, the Word did not become flesh at all, inasmuch as he never went outside of the Pleroma, but that savior became flesh who was formed by a special dispensation out of all the Aeons and was of later date than the Word. Learn then, you foolish men, that Jesus who suffered for us and who dwelt among us is himself the Word of God. For if any of the other Aeons had become flesh for our salvation, it would have been probable that the apostle spoke of another. But if the Word of the Father who descended is the same that also ascended, he, namely, the only-begotten Son of the only God, who, according to the good pleasure of the Father, became flesh for the sake of men, the apostle certainly does not speak regarding any other or concerning any ogdoad, but regarding our Lord Jesus Christ. For, according to them, the Word did not originally become flesh. For they maintain that the savior assumed an animal body, formed in accordance with a special dispensation by an unspeakable providence, so that he became visible and palpable. But flesh is that which was formed long ago for Adam by God out of the dust and it is this that John has declared that the Word of God became. Their primary and first-begotten ogdoad is thus brought to nothing. For, since Logos, and Monogenes, and Zoe, and Phōs, and Soter, and Christus, and the Son of God, and he who became incarnate for us, have been proved to be one and the same, the ogdoad which they have built up at once falls to pieces. And when this is destroyed, their whole system sinks into ruin—a system which they falsely dream into existence and thus inflict injury on the Scriptures while they build up their own hypothesis. (*Haer.* 1.9.2–3)

After this specific example from John 1:1–18, Irenaeus provides a hermeneutical reflection on the function of a "hypothesis" when reading the Scriptures. In chapter 8, Irenaeus spoke of a mosaic that helped a reader make sense of a biblical text. Here he draws a concept from literary and rhetorical studies to illustrate a similar point:

> Then, again, collecting a set of expressions and names scattered here and there in Scripture, they twist them, as we have already said, from a natural to a non-natural sense. In so doing, they act like those who bring forward any kind of hypothesis they fancy and then endeavor to support them out of the poems of Homer, so that the ignorant imagine that Homer actually composed the verses bearing upon that hypothesis, which has in fact been newly constructed. And many others are led astray by the seemingly natural sequence of the verses, so much so that they think Homer might have actually composed them. This kind of tactic is illustrated in the following sequence of sentences (and there can be no objection to this illustration because the gnostic teachers do something similar). This passage uses these Homeric verses to describe Hercules as having been sent by Eurystheus to the dog in the infernal regions:
> "Thus saying, there sent forth from his house deeply groaning." (*Od.* 10.76)
> "The hero Hercules conversant with mighty deeds." (*Od.* 21.26)
> "Eurystheus, the son of Sthenelus, descended from Perseus." (*Il.* 19.123)
> "That he might bring from Erebus the dog of gloomy Pluto." (*Il.* 8.368)
> "And he advanced like a mountain-bred lion confident of strength." (*Od.* 6.130)
> "Rapidly through the city, while all his friends followed." (*Il.* 24.327)
> "Both maidens, and youths, and much-enduring old men." (*Od.* 11.38)
> "Mourning for him bitterly as one going forward to death." (*Il.* 24.328)
> "But Mercury and the blue-eyed Minerva conducted him." (*Od.* 11.626)
> "For she knew the mind of her brother, how it labored with grief." (*Il.* 2.409)
> Now, what simple-minded person, I ask, would not be fooled by such verses as these to think that Homer actually framed them in this way with reference to the subject indicated? But he who is acquainted with the Homeric writings will recognize the verses indeed, but not the subject to which

they are applied, because he knows that some of them were spoken of Ulysses, others of Hercules himself, others still of Priam, and others again of Menelaus and Agamemnon. But if he takes them and restores each of them to its proper position, he at once destroys the narrative in question. In like manner, he who retains the rule of truth unchangeable in his heart which he received by means of baptism will doubtless recognize the names, the expressions, and the parables taken from the Scriptures but will by no means acknowledge the blasphemous use which these men make of them. For, though he will acknowledge the gems, he will certainly not receive the fox instead of the likeness of the king. But when he has restored every one of the expressions quoted to its proper position and has fitted it to the body of truth, he will lay bare and prove the figment of these heretics to be without any foundation. (*Haer.* 1.9.4)

The Rule of Faith Secures the Unity of the Testaments and the Unity of the Churches

Another key element of Irenaeus's response is to argue that the "rule of faith" is a characteristic feature of the preaching and teaching of the churches that is lacking among the gnostic groups. Irenaeus asserts that anyone who "follows out their farce to the end" will see "in what respects the very fathers of this fable differ among themselves, as if they were inspired by different spirits of error." For Irenaeus, "this very fact forms a logical proof that the truth proclaimed by the church is immoveable and that the theories of these men are but a tissue of falsehoods" (*Haer.* 1.9.5).

Irenaeus then provides an articulation of this rule of faith that guides the reading of Scripture and the preaching of the gospel among the churches:

> The church, though dispersed throughout the whole world, even to the ends of the earth, has received from the apostles and their disciples this faith: she believes in one God, the Father almighty, maker of heaven and earth and the sea and all things that are in them; and in one Christ Jesus, the Son of God, who became incarnate for our salvation; and in the Holy Spirit, who proclaimed through the prophets the dispensations of God, and the advents, and the birth from a virgin, and the passion, and the resurrection from the dead, and the ascension into heaven in the flesh of the beloved Christ Jesus, our Lord, and his future manifestation from heaven in the glory of the Father "to gather all things in one" (Eph 1:10), and to raise up anew all flesh of the whole human race in order that to Christ

Jesus our Lord and God and savior and king, according to the will of the invisible Father, "every knee should bow, of things in heaven, and things in earth, and things under the earth, and that every tongue should confess" to him (Phil 2:10–11), and that he should execute just judgment toward all; that he may send "spiritual wickedness" (Eph 6:12), and the angels who transgressed and became apostates, together with the ungodly and unrighteous and wicked and profane among men into everlasting fire; but may, in the exercise of his grace confer immortality on the righteous and holy and those who have kept his commandments and have persevered in his love, some from the beginning of their Christian course and others from the date of their repentance, and may surround them with everlasting glory.

As I have already observed, the church, having received this preaching and this faith, although scattered throughout the whole world, yet, as if occupying but one house, carefully preserves it. She also believes these points of doctrine just as if she had but one soul and one and the same heart, and she proclaims them, and teaches them, and hands them down with perfect harmony as if she possessed only one mouth. For, although the languages of the world are different, yet the import of the tradition is one and the same. For the churches which have been planted in Germany do not believe or hand down anything different, nor do those in Spain, nor those in Gaul, nor those in the East, nor those in Egypt, nor those in Libya, nor those which have been established in the central regions of the world. But as the sun, that creature of God, is one and the same throughout the whole world, so also the preaching of the truth shines everywhere and enlightens all men that are willing to come to a knowledge of the truth. Nor will any one of the rulers in the churches, however highly gifted he may be in point of eloquence, teach doctrines different from these (for no one is greater than the master); nor, on the other hand, will he who is deficient in power of expression inflict injury on the tradition. For the faith being ever one and the same, neither does one who is able at great length to discourse regarding it make any addition to it nor does one who can say but little diminish it.

It does not follow because men are endowed with greater and lesser degrees of intelligence that they should therefore change the subject-matter of the faith itself and should conceive of some other God besides him who is the framer, maker, and preserver of this universe (as if he were not sufficient for them), or of another Christ, or another only-begotten. But the fact referred to simply implies this, that one may more accurately than another bring out the meaning of those things which have been spoken in parables, and accommodate them to the general scheme of the faith; and explain with special clearness the operation and dispensation of God connected with human salvation; and show that God manifested longsuffering in regard to the apostasy of the angels who transgressed, as also with respect to the disobedience of men; and set forth why it is that one and the same God has made some things temporal and some eternal, some heavenly and others earthly; and understand for what reason God, though invisible, manifested himself to the prophets not under one form, but differently to different individuals; and show why it was that more covenants than one were given to mankind; and teach what was the special character of each of these covenants; and search out for what reason "God has consigned all to unbelief, that he may have mercy upon all" (Rom 11:32); and gratefully describe on what account the Word of God became flesh and suffered; and relate why the advent of the Son of God took place in these last times, that is, in the end, rather than in the beginning of the world; and unfold what is contained in the Scriptures concerning the end itself, and things to come; and not be silent as to how it is that God has made the gentiles, whose salvation was despaired of, fellow-heirs and of the same body and partakers with the saints; and discourse how it is that "this mortal body shall put on immortality, and this corruptible shall put on incorruption" (1 Cor 15:54); and proclaim in what sense God says, "That is a people who was not a people; and she is beloved who was not beloved" (Rom 9:25; Hos 2:23); and in what sense he says that "more are the children of her that was desolate, than of her who possessed a husband" (Isa 54:1). For in reference to these points, and others of a like nature, the apostle exclaims: "Oh! the depth of the riches both of the wisdom and knowledge of God; how unsearchable are his judgments, and his ways past finding out!" (Rom 11:33). But the superior skill spoken of is not found in this, that any one should, beyond the creator and framer of the world, conceive of the enthymesis of an erring Aeon, their mother and his, and should thus enter such a state of blasphemy; nor does it consist in this, that he should again falsely imagine, as being above this fancied being, a Pleroma at one time supposed to contain thirty, and at another time an innumerable tribe of Aeons, as these teachers who are destitute of truly divine wisdom maintain; while the catholic church possesses one and the same faith throughout the whole world, as we have already said. (*Haer.* 1.10.1–3)

At strategic places throughout Books 1–2, Irenaeus repeats aspects of this full confession of faith. For instance, before he begins responding again to heretical teachings in Book 2, Irenaeus makes this assertion:

> It is proper, then, that I should begin with the first and most important subject, that is, God the creator who made the heaven and the earth and all things that are found in this place (whom these men blasphemously style the fruit of a defect), and to demonstrate that there is nothing either above him or after him; nor that, influenced by any one, but of his own free will, he created all things since he is the only God, the only Lord, the only creator, the only Father, alone containing all things, and himself commanding all things into existence. (*Haer.* 2.1.1)

The Coherence of the Rule of Faith Exposes the Incoherence of False Teaching

One final rhetorical tactic that Irenaeus employs in his critique of the gnostic teaching is that he seeks to reduce their arguments to absurdity (*reductio ad absurdum*). He gives two central reasons why this teaching is incoherent: first, because different teachers have diverse versions of these core claims, and second, because the teachings themselves are either contradictory or mutually exclusive of one another. In this vein, Irenaeus says, "Let us now look at the inconsistent opinions of those heretics (for there are some two or three of them), how they do not agree in treating the same points, but alike, in things and names set forth opinions that are mutually discordant" (*Haer.* 1.11.1).

Some key elements are shared among these teachers (such as the multiplication of celestial beings called Aeons and the basic corruption of the material world), while the logistical details of how this works out and how it relates to biblical texts oftentimes differs (among themselves and also within a single individual's teaching).[19] Irenaeus notes first that Valentinus had "adapted the principles of the heresy called "Gnostic" to the peculiar character of his own school" (*Haer.* 1.11.1). Another teacher named Secundus agreed with Valentinus about the duality of a "right hand power" and a "left hand power" that was part of the ogdoad, but departs from him by arguing that "the power which separated from the rest, and fell away, did not proceed directly from the thirty Aeons, but from their fruits" (*Haer.* 1.11.2). Still another teacher

---

19 For example, Irenaeus notes that Valentinus sometimes "maintains that Jesus was produced from him who was separated from their mother, and united to the rest, that is, from Theletus, sometimes as springing from him who returned into the Pleroma, that is, from Christ; and at other times still as derived from Anthropos and Ecclesia" (*Haer.* 1.11.1).

who was "renowned among them" and was "struggling to reach something more sublime and to attain to a kind of higher knowledge" posited an invisible and incomprehensible entity that preceded all previously known beings (*Haer.* 1.11.3).

In light of how these speculations continued to expand and complexify with each new teacher, Irenaeus gives an extended mock response as a parody of this type of thought:

> Iu, Iu! Pheu, Pheu!—for we may well utter these tragic exclamations at such a pitch of audacity in the coining of names as he has displayed without a blush, in devising a nomenclature for his system of falsehood. For when he declares: there is a certain Proarche before all things, surpassing all thought, whom I call Monotes; and again, with this Monotes there co-exists a power which I also call Henotes—it is most manifest that he confesses the things which have been said to be his own invention and that he himself has given names to his scheme of things which had never been previously suggested by any other. It is manifest also that he himself is the one who has had sufficient audacity to coin these names; so that, unless he had appeared in the world, the truth would still have been destitute of a name. But, in that case, nothing hinders any other in dealing with the same subject to affix names after such a fashion as the following: there is a certain Proarche, royal, surpassing all thought, a power existing before every other substance, and extended into space in every direction. But along with it there exists a power which I term a Gourd; and along with this Gourd there exists a power which again I term Utter-Emptiness. This Gourd and Emptiness, since they are one, produced (and yet did not simply produce, so as to be apart from themselves) a fruit, everywhere visible, eatable, and delicious, which fruit-language calls a Cucumber. Along with this Cucumber exists a power of the same essence, which again I call a Melon. These powers, the Gourd, Utter-Emptiness, the Cucumber, and the Melon, brought forth the remaining multitude of the delirious melons of Valentinus. For if it is fitting that that language which is used respecting the universe be transformed to the primary Tetrad, and if anyone may assign names at his pleasure, who shall prevent us from adopting these names, as being much more credible than the others, as well as in general use, and understood by all? (*Haer.* 1.11.4)

Irenaeus occasionally uses this type of sarcasm at strategic points to illustrate that in his view the opinions of the gnostic teachers sometimes seem particularly extreme and are often at odds with one another.[20]

Detail and Development in the Flow of Books 1–2

These are the main lines of response that Irenaeus employs as he critically evaluates various forms of gnostic teaching and the texts and teachers of other heretical positions. In the sprawling interactions in Books 1–2, Irenaeus both drills down into the details of a position or he backs up and shows the development of a given theological assertion over time or within a specific set of theological commitments. Throughout these two lengthy sections, Irenaeus often utilizes one or more of the hermeneutical and theological responses he provides in chapters 8–11 of Book 1.

For example, the followers of a teacher named Ptolemy held that the ultimate being "first conceived the thought of producing something, and then willed to that effect." This conception and will were then thought to be separate beings that had to act together or in sequence for divine activity to occur. Irenaeus quickly contrasts this with the scriptural portrayal of God's action. "These fancied beings," Irenaeus notes, "will not appear to you, my dear friend, to be possessed of greater knowledge than he who is the God of the universe. He, as soon as he thinks, also performs what he has willed; and as soon as he wills, also thinks that which he has willed; then thinking when he wills, and then willing when he thinks, since he is all thought, all will, all mind, all light, all eye, all ear, the one entire fountain of all good things" (*Haer.* 1.12.1–2).[21] Rather than provide an extended response in cases like this one,

---

20 For example, immediately after his extended illustration in 1.11.4, Irenaeus catalogues the many different names given to the first grouping of Aeons in their system (e.g., Proarche, Anennoetos, Arrhetos, Aoratos, etc). The motivation for innovating new titles was to appear to be in possession of superior knowledge of the system: "They maintain that these powers were anterior to Bythus and Sige, that they may appear more perfect than the perfect, and more knowing than the very Gnostics! To these persons one may justly exclaim: 'O you trifling sophists!' since, even respecting Bythus himself, there are among them many and discordant opinions." These differentiations continue even to the minute anatomical details of these beings: "For some declare him to be without a consort, and neither male nor female, and, in fact, nothing at all; while others affirm him to be masculo-feminine ... others, again, name Sige as a spouse, that thus may be formed the first conjunction" (1.11.5). Cf. 1.4.4, where Irenaeus makes a similar extended rhetorical move ("I feel somewhat inclined myself to contribute a few hints toward the development of their system").

21 Irenaeus associates the gnostic notion with the Greco-Roman pantheon ("like the Jove of Homer, who is represented as passing an anxious sleepless night in devising plans for honoring Achilles and destroying numbers of Greeks"). The God of Scripture, conversely, has no anxiety and does not require uncertain deliberation in order to act.

Refuting Falsehood with the Rule of Faith

Irenaeus draws upon the textual and theological framework of the rule of faith to provide either the contrast or the refutation.

In other places, Irenaeus blends theological analysis, biblical exegesis, and pastoral reflection as he refutes a particular teaching. In response to the notion that God needed angels and intermediaries to create the world, Irenaeus puts forth the textual and theological reasons why this position is deeply incorrect:

> This manner of speech may perhaps be plausible or persuasive to those who do not know God and who compare him to needy human beings and to those who cannot produce what they intend immediately and without assistance from anything but require many external means. But it will not be regarded as at all probable by those who know that God stands in need of nothing and that he created and made all things by his Word, while he neither required angels to assist him in the production of those things which are made nor of any power greatly inferior to himself and ignorant of the Father, nor of any defect or ignorance in order that he who should know him might become man. But he himself in himself, after a fashion which we can neither describe nor conceive, predestining all things, formed them as he pleased and bestowed harmony on all things by assigning them their own place and the beginning of their creation. In this way he conferred on spiritual things a spiritual and invisible nature, on super-celestial things a celestial nature, on angels an angelical nature, on animals an animal nature, on beings that swim a nature suited to the water, and on those that live on the land one fitted for the land—on all, in short, a nature suitable to the character of the life assigned them—while he formed all things that were made by his Word that never wearies. For this is a peculiarity of the pre-eminence of God, not to stand in need of other instruments for the creation of those things which are summoned into existence. His own Word is both suitable and sufficient for the formation of all things, even as John, the disciple of the Lord, declares regarding him, "All things were made by him, and without him was nothing made" (John 1:3). Now, among the "all things" our world must be embraced. It too, therefore, was made by his Word as Scripture tells us in the book of Genesis that he made all things connected with our world by his Word. David also expresses the same truth when he says, "For he spoke, and they were made; he commanded, and they were created" (Ps 33:9). Therefore, whom shall we believe regarding the creation of the world—these heretics who have been mentioned that speak so foolishly and inconsistently

on the subject, or the disciples of the Lord, and Moses who was both a faithful servant of God and a prophet? He at first narrated the formation of the world in these words, "In the beginning God created the heaven and the earth" (Gen 1:1), and all other things in succession; but neither gods nor angels had any share in the work.

Now, that this God is the Father of our Lord Jesus Christ, Paul the apostle also has declared, saying, "There is one God, the Father, who is above all, and through all things, and in us all" (Eph 4:6). I have indeed proved already that there is only one God; but I shall further demonstrate this from the apostles themselves and from the words of the Lord. For what sort of conduct would it be, were we to forsake the utterances of the prophets, of the Lord, and of the apostles, that we might give heed to these persons, who speak not a word of sense? (*Haer.* 2.2.4–5)

At the end of his major sections, Irenaeus strategically summarizes some of his goals in writing Books 1–2. As he concludes Book 1, Irenaeus returns to themes that begin this work:

It was necessary clearly to prove that as their very opinions and regulations exhibit them, those who are of the school of Valentinus derive their origin from such mothers, fathers, and ancestors, and also to bring forward their doctrines with the hope that some of them may perhaps obtain salvation by exercising repentance and returning to the only creator and God, the former of the universe; and that from this time onward others may not be drawn away by their plausible but also wicked persuasions, imagining that they will obtain from them the knowledge of some greater and more sublime mysteries. But let them rather, learning to good effect from us the wicked tenets of these men, look with contempt upon their doctrines. While at the same time, let them pity those who, still cleaving to these miserable and baseless fables, have reached such a pitch of arrogance as to reckon themselves superior to all others on account of such knowledge, or as it should rather be called, ignorance. They have now been fully exposed; and simply to exhibit their sentiments is to obtain a victory over them.

For this reason, I have labored to bring forward and make clearly manifest the utterly ill-conditioned carcass of this miserable little fox. For many words will no longer be needed to overturn their system of doctrine when it has been made manifest to all. It is like when there is a beast hiding itself in a wooded area whose habit is to rush forth from this place and destroy multitudes. If one beats around the wooded area and thoroughly explores it in order to compel the animal to break cover, he does not strive to capture it because he sees that it is truly a ferocious beast; but those who are present can then watch and avoid its assaults and can cast darts at it from all sides, wound it, and finally slay that destructive brute. So, in our case, since we have brought to light their hidden mysteries which they keep in silence among themselves, it will no longer be necessary to use many words in destroying their system of opinions.

For it is now in your power and in the power of all your associates to familiarize yourselves with what has been said, to overthrow their wicked and undigested doctrines, and to set forth doctrines that are agreeable to the truth. Since this is the case, I shall, according to my promise and as my ability serves, labor to overthrow them by refuting them all in the following book. Even to give an account of them is a tedious affair, as you can see. But I shall furnish means for overthrowing them by meeting all their opinions in the order in which they have been described so that I may not only expose the wild beast to view, but may inflict wounds upon it from every side. (*Haer.* 1.31.3–4)

Accordingly, in the opening of Book 2, Irenaeus summarizes what he sought to accomplish in the lengthy catalogue of views in Book 1 and previews his plan to interact with the exegetical support used for these views in Book 2. He also briefly articulates the rule of truth that he introduces in Book 1.

In the first book, which immediately precedes this, exposing "knowledge falsely so called," I showed you, my very dear friend, that the whole system devised by those who are of the school of Valentinus in many and opposite ways was false and baseless. I also set forth the tenets of their predecessors, proving that they not only differed among themselves, but had long ago swerved from the truth itself. I further explained, with all diligence, the doctrine as well as the practice of Marcus the magician, since he, too, belongs to these persons; and I carefully noticed the passages which they garble from the Scriptures in order to adapt them to their own fictions. Moreover, I minutely narrated the manner in which, by means of numbers and by the 24 letters of the alphabet they boldly endeavor to establish what they regard as truth. I have also related how they think and teach that creation at large was formed after the image of their invisible Pleroma and what they believe about the Demiurge, declaring at the same time the doctrine of Simon Magus of

Samaria as their intellectual father and of all those who succeeded him. I mentioned, too, the multitude of those Gnostics that flow from him and noticed the points of difference between them, their several doctrines, and the order of their succession, while I set forth all those heresies which they have originated. I showed, moreover, that all these heretics, taking their rise from Simon, have introduced impious and irreligious doctrines into this life; and I explained the nature of their "redemption" and their method of initiating those who are rendered "perfect" along with their invocations and their mysteries. I proved also that there is one God, the creator, and that he is not the fruit of any defect nor is there anything either above him or after him. In the present book, I shall establish those points which fit in with my design insofar as time permits and overthrow their whole system by means of lengthened treatment under distinct subjects. For this reason, since it is an exposure and subversion of their opinions, I have entitled the composition of this work the way in which I have. For it is fitting, by a plain revelation and overthrow of their conjunctions, to put an end to these hidden alliances and to Bythus himself and thus to obtain a demonstration that he never existed at any previous time nor now has any existence. (*Haer.* 2.0.1)

Finally, at the close of Book 2, Irenaeus gives a synthesis of the argument he has made in the whole of Books 1–2. This concluding sequence contains the core textual and theological moves that Irenaeus makes in his response to the false teaching and is thus an appropriate place to end the current discussion:

Now, that the preaching of the apostles, the authoritative teaching of the Lord, the announcements of the prophets, the dictated utterances of the apostles, and the ministry of the law are all in harmony with our statements, has, I think, been sufficiently proved. All of these praise one and the same being, the God and Father of all, and not many diverse beings nor one deriving his substance from different gods or powers. Instead, they declare that all things were formed by one and the same Father (who nevertheless adapts his works to the natures and tendencies of the materials dealt with), things visible and invisible. In short, they declare that all things that have been made were created neither by angels nor by any other power, but by God alone, the Father. So, by these weighty arguments it has been shown that there is only one God, the maker of all things. But that I may not be thought to avoid that series of proofs which may be derived from the Scriptures of the Lord (since, indeed, these Scriptures much more evidently and clearly proclaim this very point), I shall, for the benefit of those at least who do not bring a depraved mind to bear upon them, devote a special book to the Scriptures referred to, which shall fairly follow them out and explain them, and I shall plainly set forth from these divine Scriptures proofs to satisfy all the lovers of truth. (*Haer.* 2.35.4)

The mention of a "special book" devoted to a series of biblical texts about Christ is also likely a reference to *Demonstration*.[22]

---

[22] On this possibility, see the introduction to this volume.

3

Preaching the Gospel with the Rule of Faith

Demonstration of the Apostolic Preaching

Overview

In *Demonstration*, Irenaeus presents a constructive articulation of the basic claims of the gospel and the grand storyline of the Scriptures. In the first part (1–42), Irenaeus summarizes the central elements found in the preaching of the apostles. God created the world and rules over his creation. After humankind fell into sin, the long history of Israel involves God's providence and preparation for the coming of the savior Jesus Christ. The life, ministry, death, and resurrection of Christ fulfills the Scriptures and accomplishes the redemption of God's people. In the second part (43–100), Irenaeus insists that the entire scope of the scriptural storyline prefigures and anticipates the messianic ministry of Jesus, the Christ. This testimony demonstrates that the Christ of the Scriptures is the Jesus who became incarnate.

Part One: The Storyline of Scripture and the Preaching of the Apostles

1. My beloved Marcianus, knowing your desire to walk in godliness, which alone leads to eternal life, I rejoice with you and make it my prayer that you may preserve your faith intact and so be pleasing to God who made you. I wish that it were possible for us to be together always, to help each other and to lighten the labor of our earthly life by continual discussion of profitable things. At this present time we are away from one another in the body, yet as much as it is within my power, I will seek to speak with you briefly through writing and to make plain the preaching of the truth for the confirmation of your faith.[1] I am sending you this concise manual of theological essentials so

---

1 The phrase "to make plain" corresponds to the title of the work (ἐπίδειξις, the

that by little you may attain much, learning in a short space all the members of the body of the truth and receiving in brief the demonstration of the things of God. May it be fruitful to your own salvation, and may you put to shame all those who train others in falsehood. May you also bring with all confidence our sound and pure teaching to everyone who desires to understand it. For the way that leads upwards and is visible to everyone is one. This path is illuminated by heavenly light. But the ways of those who do not see are many. These paths are dark and contrary. This one path leads to the kingdom of heaven and unites man to God; but those many other paths bring down to death and separate man from God. For this reason, it is necessary for you and for all who care for their own salvation to make your course unswerving, firm and sure by means of faith, that you might not falter, be delayed or detained by material desires, nor turn aside and wander from the proper path.

2. Now, since man is a living being made up of soul and flesh, he must exist by both of these. And, whereas from both of them offences come, purity of the flesh is the restraining abstinence from all shameful things and all unrighteous deeds, and purity of the soul is keeping the faith toward God whole, neither adding to nor subtracting from it. For godliness is obscured and dulled by the soiling and the staining of the flesh, and is broken, polluted, and no longer whole if falsehood enters into the soul. But it will keep itself in its beauty and its measure when truth is constant in the soul and purity in the flesh. For what profit is it to know the truth in words but to pollute the flesh and perform the works of evil? Or what profit can purity of the flesh bring if truth is not in the soul? For these rejoice with one another and are united and allied to bring man face to face with God. The Holy Spirit therefore says by David, "Blessed is the man who has not walked in the counsel of the ungodly" (Ps 1:1)—that is, the counsel of the nations which do not know God, for the ungodly ones are those who do not worship the God that truly is. And therefore the Word says to Moses, "I am he that is" (Exod 3:14)—but they that do not worship the God that is, these are the ungodly. "And have not stood in the way of sinners," but sinners are those who have the knowledge of God and do not keep his commandments; that is, disdainful scorners. "And have not sat in the seat of the pestilential" (Ps 1:1), now the "pestilential" are those who by wicked and perverse doctrines corrupt not only themselves but others also.[2] For the seat is a symbol of teaching. Such then are all heretics: they sit in the

---

"demonstration" of the apostolic preaching). Behr translates it as "to demonstrate, by means of summary, the preaching of the truth."

2 The term "pestilential" here translates the word λοιμῶν from the LXX of Ps 1:1. The word means something like "plaguelike" or "contagious," and Irenaeus makes use of this word picture to describe the poison of the false teachers.

seats of the pestilential, and those who receive the venom of their doctrine are likewise corrupted.

3. In order to avoid anything of this kind, we must necessarily hold fast the rule of the faith without deviation and do the commandments of God. We must believe in God, fearing him as Lord and loving him as Father. Now this "doing" is produced by faith. For Isaiah says, "If you do not believe, neither shall you understand" (Isa 7:9). And faith is produced by the truth; for faith rests on things that truly are. For in things that are, as they are, we believe; and believing in things that are, as they ever are, we keep firm our confidence in them. Since faith is the perpetuation of our salvation, we must make every effort in the maintenance of it in order that we may have a true comprehension of the things that are. Now faith occasions this for us; even as the elders, the disciples of the apostles, have handed down to us. First of all, it bids us bear in mind that we have received baptism for the remission of sins, in the name of God the Father, and in the name of Jesus Christ, the Son of God, who was incarnate and died and rose again, and in the Holy Spirit of God. And that this baptism is the seal of eternal life, and is the new birth unto God that we should no longer be the sons of mortal men but of the eternal and perpetual God; and that the eternally existing God is over all things that are made, and all things are put under him; and all the things that are put under him are made his own; for God is not ruler and Lord over the things of another, but over his own; and all things are God's; and therefore God is almighty, and all things are of God.[3]

4. For it is necessary that things that are made should have the beginning of their making from some great cause; and the beginning of all things is God. For he himself was not made by any, and by him all things were made. And therefore it is right, first of all, to believe that there is one God, the Father, who made and fashioned all things, and made what was not that it should be, and who, containing all things, alone is uncontained. Now among all things is this world of ours, and in the world is man. So then, this world was also formed by God.

5. There is therefore one God, the Father, not made, invisible, creator of all things; above whom there is no other God, and after whom there is no other God. Since God is rational, therefore by the Word he created the things that were made.[4] And God is Spirit, and by the Spirit he adorned all things. As the

---

3 Robinson notes the difficulty of the Armenian phrasing of these last two sentences and gives a possible solution (see 73n2). The rendering here follows Behr (42).

4 Robinson notes the wordplay in this sentence: "God is λογικός, therefore by λόγος he created the world" (74n1). Cf. Behr's translation: "And as God is verbal, therefore He made created things by the Word" (43).

prophet also says, "By the word of the Lord were the heavens established, and by his spirit all their power" (Ps 33:6). Since the Word establishes, that is to say, gives body and grants the reality of being, and the Spirit gives order and form to the diversity of the powers; rightly and fittingly is the Word called the Son and the Spirit called the Wisdom of God. Rightly also does Paul his apostle say, "One God, the Father, who is over all and through all and in all" (Eph 4:6). For "over all" is the Father; and "through all" is the Son, for through him all things were made by the Father; and "in us all" is the Spirit, who cries "Abba Father" (cf. Gal 4:6) and fashions man into the likeness of God. Now the Spirit shows forth the Word, and therefore the prophets announced the Son of God; and the Word utters the Spirit, and therefore is himself the announcer of the prophets and leads and draws man to the Father.

6. This then is the order of the rule of our faith, and the foundation of the building, and the stability of our discourse: God, the Father, not made, not material, invisible; one God, the creator of all things—this is the first point of our faith. The second point is this: the Word of God, Son of God, Christ Jesus our Lord, who was manifested to the prophets according to the form of their prophesying and according to the method of the economy of the Father—through whom all things were made; who also at the end of times, to complete and gather up all things, was made man among men, visible and tangible, in order to abolish death and bring forth life and produce a community of union between God and man. And the third point is this: the Holy Spirit, through whom the prophets prophesied, the fathers learned the things of God, and the righteous were led forth into the way of righteousness; and who in the end of times was poured out in a new way upon mankind in all the earth, renewing man unto God.

7. For this reason the baptism of our regeneration proceeds through these three points: God the Father bestowing on us regeneration through his Son by the Holy Spirit. For as many as carry in them the Spirit of God are led to the Word, that is to the Son; and the Son brings them to the Father; and the Father causes them to possess incorruption. Without the Spirit it is not possible to behold the Word of God, nor without the Son can any draw near to the Father, for the knowledge of the Father is the Son, and the knowledge of the Son of God is through the Holy Spirit; and, according to the good pleasure of the Father, the Son ministers and dispenses the Spirit to whomsoever the Father wills and as he wills.

8. And by the Spirit the Father is called most high and almighty and Lord of hosts; that we may learn concerning God that it is he who is creator of heaven and earth and all the world, and maker of angels and men, and Lord of

all, through whom all things exist and by whom all things are sustained; merciful, compassionate and very tender, good, just, the God of all, both of Jews and of gentiles, and of them that believe. To them that believe he is as Father, for in the end of times he opened up the covenant of adoption; to the Jews as Lord and lawgiver, for in the intermediate times, when man forgot God and departed and revolted against him, he brought them into subjection by the law, that they might learn that they had for Lord the maker and creator, who also gives the breath of life, and whom we ought to worship day and night; and to the gentiles as maker and creator and almighty; and to all alike sustainer and nourisher and king and judge; for none shall escape and be delivered from his judgment, neither Jew nor gentile, nor believer that has sinned, nor angel. But they who now reject his goodness shall know his power in judgment, according to that which the blessed apostle says, "Not knowing that the goodness of God leads you to repentance; but according to your hardness and penitent heart you treasure up for yourself wrath in the day of wrath and of the revelation of the righteous judgment of God, who shall render to every man according to his works" (Rom 2:4–6). This is he who is called in the Law the God of Abraham, Isaac and Jacob, the God of the living; although the sublimity and greatness of this God is unspeakable.

9. Now this world is encompassed by seven heavens, in which powers, angels, and archangels dwell, doing service to God, the Almighty and maker of all things—not as though he was in need, but that they may not be idle and unprofitable and ineffectual. For this reason also, the Spirit of God is manifold in his actions.[5] In seven forms of service he is reckoned by the prophet Isaiah as resting on the Son of God, that is the Word, in his coming as man. "The Spirit of God," he says, "shall rest upon him, the Spirit of wisdom and of understanding, the Spirit of counsel and of might, the Spirit of knowledge and of godliness; the Spirit of the fear of God shall fill him" (Isa 11:2). Now the heaven which is first from above and encompasses the rest is that of wisdom; and the second from it, of understanding; and the third, of counsel; and the fourth, reckoned from above, is that of might; and the fifth, of knowledge; and the sixth, of godliness; and the seventh, this firmament of ours, is full of the fear of that Spirit which gives light to the heavens. For, as the pattern of this, Moses received the seven-branched candlestick that shined continually in the holy place; for as a pattern of the heavens he received this service, according to that which the Word spoke to him, "You shall make it according to all the pattern of the things which you have seen on the mountain" (Exod 25:40).

---

5 Robinson gives the translation here as "indwelling" but notes that this word should perhaps be rendered as "operation" (ἐνέργεια) or "action" (78n2). Behr gives this phrase as "thus the Spirit of God is active in manifold ways" (45).

10. Now this God is continually glorified by his Word who is his Son, and by the Holy Spirit who is the Wisdom of the Father of all. And the powers of these, namely of the Word and Wisdom, which are called Cherubim and Seraphim, glorify God with unceasing voices. And every created thing that is in the heavens offers glory to God the Father of all. By his Word, he has created the whole world, and in the world are the angels; and to all the world he has given laws in which each thing should abide, and according to that which is determined by God should not pass their bounds, each fulfilling his appointed task.

11. But he formed man with his own hands, taking from the earth that which was purest and finest, and mingling in measure his own power with the earth. For he traced his own form on the formation, that that which should be seen should be of divine form. For man was formed as the image of God and set on the earth. And that he might become living, he breathed on his face the breath of life; that both for the breath and for the formation man should be similar to God. Moreover, he was free and self-controlled, being made by God for this end, that he might rule all those things that were upon the earth. And this great created world, prepared by God before the formation of man, was given to man as his place, containing all things within itself. And in this place there were also with their tasks the servants of that God who formed all things; and the steward, who was set over all his fellow servants received this place. The servants were angels, and the steward was the archangel.

12. Having made man lord of the earth and all things in it, he secretly appointed him lord also of those who were servants in it. They however were in their perfection; but the lord, that is, man, was but small; for he was a child; and it was necessary that he should grow, and so come to his perfection. And, that he might have his nourishment and growth with festive and delicious meats, he prepared him a place better than this world, excelling in air, beauty, light, food, plants, fruit, water, and all other necessities of life, and its name is paradise. And so fair and good was this paradise, that the Word of God continually resorted there, and walked and talked with the man, figuring beforehand the things that should be in the future, namely, that he should dwell with him and talk with him, and should be with men, teaching them righteousness. But man was a child, not yet having his understanding perfected; for this reason also he was easily led astray by the deceiver.

13. While man dwelled in paradise, God brought before him all living things and commanded him to give names to all of them. "And whatever Adam called a living soul, that was its name" (Gen 2:9). And he determined also to make a helper for the man. For God said, "It is not good for the man to be alone, let us make for him a helper suitable for him" (Gen 2:8). For among

all the other living things there was not found a helper equal and comparable and similar to Adam. But God himself caused Adam to go into a deep sleep (Gen 2:21); and, that work might be accomplished from work, since there was no sleep in paradise, this was brought upon Adam by the will of God; and God "took one of Adam's ribs and filled up the flesh in its place, and the rib which he took he fashioned into a woman; and so he brought her to Adam" (Gen 2:21–22); and seeing her, he said, "this is now bone of my bone, flesh of my flesh. She shall be called woman, because she was taken from her husband" (Gen 2:23).

14. And Adam and Eve (for that is the name of the woman) "were naked and were not ashamed" (Gen 2:25). For there was in them an innocent and childlike mind, and it was not possible for them to conceive and understand anything of that which is born in the soul by wickedness through lusts and shameful desires. For they were at that time whole, preserving their own nature; since they had the breath of life which was breathed on their creation. And, while this breath remains in its place and power, it has no comprehension and understanding of things that are debased. And therefore they were not ashamed, kissing and embracing each other in purity after the manner of children.

15. But, in order that man might not entertain thoughts of grandeur nor exalt himself, as though he had no lord due to the authority and freedom that had been granted to him, and by doing so transgress against God his maker, overstep his measure, and selfishly contemplate prideful opposition to God, a law was given to him so that he might perceive that he had as lord the Lord of all. And God set for him certain limitations, so that if he should keep the commandment of God, he should ever remain such as he was, that is to say, immortal; but, if he should not keep it, he should become mortal and be dissolved back into the earth, the very place from which his formation had been taken. Now the commandment was this, "Of every tree that is in the paradise you shall freely eat; but of that tree alone from which is the knowledge of good and evil, of it you shall not eat; for in the day you eat, you shall surely die" (Gen 2:16–17).

16. The man did not keep this commandment but was disobedient to God. In this he was led astray by the angel who was envious and jealous because of the great gifts that God had given to mankind. This angel both brought himself to nothing and also made man sinful by persuading him to disobey the commandment of God. Due to his falsehood, the angel became the author and originator of sin and was himself struck down because he had offended God. And he caused man to be cast out from paradise. Because through the

guidance of his disposition he apostatized and departed from God, he was called Satan, according to the Hebrew word; that is, apostate; but he is also called slanderer. Now God cursed the serpent which carried and conveyed the slanderer; and this curse came on the beast himself and on the angel hidden and concealed in him, even on Satan; and he put away man from his presence, removing him and then making him dwell on the path to paradise, because paradise does not receive the sinful.

17. And when they were put out of paradise, Adam and his wife Eve encountered many troubles of anxious grief, and they went about with sorrow, toil, and lamentation in this world. For under the beams of this sun man tilled the earth, and it put forth thorns and thistles which was the punishment for sin. Then that which was written was fulfilled, "Adam knew his wife, and she conceived and bore Cain," and after him "she bore Abel" (Gen 4:1–2). Now the apostate angel who had led man into disobedience, made him sinful, and caused his expulsion from paradise was not content with this first evil but also brought about a second evil on these two brothers. For filling Cain with his spirit, he made him a murderer of his brother. And so Abel died, slain by his brother; signifying from that time onward that certain ones would be persecuted and oppressed and slain, the unrighteous slaying and persecuting the righteous. And God was angered at this even more and cursed Cain; and it happened that everyone of that race in successive generations was made in the likeness of their father. And God "raised up" another son to Adam, "instead of Abel" who was slain (Gen 4:25).

18. For a very long time, wickedness then extended and spread until it reached and laid hold of the whole race of mankind. Then only a very small seed of righteousness remained among them. Illicit unions also took place upon the earth when angels were united with the daughters of the race of mankind. They had sons with them who were called giants due to their exceeding greatness. And the angels brought teachings of wickedness as presents to their wives; they brought them the virtues of roots and herbs, dyeing in colors and cosmetics, the discovery of rare substances, love-potions, aversions, secret affairs, lusts, constraints of love, spells of bewitchment, and all sorcery and idolatry hateful to God; by the entry of these things into the world, evil extended and spread while righteousness was diminished and enfeebled.[6]

19. This continued until judgment came upon the world from God by means of a flood, in the tenth generation from the first-formed man. Noah

---

[6] Behr notes that "the expanded material in this chapter derives from *1 Enoch* 6–8, perhaps by way of Justin, cf. *Second Apology* 5" (105n54).

alone was found righteous. Because of his righteousness, he himself was delivered in the ark along with his wife, his three sons, and the three wives of his sons. And when destruction came upon everyone, both man and also animals that were on the earth, those who were preserved in the ark escaped. Now the three sons of Noah were Shem, Ham, and Japheth, from whom the race was multiplied again. These were the beginning of mankind after the flood.

20. Now of these sons, one fell under a curse, and the two others inherited a blessing by reason of their works. For the younger of them, who was called Ham, having mocked his father, and having been condemned of the sin of impiety because of his outrage and unrighteousness against his father, received a curse.[7] This curse further extended to all of his descendants. It came about that after him his whole race was cursed, and they increased and multiplied in sins. But his brothers Shem and Japheth obtained a blessing because of their piety toward their father. Now the curse of Ham, with which his father Noah cursed him, is this, "Cursed be Ham the child; he shall be a servant to his brothers" (Gen 9:25). This having come upon his race, he produced many descendants upon the earth, even for fourteen generations, who grew up in a wild condition. And then his race was cut off by God and delivered over to judgment. For the Canaanites, the Hittites, the Perizzites, the Hivites, the Amorites, the Jebusites, the Girgashites, the Sodomites, the Arabians also and the dwellers in Phoenicia, all the Egyptians and the Libyans, these are of the offspring of Ham who have fallen under the curse; for the curse is of long duration over the ungodly.

21. And even as the curse passed on, so also the blessing passed on to the race of him who was blessed, to each in his own order. For Shem was blessed first in these words, "Blessed be the Lord, the God of Shem; and Ham shall be his servant" (Gen 9:26). The power of the blessing lies in this, that the God and Lord of all should be to Shem a peculiar possession of worship. And the blessing extended and reached Abraham who was reckoned as a descendant in the tenth generation from the race of Shem. And therefore, the Father and God of all was pleased to be called the God of Abraham, the God of Isaac, and the God of Jacob, because the blessing of Shem reached out and attached itself to Abraham. Now the blessing of Japheth is indicated by these words, "God shall enlarge unto Japheth, and he shall dwell in the house of Shem, and Ham shall be his servant" (Gen 9:27). That is to say, in the end of the ages he blossomed forth at the appearing of the Lord through the calling of the gentiles,

---

7 Robinson and Behr note the textual difficulty with "Ham" here and throughout this section (as the MT and most LXX manuscripts of Gen 9:25 indicate Canaan is cursed rather than Ham). See Behr, 105n56.

when God included them in the fulfillment of this promise; and "their sound went out into all the earth, and their words to the end of the world" (Ps 19:4). The enlarging, then, is the calling from among the gentiles, that is to say, the church. "And he dwells in the house of Shem" (Gen 9:27); that is, in the inheritance of the fathers, receiving in Christ Jesus the right of the firstborn. So according to the rank in which each was blessed, in that same order he received the fruit of the blessing through his offspring.

22. Now after the flood, God made a covenant with all the world, even with every living thing of animals and of men, that he would not destroy again with a flood all that grew upon the earth. And he gave them a sign, saying, "When the sky shall be covered with a cloud, the bow shall be seen in the cloud; and I will remember my covenant, and will not destroy again by water every moving thing upon the earth" (Gen 9:14–15). And he changed the food of men by allowing them to eat meat. For from Adam the first-formed until the flood, men ate only of seeds and the fruit of trees, and to eat meat was not permitted. But since the three sons of Noah were the beginning of a race of men, God blessed them for multiplication and increase, saying, "Increase and multiply, and replenish the earth and rule it; and the fear and dread of you shall be upon every living thing of animals and upon all the birds of the air; and they shall be meat for you, even as the green herb. But the flesh with the blood of life you shall not eat; for your blood also will I require at the hand of all beasts and at the hand of man. Whoever sheds a man's blood, his blood shall be shed in return" (Gen 9:1–6). For he made man the image of God; and the image of God is the Son, after whose image man was made. And for this reason, he appeared in the end of times that he might show the image to be in his likeness. According to this covenant, the race of man multiplied, springing up from the seed of the three. And "upon the earth was one set of words" (Gen 11:1), that is to say, one language.

23. And they arose and came from the land of the east; and, as they went through the land, they came to the land of Shinar, which was exceedingly broad, where they decided to build a tower. They were looking for a way to go up to heaven and be able to leave their work as a memorial to those men who should come after them. And the building was made with burnt bricks and tar. And the boldness of their audacity went forward, as they were all of one mind and consent, and by means of one speech they served the purpose of their desires. But that the work should advance no further, God divided their tongues so that they should no longer be able to understand one another. And so they were scattered and planted out, and took possession of the world, and dwelt in groups and companies each according to his own

language. From this place came the diverse tribes and various languages upon the earth. So then, whereas three races of men took possession of the earth, and one of them was under the curse, and two under the blessing, the blessing first of all came to Shem, whose race dwelt in the east and held the land of the Chaldeans.

24. In the progress of time, that is to say, in the tenth generation after the flood, Abraham appeared, seeking the God who by the blessing of his ancestor was due and proper to him. And when, urged by the eagerness of his spirit, he went all about the world searching for where God was but failed to find out, God took pity on him who alone was silently seeking him. And he appeared to Abraham, making himself known by the Word, as by a beam of light. For he spoke with him from heaven and said to him, "Leave your country, and your kindred, and your father's house; and come into the land that I will show you" (Gen 12:1; Acts 8:3), and dwell there. And he believed the heavenly voice, being then of old age, even seventy years old, and having a wife; and together with her he left Mesopotamia, taking with him Lot, the son of his brother who was dead. And when he came into the land which is now called Judea, in which at that time dwelt seven tribes descended from Ham, God appeared to him in a vision and said, "To you I will give this land, and to your seed after you, for an everlasting possession" (Gen 17:8), and he said that his seed should be a stranger in a land not their own, and should experience evil there, being afflicted and in bondage four hundred years; and in the fourth generation should return to the place that was promised to Abraham; and that God would judge that race which had brought his descendants into bondage. And, that Abraham might know that the greatness of his offspring would become a multitude, God brought him out by night and said, "Look upon the heaven, and behold the stars of the heaven, if you are able to number them, so shall your seed be" (Gen 15:5). And when God saw the undoubting and unwavering certainty of his spirit, he bore witness to him by the Holy Spirit, saying in the Scripture, "And Abraham believed, and it was counted to him for righteousness" (Gen 15:6; Rom 4:3). Now he was uncircumcised when he received this promise. That the excellency of his faith should be made known by a sign, he therefore gave him the sign of circumcision, "a seal of the righteousness of that faith which he had in uncircumcision" (Rom 4:11). After this, Abraham had a son named Isaac from Sarah who was barren, according to the promise of God; and he circumcised him according to the covenant God had made with him. Isaac had a son named Jacob. In this way, the original blessing of Shem reached to Abraham, and from Abraham to Isaac, and from Isaac to Jacob, the inheritance of the Spirit being imparted to them. For

he was called the God of Abraham, the God of Isaac, and the God of Jacob. Jacob then had twelve sons, from whom the twelve tribes of Israel were named.

25. When famine had come upon all the earth, it happened that there was only food in Egypt. So Jacob along with all his descendants left their land and came to dwell in Egypt. The number of all who migrated was 75 (Acts 8:14). Four hundred years later, they became 60,600, just as the oracle had declared beforehand. Moreover, because they were grievously afflicted and oppressed through evil bondage, they sighed and groaned to the God of their fathers, the God of Abraham, Isaac, and Jacob. Accordingly, God brought them out of Egypt by the hand of Moses and Aaron, striking the Egyptians with ten plagues. In the last plague, he sent a destroying angel that killed their firstborn, both of man and of beast. The children of Israel, though, were saved from this plague. This revealed in a mystery the sufferings of Christ by the sacrifice of a lamb without spot that gave its blood to be smeared on the houses of the Hebrews as a sure precaution. The name of this mystery is "passion," the source of deliverance. Dividing the Red Sea, he also brought the children of Israel with all security to the wilderness. As to the pursuing Egyptians who followed them and entered into the sea, they were all overwhelmed. This judgment of God thus came upon those who had sinfully oppressed the seed of Abraham.

26. In the wilderness, Moses then received the law from God, "the ten words on tables of stone, written with the finger of God" (Exod 31:18; 34:28). Now the finger of God is that which is stretched forth from the Father in the Holy Spirit; and the commandments and ordinances which he delivered to the children of Israel to observe. And he constructed the tabernacle of witness by the command of God as the visible form on earth of those things which are spiritual and invisible in the heavens. This tabernacle also served as a figure of the form of the church and a prophecy of things to come; in which were also the vessels and the altars of sacrifice and the ark in which he placed the tables of the law. Moses also appointed Aaron and his sons as priests, assigning the priesthood to all their tribe. The members of this tribe were the descendants of Levi. Moreover, Moses summoned this whole tribe by the word of God to accomplish the work of service in the temple of God and gave them the Levitical law to show them what manner of men they ought to be who are continually employed in performing the service of the temple of God.

27. And when they were near to the land which God had promised to Abraham and his seed, Moses chose a man from every tribe and sent them to search out the land, its cities, and those who dwelled within those cities.

At that time God revealed to him the Name which alone is able to save them that believe upon it. And Moses changed the name of Hoshea the son of Nun, one of them that were sent, and named him Jesus; and so he sent them forth with the power of the Name, believing that he should receive them back safe and sound through the guidance of the Name which came to pass. Now when they had gone and searched and inquired, they returned bringing with them a bunch of grapes; and some of the twelve who were sent caused the whole multitude to fear and be dismayed by saying that the cities were exceedingly great and walled and that the sons of the giants dwelled within them. They concluded that it was not possible for them to take the land. Immediately, the whole multitude wept while failing to believe that it was God who should grant them power and subjugate all to them. They also spoke evil of the land, as not being good, and as though it were not worthwhile to undergo the danger for the sake of such a land. But two of the twelve, Jesus the son of Nun, and Caleb the son of Jephunneh, tore their clothes for the evil that was done, and implored the people not to be disheartened nor lose their courage; for God had given all into their hands, and the land was exceedingly good. And when they did not believe, but the people still continued in the same unbelief, God changed and altered their path, that they should wander desolate and sore stricken in the desert. And according to the number of days it took the spies to go into and return from the land (which was 40 in number) setting a year for a day, he kept them in the wilderness for the space of 40 years; and none of those who were fully grown and had understanding did he count worthy to enter into the land because of their unbelief, except the two who had testified of the inheritance, Jesus the son of Nun and Caleb the son of Jephunneh, and those who were quite young and did not know the right hand from the left. So all the unbelieving multitude perished and were consumed in the wilderness, receiving one by one the due reward for their lack of faith. But the children, growing up in the course of 40 years, filled up the number of the dead.

28. When the 40 years were fulfilled, the people drew near to the Jordan and were assembled and positioned for the purpose of overtaking Jericho. Here Moses gathered the people together and summed up all of his previous words, proclaiming the mighty works of God even up until that day, fashioning and preparing those who had grown up in the wilderness to fear God and keep his commandments, imposing on them as it were a new legislation, adding to that which was made before. This was called Deuteronomy, and in it were written many prophecies concerning our Lord Jesus Christ and concerning the people, and also concerning the calling of the gentiles and the kingdom.

29. When Moses had finished his course, God said to him, "Go up the mountain and die," for you shall not bring my people into the land (Deut 32:49–50). So he "died according to the word of the Lord" (Deut 34:5); and Jesus the son of Nun succeeded him. He divided the Jordan and made the people pass over into the land. And when he had overthrown and destroyed the seven races that dwelled within the land, he assigned to the people the temporal Jerusalem, in which David was king, and also Solomon his son, who built the temple to honor the name of God, according to the likeness of the tabernacle which had been made by Moses after the pattern of the heavenly and spiritual things.

30. The prophets were sent to this place by God through the Holy Spirit. They instructed the people and turned them to the God of their fathers, the almighty; and they became messengers of the revelation of our Lord Jesus Christ, the Son of God, declaring that from the offspring of David his flesh should blossom forth; that after the flesh he might be the son of David who was the son of Abraham by a long succession; but according to the Spirit, Son of God, pre-existing with the Father, begotten before all the creation of the world, and at the end of times appearing to all the world as man, the Word of God "gathering up in himself all things that are in heaven and that are on earth" (Eph 1:10).

31. So then he united man with God and established a community of union between God and man; since we could not in any other way participate in incorruption, except by his coming among us. For so long as incorruption was invisible and unrevealed, it did not help us at all. Therefore, it became visible, that in all respects we might participate in the reception of incorruption. Because in the original formation of Adam all of us were tied and bound up with death through his disobedience, it was right that through the obedience of him who was made man for us we should be released from death. And because death reigned over the flesh, it was right that through the flesh it should lose its force and let man go free from its oppression. So "the Word was made flesh" (John 1:14), that, through that very flesh which sin had ruled and dominated, it should lose its force and no longer be in us. And therefore our Lord took that same original formation as his entry into flesh, so that he might draw near and contend on behalf of the fathers, and conquer by Adam that which by Adam had stricken us down.

32. From what then is the substance of the first-formed man? From the Will and the Wisdom of God, and from the virgin earth. "For God had not sent rain," the Scripture says, "upon the earth," before man was made, "and there was no man to till the earth" (Gen 2:5). From this, then, while it was

still virgin, God took dust of the earth and formed the man, the beginning of mankind. So then the Lord, summing up afresh this man, took the same order of entry into flesh, being born from the virgin by the Will and the Wisdom of God; that he also should demonstrate the likeness of Adam's entry into flesh and there should be that which was written in the beginning, "man after the image and likeness" of God (Gen 1:26).

33. Just as through a disobedient virgin man was struck down and fell into death, so through the virgin who was obedient to the Word of God man was revived and received life. For the Lord came to seek again the sheep that was lost; and it was man that was lost. For this reason, there was not made some other formation, but in that same formation which had its descent from Adam he preserved the likeness of the first formation. For it was necessary that Adam should be summed up in Christ, that mortality might be swallowed up and overwhelmed by immortality (cf. 1 Cor 15:53); and Eve summed up in Mary, that a virgin should be a virgin's intercessor, and by a virgin's obedience undo and put away the disobedience of a virgin.

34. And the trespass which came by the tree was undone by the tree of obedience, when, obeying God, the Son of man was nailed to the tree; thereby putting away the knowledge of evil and bringing in and establishing the knowledge of good. Now it is evil to disobey God, even as obeying God is good. For this reason, the Word spoke by Isaiah the prophet, announcing beforehand that which was to come—for this is why they are prophets, because they proclaim what is to come. By him then the Word spoke thus, "I refuse not, nor deny; I gave my back to scourging and my cheeks to smiting; and I did not turn my face away from the shame of spitting" (Isa 50:5–6). So then by the obedience with which he obeyed "even unto death," hanging on the tree, he put away the old disobedience which was brought about by the tree. Now seeing that he is the Word of God almighty, who in an unseen manner in our midst is universally extended in all the world, and encompasses its length and breadth and height and depth—for by the Word of God the whole universe is ordered and disposed—in it is crucified the Son of God, inscribed crosswise upon it all. For it is right that being made visible, he should set upon all visible things the sharing of his cross, that he might show his operation on visible things through a visible form. For it is he who illuminates the height, that is the heavens; and encompasses the deep which is beneath the earth; and stretches and spreads out the length from east to west; and steers across the breadth of north and south; summoning all that are scattered in every quarter to the knowledge of the Father.

35. Moreover, he fulfilled the promise made to Abraham, which God had

promised him, to make his descendants as the stars of heaven. For this Christ did, who was born of the virgin who was of Abraham's seed, and constituted those who have faith in him as "lights in the world" (Phil 2:15), and by the same faith as with Abraham justified the gentiles. For "Abraham believed God, and it was counted to him as righteousness" (Gen 15:6; Rom 4:3). In like manner we are also justified by faith in God, for "the just shall live by faith" (Rom 1:17). Now "the promise to Abraham is not by the law, but by faith" (Rom 4:13) for Abraham was justified by faith; and "the law is not made for a righteous man" (1 Tim 1:9). In the same way, we are also justified not by the law, but by faith, which is witnessed to in the Law and in the Prophets, whom the Word of God presents to us.

36. He also fulfilled the promise to David. For to him God had promised that of the "fruit of his body" he would raise up an eternal king, whose kingdom should have no end (Ps 132:11). And this king is Christ, the Son of God, who became the Son of Man; that is, who became the fruit of that virgin who had her descent from David. For this reason, the promise was, "of the fruit of your body," that he might declare the peculiar uniqueness of him who was the fruit of the virgin body that was of David, even of him who was king over the house of David, and of whose kingdom there shall be no end.

37. Accordingly, he gloriously achieved our redemption and fulfilled the promise of the fathers and abolished the old disobedience. The Son of God became son of David and son of Abraham; perfecting and summing this up in himself, that he might make us to possess life. The Word of God was made flesh by the economy of the virgin to abolish death and make man live. For we were imprisoned by sin, being born in sinfulness and living under death.

38. But God the Father was very merciful. He sent his creative Word, who in coming to deliver us came to the very place and spot in which we had lost life. There he broke the bonds of our chains. His light appeared and made the darkness of the prison disappear, and hallowed our birth and destroyed death, loosing those same chains by which we were bound. And he manifested the resurrection, himself becoming "the first begotten of the dead" (Rev 1:5), and in himself raising up man that was fallen, lifting him up far above the heaven to the right hand of the glory of the Father; even as God promised by the prophet, saying, "and I will raise up the tabernacle of David that is fallen" (Amos 9:11); that is, the flesh that was from David. And this our Lord Jesus Christ truly fulfilled when he gloriously achieved our redemption, that he might truly raise us up, setting us free unto the Father. And if any man will not receive his birth from a virgin, how shall he receive his

resurrection from the dead? For it is nothing wonderful and astonishing and extraordinary, if one who was not born rose from the dead. Indeed, we cannot speak of a resurrection of him who came into being without birth. For one who is unborn and immortal and has not undergone birth will also not undergo death. For he who did not take the beginning of man, how could he receive his end?

39. Now, if he was not born, neither did he die; and if he did not die, neither did he rise from the dead; and if he did not rise from the dead, neither did he conquer death and bring its reign to nothing; and if death has not been conquered, how can we ascend to life, who from the beginning have fallen under death? So then those who take away redemption from man, and do not believe God that he will raise them from the dead, these also despise the birth of our Lord, which he underwent on our behalf, that the Word of God should be made flesh in order that he might manifest the resurrection of the flesh, and might have pre-eminence over all things in the heavens, as the first-born and eldest offspring of the thought of the Father, the Word, fulfilling all things, and himself guiding and ruling upon earth. For he was the virgin's first-born, a just and holy man, God-fearing, good, well-pleasing to God, perfect in all his ways, and delivering from hell all who follow after him. For he himself was "the first-begotten of the dead," the prince and author of life unto God (Rev 1:5).

40. Thus then the Word of God "has pre-eminence in all things" (Col 1:18); for that he is true man and "wonderful counselor and mighty God" (Isa 9:6); calling men anew to fellowship with God, that by fellowship with him we may partake of incorruption. So then he who was proclaimed by the law through Moses, and by the prophets of the most high and almighty God, as Son of the Father of all; he from whom are all things, he who spoke with Moses—he came into Judea, generated from God by the Holy Spirit, and born of the virgin Mary, even of her who was of the seed of David and of Abraham, Jesus the anointed of God, showing himself to be the one who was proclaimed beforehand by the prophets.

41. And his forerunner was John the Baptist, who prepared and made ready the people beforehand for the reception of the Word of life; declaring that he was the Christ, on whom the Spirit of God rested, mingling with his flesh. His disciples, the witnesses of all his good deeds, and of his teachings and his sufferings and death and resurrection, and of his ascension into heaven after his bodily resurrection—these were the apostles, who after receiving the power of the Holy Spirit were sent forth by him into all the world, and brought about the calling of the gentiles, showing to mankind the way of life, to turn them

from idols and fornication and covetousness, cleansing their souls and bodies by the baptism of water and of the Holy Spirit; which Holy Spirit they had received of the Lord, and they distributed and imparted the Holy Spirit to them that believed; and thus they ordered and established the churches. By faith and love and hope they established that which was foretold by the prophets, the calling of the gentiles, according to the mercy of God which was extended to them; bringing it to light through their service and admitting them to the promise of the fathers. To those who thus believed in and loved the Lord, and continued in holiness and righteousness and patient endurance, the God of all had promised to grant eternal life by the resurrection of the dead; through him who died and rose again, Jesus Christ, to whom he has delivered over the kingdom of all existing things, and the rule of the quick and the dead and also the judgment. And they counseled them by the word of truth to keep their soul unstained and their flesh undefiled until the resurrection.

42. For such is the state of those who have believed, since in them the Holy Spirit continually abides, who was given by him in baptism and is retained by the receiver if he walks in truth, holiness, righteousness, and patient endurance. For this soul has a resurrection in them that believe, the body receiving the soul again, and along with it, by the power of the Holy Spirit, being raised up and entering into the kingdom of God. This is the fruit of the blessing of Japheth, in the calling of the gentiles, made manifest through the church, standing in readiness to receive its "dwelling in the house of Shem" according to the promise of God. That all these things would so come to pass, the Spirit of God declared beforehand by the prophets; that in respect of them, the faith of those who worship God in truth should be confirmed. For what was an impossibility to our nature, and therefore ready to cause incredibility to mankind, this God caused to be made known beforehand by the prophets; in order that, through its having been foretold in times long before, and then at last finding effect in this way even as it was foretold, we might know that it was God who thus proclaimed to us beforehand our redemption.

Part Two: The Gospel according to the Scriptures

43. So then we must believe God in all things, for in all things God is true. Now that there was a Son of God, and that he existed not only before he appeared in the world, but also before the world was made, Moses, who was the first that prophesied says in Hebrew, *Baresith bara Elowin basan benuam samenthares*. And this translated into our language is, "The Son in the

beginning: God established then the heaven and the earth" (Gen 1:1).[8] Jeremiah the prophet also testified, saying thus, "Before the morning-star I begat you; and before the sun is your name,"[9] and that is, before the creation of the world; for together with the world the stars were made. And again the same says, "Blessed is he who was, before he became man."[10] Because, for God, the Son was at the beginning before the creation of the world; but for us he was then, when he appeared; and before that he was not for us, who did not know him. For this reason also his disciple John, in teaching us who the Son of God is, who was with the Father before the world was made, and that all the things that were made were made by him, says thus, "In the beginning was the Word, and the Word was with God, and the Word was God. The same was in the beginning with God. All things were made by him, and without him nothing was made" (John 1:1–3), showing with certainty that the Word, who was in the beginning with the Father, and by whom all things were made, this is his Son.

44. And again Moses tells how the Son of God drew near to speak with Abraham. "And God appeared to him by the oak of Mamre in the middle of the day. And looking up with his eyes, behold, he saw three men standing across from him. And he bowed himself down to the earth, and said, Lord, if indeed I have found favor in your sight" (Gen 18:1–3). In what follows here, he spoke with the Lord, and the Lord spoke with him. Two of the three were angels, but one was the Son of God, with whom also Abraham spoke, pleading on behalf of the men of Sodom, that they should not perish if at least ten righteous should be found there. And, while these were speaking, the two angels entered into Sodom, and Lot received them. Then the Scripture says, "and the Lord rained upon Sodom and Gomorrah brimstone and fire from the Lord out of heaven" (Gen 19:24). That is to say, the Son, who spoke with Abraham, being "Lord," received power to punish the men of Sodom "from the Lord out of heaven," even from the Father who rules over all. So Abraham was a prophet and saw things to come, which were to take place in human form; even the Son of God, that he should speak with men and eat with them, and then

---

8 On the text-critical issues here, see Behr (109n121). Behr notes that there is an ambiguity in the Armenian of this sentence which makes punctuation difficult to determine. Robinson divides the sentence with a colon ("The Son in the beginning: God established then the heaven and the earth") and Behr omits punctuation at this point ("and this is translated . . . "A Son [in] the beginning God established then heaven and earth"). From the context of the paragraph, it is clear that Irenaeus interprets Gen 1:1 in light of the wording of John 1:1–3 in addition to any linguistic argument from the opening phrases of Genesis.

9 The quotation here attributed to Jeremiah is a composite quotation drawn from Ps 109:3 and Ps 71:17.

10 The source of this quotation is unknown.

should bring in the judgment from the Father, having received from him who rules over all the power to punish the men of Sodom.

45. When Jacob went into Mesopotamia, he also saw him in a dream, "standing upon the ladder" (Gen 28:13), that is the tree which was set up from earth to heaven; for in this way those who believe in him go up to the heavens. For his sufferings are our ascension on high. And all such visions point to the Son of God, speaking with men and being in their midst. For it was not the Father of all, who is not seen by the world, the maker of all who has said, "Heaven is my throne, and earth is my footstool; what house will you build me, or what is the place of my rest? And who comprehends the earth with his hand, and with his span the heaven?" (Isa 66:1; Acts 7:49). It was not he that came and stood in a very small space and spoke with Abraham; but the Word of God, who was ever with mankind, and made known beforehand what should come to pass in the future and taught men the things of God.

46. This is he who spoke with Moses in the bush, and said, "I have surely seen the affliction of my people who are in Egypt; and I have come down to deliver them" (Exod 3:7). He it is who came forth and came down for the deliverance of the oppressed, bringing us out from the power of the Egyptians, that is, from all idolatry and impiety; and delivering us from the Red Sea, that is, delivering us from the deadly confusion of the gentiles and the grievous vexation of their blasphemy. For in them the Word of God prepared and rehearsed beforehand the things concerning us. Then he set forth in types beforehand that which was to be; how in very truth he has brought us out from the cruel service of the gentiles, and he has made a stream of water in the desert to flow forth in abundance from a rock; and that rock is himself; and has given twelve fountains, that is, the teaching of the twelve apostles. And the obstinate unbelievers he brought to an end and consumed in the wilderness; but those who believed on him, and "in malice" were "children" (1 Cor 14:20), he made to enter into the inheritance of the fathers; whom not Moses, but Jesus puts in possession of the heritage; who also delivers us from Amalek by the expansion of his hands and brings us to the kingdom of the Father.

47. So then the Father is Lord and the Son is Lord, and the Father is God and the Son is God; for he who is begotten of God is God. In the substance and power of his being, therefore, there is shown forth one God; but according to the economy of our redemption, there is also both Son and Father. Because the Father of all is invisible and unapproachable to created things, those who are to draw near to God must therefore have their access to the Father through the Son. Yet more plainly and evidently does David speak concerning the Father and the Son as follows, "Your throne, O God is for ever and ever.

You have loved righteousness and hated unrighteousness. Therefore, God has anointed you with the oil of gladness above your companions" (Ps 45:6; Heb 1:8). For the Son, being God, receives from the Father, that is, from God, the throne of the everlasting kingdom and the oil of anointing above his companions. The "oil of anointing" is the Spirit, with which he has been anointed; and his "companions" are prophets and righteous men and apostles, and all who receive the fellowship of his kingdom, that is to say, his disciples.

48. And again David says, "The Lord said to my Lord, 'Sit at my right hand, until I make your enemies your footstool. The rod of your strength the Lord shall send forth from Zion; and you shall rule in the midst of your enemies. With you in the beginning in the day of your power, in the brightness of the holy ones; from the womb before the morning-star I begat you.' The Lord swore and will not repent, 'You are a priest forever after the order of Melchizedek.' And the Lord on your right hand has broken in pieces kings in the day of wrath; he shall judge among the gentiles, he shall fill up the ruins, and shall break in pieces the heads of many on the earth. He shall drink of the stream in the way. Therefore, he shall lift up the head" (Ps 110:1–7). Now through this he proclaimed that he came into being before all, and that he rules over the gentiles and judges all mankind and the kings who now hate him and persecute his name; for these are his enemies. And in calling him God's priest forever, he declared his immortality. And therefore, he said, "He shall drink of the stream in the way; therefore, he shall lift up the head," proclaiming the exaltation with glory that followed the humiliation and ingloriousness according to his humanity.

49. And again Isaiah the prophet says, "Thus says the Lord God to my anointed the Lord, whose right hand I have held, that the gentiles should listen to him" (Isa 45:1). How the Christ is called Son of God and king of the gentiles, that is, of all mankind; and that he is not only called but is Son of God and king of all, David declares thus, "The Lord said to me, 'You are my Son, today I have begotten you. Ask of me and I will give you the gentiles for your inheritance, and the utmost parts of the earth for a possession'" (Ps 2:7). These things were not said of David; for neither over the gentiles nor over the utmost parts did he rule, but only over the Jews. So then it is plain that the promise to the anointed to reign over the utmost parts of the earth is to the Son of God, whom David himself acknowledges as his Lord, saying thus, "The Lord said to my Lord, 'Sit at my right hand'" (Ps 110:1), and so forth, as we have said above. For he means that the Father speaks with the Son; as we showed a little before from Isaiah, that he said thus, "God says to my anointed the Lord, that the gentiles should obey him" (Isa 45:1). For the promise is the

same by the two prophets, that he should be king; so that the speech of God is addressed to one and the same, I mean, to Christ the Son of God. Because David says, "The Lord said to me" (Ps 2:7), it is necessary to say that it is not David who speaks in his own person, nor any one of the prophets. For it is not a man who speaks the prophecies, but the Spirit of God, assimilating and likening himself to the persons represented, speaks in the prophets and utters the words sometimes from Christ and sometimes from the Father.

50. So then it is fitting that Christ says through David that he converses with the Father; and it is likewise proper that he says other things concerning himself through the prophets; as in other instances, so also after this manner by Isaiah, "And now thus says the Lord, who formed me as his servant from the womb, to gather Jacob and to gather Israel unto him; and I shall be glorified before the Lord, and my God shall be a strength to me. And he said, 'A great thing shall it be to you to be called my servant, to establish and confirm the tribe of Jacob, and to restore again the dispersion of Israel; and I have set you for a light of the gentiles, that you should be for salvation to the end of the earth'" (Isa 49:5–6).

51. Here, first of all, is seen that the Son of God pre-existed, from the fact that the Father spoke with him, and before he was born revealed him to men. Next, that he must necessarily be born a man among men; and that the same God "forms" him "from the womb," that is, that of the Spirit of God he should be born; and that he is Lord of all men and savior of them that believe in him, both Jews and others. For the people of the Jews is called "Israel" in the Hebrew language, from Jacob their father, who was the first to be called Israel. And "gentiles" he calls the whole of mankind. And that the Son of the Father calls himself "servant," this is on account of his obedience to the Father; for among men also, every son is servant of his father.

52. That Christ, then, being Son of God before all the world, is with the Father; and being with the Father is also near and close and joined with mankind; and is king of all, because the Father has subjected all things to him; and savior of them that believe in him—such things do the Scriptures declare. For it is not feasible and possible to enumerate every Scripture in order; and from these you may understand the others also which have been spoken in a similar manner, believing in Christ and seeking understanding and comprehension from God, so as to understand what has been spoken by the prophets.

53. And that this Christ, who was with the Father, being the Word of the Father, was thereafter to be made flesh and become man and undergo the process of birth and be born of a virgin and dwell among men, the Father of all bringing about his incarnation—Isaiah says thus, "Therefore, the Lord

himself shall give you a sign; behold, the virgin shall conceive and shall bring forth a son, and you shall call him Emmanuel; butter and honey he shall eat; before he knows or selects the evil, he chooses the good; for, before the child knows good or evil, he rejects wickedness to choose the good" (Isa 8:14–15). So he proclaimed his birth from a virgin; and that he was truly man he declared beforehand by his eating; and also because he called him the child; and further by giving him a name; for this is the custom also for one that is born. And his name is two-fold: in the Hebrew tongue, Messiah Jesus, and in ours, Christ Savior. And the two names are names of works actually accomplished. For he was named Christ, because through him the Father anointed and adorned all things; and because on his coming as man he was anointed with the Spirit of God and his Father. As also he says of himself by Isaiah, "The Spirit of the Lord is upon me; for this reason he has anointed me to preach good tidings to the poor" (Isa 61:1). And he was named Savior for this, that he became the cause of salvation to those who at that time were delivered by him from all sicknesses and from death, and to those who afterwards believed on him the author of salvation in the future and forevermore.

54. For this reason then, he is Savior. Now Emmanuel is, being interpreted, "God with you," or as a yearning cry uttered by the prophet, such as this, "God shall be with us," according to which it is the explanation and manifestation of the good tidings proclaimed (cf. Matt 1:23). For "Behold," he says, "the virgin shall conceive and shall bring forth a son" (Isa 7:14); and he, being God, is to be with us. And, as if altogether astonished at these things, he proclaims in regard to these future events that "God shall be with us." And yet again concerning his birth the same prophet says in another place, "Before she who labored gave birth, and before the pains of labor came on, she escaped and delivered a son" (Isa 66:7). Thus he showed that his birth from the virgin was unforeseen and unexpected. And again the same prophet says, "Unto us a son is born, and unto us a child is given; and his name shall be called Wonderful Counselor, Mighty God" (Isa 9:6).

55. He calls him "wonderful counselor," meaning of the Father; by this it is declared that the Father works all things together with him; as is contained in the first book of Moses which is entitled Genesis, "And God said, 'Let us make man after our image and likeness'" (Gen 1:26). For there is seen in this place the Father speaking to the Son, the wonderful counselor of the Father. Moreover, he is also our counselor, giving advice; not compelling as God, even though he is "mighty God," as he says; but giving advice that we should forsake ignorance and acquire knowledge, and depart from error and come to the truth, and put away corruption and receive incorruption.

56. Again Isaiah says, "And they shall wish that they had been burned with fire; for unto us a child is born, and unto us a son is given; whose government is upon his shoulders, and his name is called angel of great counsel. For I will bring peace upon the rulers, again peace and health unto him. Great is his rule, and of his peace there is no end, upon the throne of David and upon his kingdom, to prosper and complete, to aid and undertake, in righteousness and judgment from this time forth and forevermore" (Isa 9:5–7). For through this the Son of God is proclaimed both as being born and also as an eternal king. But "they shall wish that they had been burned with fire" is said of those who do not believe in him, and who have done to him all that they have done; for they shall say in the judgment, "How much better that we had been burned with fire before the Son of God was born, than that, when he was born, we should not have believed on him." For there is hope that when those who have been raised are judged, those who died before Christ appeared might obtain salvation; even for those who feared God and died in righteousness and had in them the Spirit of God, such as the patriarchs, prophets, and righteous men. But for those who after Christ's appearing did not believe in him, there is a vengeance without pardon in the judgment. Now in this, "whose government is upon his shoulder," the cross on which he was nailed is declared in a figure. For that which was and is a reproach to him (and for his sake to us), even the cross, this is his "government" which is also a sign of his kingdom. And "angel of great counsel," he says; that is, of the Father whom he has declared to us.

57. That the Son of God should be born, and in what way he was to be born, and that he should be shown to be the Christ—from what has been said it is plain how this was made known beforehand by the prophets. In addition to this, in what land and among whom of mankind he was to be born and to appear, this also was proclaimed beforehand with words such as these. Accordingly, Moses in Genesis says, "A prince shall not be lacking from Judah, nor a leader from his loins, until he comes to whom it belongs; and he shall be the expectation of the gentiles; washing his robe in wine, and his garment in the blood of the grape" (Gen 49:10–11). Now Judah was the ancestor of the Jews, the son of Jacob; from whom also they obtained the name. And they never failed to have a prince or a leader among them until the coming of Christ. But from the time of his coming, the land of the Jews was given over into subjection to the Romans, and they no longer had a prince or king of their own. For he had come, "to whom it belongs" in heaven, the kingdom; who also "washed his robe in wine, and his garment in the blood of the grape." His robe as well as his garment are those who believe in him, whom he also

cleansed, redeeming us by his blood. And his blood is said to be blood of the grape; for even as no man makes the blood of the grape, but God produces and makes the ones who drink it glad, so also no man brought about his flesh and blood, but God made it. "The Lord himself gave the sign" of the virgin, even that Emmanuel which was from the virgin (Isa 7:14); who also "makes glad" them that drink of him, that is to say, who receive his Spirit, even "everlasting gladness." For this reason also, he is the "expectation of the gentiles," of those who "hope in him," because we expect that he will establish again the kingdom.

58. And again Moses says, "A star shall rise out of Jacob; and a leader shall be raised up out of Israel" (Num 24:1); showing yet more plainly that the economy of his advent in the flesh should be among the Jews. From Jacob and from the tribe of Judah he who was born, coming down from heaven, took upon himself this economy; for the star appeared in heaven. By "leader" he means king, because he is the king of all the redeemed. At his birth the star appeared to the Magi who dwelled in the east; and by this they learned that Christ was born; and they came to Judea, led by the star; until the star came to Bethlehem where Christ was born, and entered the house where the child was laid, wrapped in swaddling clothes; and the star then remained over his head, declaring to the Magi the Son of God, the Christ.

59. Moreover, Isaiah himself says further, "And a rod shall come forth from the roots of Jesse, and a flower shall come forth from his root. And the spirit of God shall rest upon him; the spirit of wisdom and of understanding, the spirit of counsel and of might, the spirit of knowledge and of godliness; the spirit of the fear of God shall fill him. He shall not judge according to opinion, and he shall not reprove according to speech; but he shall execute judgment for the humble and show mercy to the humble of the earth. And he shall smite the earth with the word of his mouth, and he shall slay the impious man with the breath of his lips. And he shall gird his loins with righteousness, and with truth encompassed about his reins. And the wolf shall feed with the lamb, and the leopard with the young goat, and the calf and the lion shall pasture together. And a nursing child shall put his hand on the hole of the vipers and on the lair of the offspring of the vipers, and they shall not hurt him. And in that day there shall be a root of Jesse, and he that rises up to rule the gentiles; in him shall the gentiles hope; and his rising up shall be honor" (Isa 11:1–10, LXX). By these words he states that he was born from her who was of the race of David and of Abraham. For Jesse was the descendant of Abraham, and the father of David; and David's descendant was the virgin who conceived Christ. Now as to the "rod," for this reason also Moses showed the mighty works to

Pharaoh with a rod; and with other men also the rod is a sign of rule. And by "flower" he means his flesh; for by the Spirit it budded forth, as we have said before.

60. Now, "He shall not judge according to opinion, and he shall not reprove according to speech; but he shall execute judgment for the humble and show mercy to the humble of the earth"—by this he establishes and declares his godhead. For to judge without respect of persons and partiality, not favoring the illustrious but affording to the humble treatment that is similar, equal, and fair, accords with the height and summit of the righteousness of God. For God is influenced and moved by none, except for the righteous. To show mercy is the peculiar attribute of God who is able to save by mercy. And "He shall smite the earth with a word," and "slay the impious" with a word only. This belongs to God who works all things with a word. In saying, "He shall gird his loins with righteousness, and with truth encompassed about his reins," he declares his human form and aspect in addition to his own surpassing righteousness.

61. Now as to the union, concord, and peace of the animals of different kinds, which by nature are opposed and hostile to each other, the elders say that so it will be in truth at the coming of Christ, when he is to reign over all.[11] For already in a symbol he announces the gathering together in peace and concord, through the name of Christ, of men of different races and yet of similar dispositions. For the righteous are likened to calves, lambs, young goats, and nursing children. In the former time, there were other men and women who had aggressive greed and were thus like wild beasts in both manner and disposition. Some of them were even like wolves and lions who would ravage the weak and war against their equals. Some of the women among them were also like leopards or vipers who killed even their loved ones with deadly poison or by reason of their lustful desire. But now, having come together in one name, these two groups of people have acquired righteous habits by the grace of God and have changed their wild and untamed nature. And this has come to pass already. For those who were before exceedingly wicked, so that they left no work of ungodliness undone, learning of Christ and believing on him, have at once believed and been changed, so as to leave no excellency of righteousness undone. This is the kind of great transformation that faith in Christ the Son of God brings about for those who believe in him. And he says, "Rising up to rule the gentiles," because he is to die and rise again, and be confessed and believed as the Son of God and king. On this account he says, "And

---

11 Irenaeus often uses "the elder" or "the elders" to refer to tradition received from Papias (see *Haer.* 5.33.4).

Preaching the Gospel with the Rule of Faith

his rising up shall be honor," that is, glory; for then was he glorified as God, when he rose.

62. For this reason again the prophet says, "In that day I will raise up the tabernacle of David that is fallen" (Amos 9:11); that body of Christ, which, as we have said before, is born of David, he plainly declares as rising from the dead after death. For the body is called a tabernacle. By these words he says that he who according to the flesh is of the race of David will be Christ the Son of God; and that he will die and rise again, and that he is in aspect a man, but in power God; and that he himself will be the judge of all the world and the only redeemer and worker of righteousness—all this the Scripture declared.

63. The prophet Micah also speaks of the place where Christ should be born, that it should be in Bethlehem of Judea, saying thus, "And you, Bethlehem of Judea, are you the least among the princes of Judah? For from you shall come a prince who shall feed my people Israel" (Micah 5:2; Matt 2:6). But Bethlehem is the native place of David; so that not only with respect to the virgin who bore him is he of David's lineage, but also with respect to his birth in Bethlehem the native place of David.

64. And again David says that Christ is to be born of his lineage, speaking after this manner, "For David your servant's sake, do not turn away the face of your Christ. The Lord swore truth unto David, and he will not disappoint him. I will set on your throne one from the fruit of your body. If your children shall keep my covenant and my testimonies, which I covenanted with them, their sons shall sit upon your throne forevermore" (Ps 132:10–12). But none of the sons of David reigned forevermore, nor was their kingdom forevermore; for it was brought to nothing. But the king that was born of David, he is the Christ. All these testimonies declare in plain terms his descent according to the flesh, and the lineage and place where he was to be born; so that no man should seek among the gentiles or anywhere else for the birth of the Son of God, but in Bethlehem of Judea from Abraham and from David's offspring.

65. Regarding the manner of his entry into Jerusalem, which was the capital of Judea, where his royal seat and the temple of God also were, the prophet Isaiah declares, "Say to the daughter of Zion, 'Behold a king comes to you meek and sitting upon a donkey, a colt the foal of a donkey'" (Isa 62:11; Zech 9:9; Matt 21:5).[12] For he entered Jerusalem while sitting on a donkey's colt, and the multitudes spread and put down their garments for him. By the "daughter of Zion," he means Jerusalem.

---

12 Robinson notes that this passage "is quoted in the Matthaean form and ascribed to Isaiah from whom the first words come. In St Matthew's Gospel it is ascribed to 'the prophet,' though some codices insert 'Zechariah'" (127n2).

66. So then, that the Son of God should be born, and in what manner he should be born, and where he was to be born, and that Christ is the one eternal king, the prophets thus declared. That they also spoke beforehand about him who came forth from mankind, how he should heal those whom he healed, and raise the dead whom he raised, and be hated and despised and undergo sufferings and be put to death and crucified, even as he was hated and despised and put to death, let us now speak.

67. Concerning his healings, Isaiah says, "He took our infirmities and bore our sicknesses" (Isa 53:4; Matt 8:17), that is to say, he shall take and shall bear. For there are passages in which the Spirit of God recounts things through the prophets that are spoken of as having already taken place. For that which God has approved and conceived of as determined to take place is reckoned as having already taken place. The Spirit, regarding and seeing the time in which the issues of the prophecy are fulfilled, utters the words accordingly. Concerning the kind of healing, he will thus say, "In that day the deaf shall hear the words of the book, and in darkness and in me the eyes of the blind shall see" (Isa 29:18). And the same says again, "Be strong, you weak hands and feeble and trembling knees; be comforted, you that are of a fearful mind. Be strong, fear not. Behold, our God will recompense judgment; he will come and save us. Then the eyes of the blind shall be opened, and the ears of the deaf shall hear; then the lame man shall leap as a deer, and the tongue of the stammerers shall be plain" (Isa 35:3–6). And concerning the dead, that they shall be raised, he says, "The dead shall be raised, and they that are in the tombs shall be raised" (Isa 26:19). In bringing these things to pass, he shall be believed to be the Son of God.

68. And that he shall be despised and tormented and in the end put to death, Isaiah thus says, "Behold, my son shall understand, and shall be exalted and glorified greatly. Even as many shall be astonished at you, so without glory shall your form be from men. And many races shall be astonished, and kings shall shut their mouths. For they to whom it was not declared concerning him shall see, and they who have not heard shall consider. Lord, who has believed our report? and to whom has the arm of the Lord been revealed? We declared before him as a child, as a root in a dry ground; and there is to him no form nor glory; and we saw him, and he had no form nor beauty ... for his face was turned away, he was dishonored and made of no account. He bears our sins, and for our sakes endures pain; and we accounted him to be in pain and chastisement and affliction. But he was wounded for our iniquities and was tormented for our sins. The discipline of our peace was upon him; by his stripes we were healed" (Isa 52:13–53:5). By these words it is declared that he

was tormented; as David also says, "and I was tormented" (cf. Ps 38:8; Ps 72:14). Now David was never tormented, but Christ was, when the command was given that he should be crucified. By Isaiah his Word also says, "I gave my back to scourging, and my cheeks to smiting; and I did not turn my face away from the shame of spitting" (Isa 50:6). And Jeremiah the prophet says the same, "he shall give his cheek to the one who smites; he shall be filled with reproaches" (Lam 3:30). All these things Christ suffered.

69. Now what follows in Isaiah is this, "By his stripes we were healed. All we like sheep went astray; a man in his own way went astray; and the Lord delivered him up for our sins" (Isa 53:5–6). It is manifest therefore that by the will of the Father these things occurred to him for the sake of our salvation. Then he says, "And by reason of his suffering he did not open his mouth; he was brought as a sheep to the slaughter, as a lamb who is silent before the shearer" (Isa 53:7). Behold how he declares his voluntary coming to death. When the prophet says, "In the humiliation his judgment was taken away" (Isa 53:8), he signifies the appearance of his humiliation; according to the form of the abasement was the taking away of judgment. The taking away of judgment is for some unto salvation and for others unto the torments of perdition. For there is a taking away *for* a person and also a taking away *from* a person. So also with the judgment. Those for whom it is taken away have it unto the torments of their perdition; but those from whom it is taken away are saved by it. Now those who crucified him took away to themselves the judgment, and when they had done this to him did not believe in him. For through that judgment which was taken away by them, they shall be destroyed with torments. And from them that believe in him, the judgment is taken away, and they are no longer under it. The judgment is that which will be the destruction of the unbelievers by fire at the end of the world.

70. Then he says, "His generation who shall declare?" (Isa 53:8). This was said to warn us, lest on account of his enemies and the outrage of his sufferings we should despise him as a lowly and disgraceful man. For he who endured all this has an undeclarable generation; for by "generation" he means his lineage; for he who is his Father is undeclarable and inexpressible. Know therefore that such lofty lineage was his who endured these lowly sufferings. Do not despise him because of the sufferings that he purposefully endured for your sake, but fear him because of his lineage.

71. And in another place Jeremiah says, "The Spirit of our face, the Lord Christ; and how he was taken in their snares, of whom we said, 'Under his shadow we shall live among the gentiles'" (Lam 4:20). That, being the Spirit of God, Christ was to become a suffering man the Scripture declares; and is,

as it were, amazed and astonished at his sufferings, that in such manner he was to endure sufferings, "under whose shadow we said that we should live." And by "shadow" he means his body. For just as a shadow is made by a body, so also Christ's body was made by his Spirit. But, further, the humiliation and lowliness of his body he indicates by the shadow. For, as the shadow of bodies standing upright is upon the ground and is trodden upon, so also the body of Christ fell upon the ground by his sufferings and was trodden on indeed. And he named Christ's body a shadow, because the Spirit overshadowed it, as it were, with glory and covered it. Moreover, oftentimes when the Lord passed by, they laid those who were held by different kinds of diseases in the way, and whoever his shadow fell upon, they were healed.

72. Concerning the sufferings of Christ, the same prophet also says, "Behold how the righteous is destroyed, and no man lays it to heart; and righteous men are taken away, and no man understands. For from the face of iniquity is the taking away of the righteous. Peace shall be his burial, he has been taken away from the midst" (Isa 57:1–2). And who else is perfectly righteous, but the Son of God, who makes righteous and perfects them that believe in him, who like him are persecuted and put to death? But in saying, "Peace shall be his burial," he declares how on account of our redemption he died; for it is in the peace of redemption. He also declares that by his death those who were formerly enemies and opposed to one another, believing him with one accord, should have peace with one another, becoming friends and beloved on account of their common faith in him; as indeed they have become. But in saying, "He has been taken away from the midst," he signifies his resurrection from the dead. Moreover, because he appeared no more after his death and burial, the prophet declares that after dying and rising again he was to remain immortal, saying thus, "He asked life and you gave it to him, and length of days for ever and ever" (Ps 21:4). Now what is this that he says, "He asked life," since he was about to die? He proclaims his resurrection from the dead, and that being raised from the dead he is immortal. For he received both life, that he should rise, and "length of days for ever and ever," that he should be incorruptible.

73. Concerning the death and resurrection of Christ, David says, "I laid down and slept; I awaked, for the Lord received me" (Ps 3:5). David said this not of himself, for he was not raised after death; but the spirit of Christ, who spoke also in other prophets concerning him, says here by David, "I laid down and slept; I awaked, for the Lord received me." By sleep he means death; for he arose again.

74. Concerning the sufferings of Christ, David also says, "Why did the gentiles rage, and the people imagine vain things? Kings rose up on the earth, and

princes were gathered together, against the Lord and his anointed" (Ps 2:1–2). For Herod, the king of the Jews and Pontius Pilate, the governor of Claudius Caesar,[13] came together and condemned him to be crucified. For Herod feared that Christ was going to be an earthly king who would expel him from the kingdom. But Pilate was constrained against his will by Herod and the Jews that were with him to deliver Christ to death. For they threatened Pilate, arguing that if he did not do this to Christ, then he would be acting contrary to Caesar by releasing a man who was called a king.

75. Concerning the sufferings of Christ, the same prophet says further, "You have repelled and despised us; and have cast away your anointed. You have broken the covenant of my servant; You have cast his holiness to the ground. You have overthrown all his hedges; you have made his strongholds tremble. Those who pass on the way have ravaged him. He has become a reproach to his neighbors. You have exalted the right hand of his oppressors. You have made his enemies rejoice over him. You have turned away the help of his sword and did not give him a hand in the battle. You have removed and thrown him down from purification. You have overturned his throne upon the ground. You have shortened the days of his time and have poured forth shame upon him" (Ps 139:39–45). That he should endure these things, and that too by the will of the Father, he manifestly declared. For by the will of the Father he was to endure sufferings.

76. And Zechariah says thus, "Sword, awake against my shepherd, and against the man that is my companion. Strike the shepherd, and the sheep of the flock shall be scattered" (Zech 13:7). And this came to pass when he was taken by the Jews; for all the disciples abandoned him, fearing that they should die with him. For they did not yet steadfastly believe in him until they had seen him risen from the dead.

77. Again he says in the Twelve Prophets, "And they bound him and brought him as a present to the king" (Hos 10:6). For Pontius Pilate was governor of Judea, and he had at that time resentful enmity against Herod the king of the Jews. But then, when Christ was brought to him bound, Pilate sent him to Herod, giving command to enquire of him, that he might know with certainty what he should desire concerning him, thus making Christ a convenient occasion of reconciliation with the king.

78. And in Jeremiah he thus declares his death and descent into hell, saying, "And the Lord the Holy One of Israel, remembered his dead, which formerly fell asleep in the dust of the earth. And he went down unto them, to

---

13 On the reference to Claudius here, see the discussion of chronology and Irenaeus's belief that Jesus lived into his 50s in Robinson (134n1) and Behr (116n197).

bring the tidings of his salvation, to deliver them."[14] In this place he also renders the cause of his death; for his descent into hell was the salvation of them that had passed away.

79. Concerning his cross, Isaiah says thus, "I have stretched out my hands all day long to a disobedient and contrary people" (Isa 65:2). For this is an indication of the cross. Even more manifestly David says, "Hunting dogs encompassed me; the assembly of evil doers came about me. They pierced my hands and my feet" (Ps 22:16). He also says, "My heart became even as wax melting in the midst of my body; and they pulled apart my bones," and again he says, "Spare my soul from the sword and nail my flesh, for the assembly of evil doers has risen up against me" (Ps 22:14, 17). In these words, he signifies with manifest clearness that he should be crucified. Moses says this same thing to the people, "And your life shall be hanged up before your eyes, and you shall fear by day and by night, and you shall not believe in your life" (Deut 28:66).

80. David continues by saying, "They looked upon me; they divided my garments among them, and for my clothing they cast lots" (Ps 22:17–18). For at his crucifixion, the soldiers divided his garments as was their custom; and the garments they divided by tearing; except for the clothing, because it was woven from the top and was not sewn, they cast lots, that to whomsoever it should fall, he should take it.

81. Jeremiah the prophet also says, "And they took the thirty pieces of silver, the price of him that was sold, whom they bought from the children of Israel. Then they gave them for the potter's field, as the Lord commanded me" (Matt 27:9; Zech 11:12–13). For Judas, being one of Christ's disciples, agreed with the Jews and covenanted with them, when he saw they desired to kill him, because he had been reproved by him; and he took the thirty coins of the province and betrayed Christ. And then, repenting of what he had done, he gave the silver back again to the rulers of the Jews and hanged himself. But they, thinking it not right to cast it into their treasury because it was the price of blood, bought with it the ground that was a certain potter's for the burial of strangers.

82. At his crucifixion, when he asked for a drink, they gave him vinegar mixed with gall to drink. This too was declared through David, "They gave me gall to eat, and in my thirst they gave me vinegar to drink" (Ps 69:21; John 19:29).

---

14 Note the discussion of this difficult quotation in Robinson (136n1) and Behr (116n199). Behr notes that this is "an apocryphal quotation, found previously in Justin, who claims that it has been erased" by Jewish scribes.

83. That he was to ascend into heaven after being raised from the dead, David says, "The chariot of God is ten-thousandfold, thousands are the drivers; the Lord is among them in Sinai in his sanctuary. He ascended on high, he led captivity captive; he received, he gave gifts to men" (Ps 68:17–18; Eph 4:8). By "captivity," he means the destruction of the rule of the apostate angels. He declares also the place where he was to ascend into heaven from the earth. For "the Lord," he says, "from Zion ascended on high." For after he was risen from the dead, on the mount above Jerusalem which is called the Mount of Olives, he assembled his disciples and explained to them the things concerning the kingdom of heaven; and they saw that he ascended and how the heavens were opened and received him.

84. David also says, "Lift up your gates, you rulers; and be lifted up, you everlasting gates, and the king of glory shall come in" (Ps 24:7). For the everlasting gates are the heavens. But because the Word descended invisible to created things, he was not made known in his descent to them. Because the Word was made flesh, he was visible in his ascension. And when the powers saw him, the angels below cried out to those who were in the heavens, "Lift up your gates; and be lifted up, you everlasting gates, that the king of glory may come in." And when they marveled and said, "Who is this?" those who had already seen him testified a second time, "The Lord, strong and mighty, he is the king of glory" (Ps 24:8).

85. Being raised from the dead and exalted at the Father's right hand, he awaits the time appointed by the Father for the judgment, when all enemies shall be put under him. Now the enemies are all those who were found in apostasy, angels and archangels and powers and thrones, who despised the truth. The prophet David himself says, "The Lord said to my Lord, 'Sit at my right hand, until I make your enemies your footstool'" (Ps 110:1). That he indeed ascended to that place from which he had come down, David says, "His going forth is from the end of the heavens, and his resting place also the end of the heavens" (Ps 19:6). Then he signifies his judgment, "and there is none that shall be hidden from his heat."

86. If then the prophets prophesied that the Son of God was to appear upon the earth, and prophesied also where on the earth and how and in what manner he should make known his appearance, and all these prophecies the Lord took upon himself, then our faith in him is well-founded, and the tradition of the preaching is true. That is to say, the testimony of the apostles, who being sent forth by the Lord preached in all the world the Son of God, who came to suffer and endured to the destruction of death and the quickening of the flesh. Thus, by putting away the enmity toward God, which is

unrighteousness, we may obtain peace with him, doing that which is pleasing to him. And this was declared by the prophets in the words, "How beautiful are the feet of them that bring tidings of peace, and of them that bring tidings of good things" (Rom 10:15; Isa 52:7). And that these were to go forth from Judea and from Jerusalem, to declare to us "the word" of God, which is "the law" for us, Isaiah says thus, "For from Zion shall come forth the law, and the word of the Lord from Jerusalem" (Isa 2:3). And that in all the earth they were to preach, David says, "Into all the earth went forth their speech, and their words to the ends of the world" (Ps 19:4).

87. That men were to be saved not by the many words of the law, but by the brevity of faith and love, Isaiah says thus, "A word brief and short in righteousness; for God will make a concise word in the whole world" (Isa 10:22–23; Rom 10:18). Therefore, the apostle Paul also says, "Love is the fulfilling of the law" (Rom 13:10), for he who loves God has fulfilled the law. Moreover, the Lord, when he was asked which is the first commandment, said, "You shall love the Lord your God with all your heart and with all your strength. And the second is like it, 'You shall love your neighbor as yourself.' On these two commandments," he says, "hangs all the Law and the Prophets" (Matt 22:37–40). So then by our faith in him he has made our love toward God and our neighbor grow, making us godly, righteous, and good. Therefore, God has made a concise word in the world.

88. And that after his ascension he was to be exalted above all, and that there shall be none to be compared and equaled to him, Isaiah says thus, "Who is he that enters into judgment with me? Let him stand up against me. And who is he who is justified? Let him draw near to the Lord's Son. Woe unto you, for you shall grow old as a garment, and the moth shall devour you. And all flesh shall be humbled and abased, and the Lord alone shall be exalted in the highest" (Isa 50:8–9). That in the end by his name they should be saved who served God, Isaiah also says, "And on those who serve me a new name shall be called, which shall be blessed upon the earth; and they shall bless the true God" (Isa 65:15–16). That this blessing he himself should bring about, and should himself redeem us by his own blood, Isaiah further declared, saying, "No mediator, no angel, but the Lord himself saved them, because he loved them and spared them. He himself redeemed them" (Isa 63:9).

89. That he would not send back the redeemed to the legislation of Moses—for the law was fulfilled in Christ—but would have them live in newness by the Word, through love and faith in the Son of God, Isaiah declared, saying, "Remember not the former things, nor bring to mind the things that were in the beginning. Behold I make new things, which shall now spring up, and you

shall know them. And I will make a way in the wilderness, and streams in the waterless place, to give drink to my chosen race, and to my people whom I have purchased to declare my virtues" (Isa 43:18–21). Now a "wilderness" and a "waterless place" was at first the calling of the gentiles, for the Word had not passed through them, nor given them the Holy Spirit to drink. It is he who fashioned the new way of godliness and righteousness, and made copious streams to spring forth, disseminating the Holy Spirit over the earth, even as it had been promised through the prophets, that in the end of days he should pour out the Spirit upon the face of the earth.

90. Therefore, "by newness of the spirit" is our calling, and not "in the oldness of the letter" (Rom 7:6). In the same way, Jeremiah prophesied, "Behold the days are coming, says the Lord, when I will accomplish a new covenant for the house of Israel and for the house of Judah. This is not like the testament which I covenanted with their fathers in the day when I took them by the hand to lead them out of the land of Egypt. Because they did not continue in the covenant, I no longer regarded them, says the Lord. But this is the covenant of the testament that I will covenant with the house of Israel after those days, says the Lord. I will put my laws into their minds and write them in their hearts. I will be to them a God, and they shall be to me a people. No longer will anyone have to teach his neighbor or his brother, saying, 'Know the Lord,' for all shall know me, from the least to the greatest of them. For I will pardon and be merciful with respect to their iniquities, and their sins will I remember no more" (Jer 31:31–34, LXX 38:31–34; Heb 8:8–12).

91. That the calling from among the gentiles should inherit these promises, to whom also the new testament was opened up, Isaiah says thus, "These things says the God of Israel: 'In that day a man shall trust in his maker, and his eyes shall look to the Holy One of Israel; and they shall not trust in altars, nor in the work of their own hands, which their fingers have made'" (Isa 17:6–8). For very plainly this was said of those who have forsaken idols and believed in God our maker through the Holy One of Israel. And the Holy One of Israel is Christ. He became visible to men, and to him we look eagerly and behold him; and we trust not in altars, nor in the works of our hands.

92. And that he should become visible among us—for the Son of God became the Son of man—and be found among us who had no prior knowledge of him, the Word himself says thus in Isaiah, "I became manifest to those who did not seek me. I was found by those who did not ask for me. I said, 'Behold, here am I, to a people that did not call on my name'" (Isa 65:1).

93. And that this race was to become a holy people was thus declared in the Twelve Prophets by Hosea, "I will call that which was not my people, my

people; and her that was not beloved, beloved. It shall come to pass that in the place where it was called not my people, there shall they be called sons of the living God" (Hos 2:23; 1:10; Rom 9:25–26). This is also that which was said by John the Baptist, "That God is able to raise up sons to Abraham from these stones" (Matt 3:9). For our hearts being withdrawn and taken away from the stony worship by means of faith behold God and become sons of Abraham, who was justified by faith. Therefore, God says by Ezekiel the prophet, "I will give them another heart, and a new spirit I will give them; and I will withdraw and take away the stony heart from their flesh, and I will give them another heart of flesh. They will then walk in my precepts and keep my ordinances and do them. And they shall be a people to me, and I will be God to them" (Ezek 11:19–20).

94. So then by the new calling, a change of hearts in the gentiles came to pass through the Word of God, when he was incarnate and tabernacled with men, just as his disciple John says, "And the Word was made flesh and dwelled among us" (John 1:14). For this reason, the church bears much fruit of the redeemed. For Moses no longer serves as mediator nor Elijah as messenger, but the Lord himself has redeemed us, granting many more children to the church than to the first synagogue, as Isaiah declared, saying, "Rejoice you barren, that did not bear" (Isa 54:1). The "barren" is the church, which never at all in former times presented sons to God. "Cry out and call, you that did not travail, for the children of the desolate are more than of her which has a husband" (Isa 54:1; Gal 4:27). Now the first synagogue had the law as husband.

95. Moreover, Moses in Deuteronomy says that the gentiles should be "the head," and the unbelieving people "the tail" (cf. Deut 28:44). And again he says, "You provoked me to jealousy with those that are no gods, and angered me with your idols. So I will provoke you to jealousy with that which is no nation, and with a foolish nation I will anger you" (Deut 32:21; Rom 10:19). For they forsook the God who is, and worshipped and served the gods who are not. They also killed the prophets of God and "prophesied for Baal" (Jer 2:8), who was the idol of the Canaanites. They despised and condemned the Son of God, the one who is, but they chose Barabbas the robber who had been taken for murder. They disavowed the eternal king, and they acknowledged the temporal Caesar as their king. So, it pleased God to grant their inheritance to the foolish gentiles who were neither citizens of God nor had any prior knowledge of who God is. Since, then, life has been given us by this calling, and God has summed up again for himself in us the faith of Abraham, we ought not to turn back anymore—that is, to the first legislation. For we have

received the Lord of the law, the Son of God, and by faith in him we learn to love God with all our heart, and our neighbor as ourselves. Now the love of God is far from all sin, and the love of neighbor does not work against the neighbor.

96. For this reason also we do not need the law as a tutor. Behold, we speak with the Father, and in his presence we stand, being "children in malice," and grown strong in all righteousness and soberness (cf. 1 Cor 14:20). For, to him who counts no man his enemy, but all men his neighbors, no longer shall the law say, "Do not commit adultery," to him who has no desire at all for another's wife; and "You shall not kill," to him who has put away from himself all anger and enmity; and "You shall not covet your neighbor's field or ox or donkey," to those who have no care at all for earthly things, but store up the heavenly fruits; nor "an eye for an eye, and a tooth for a tooth." Therefore, he cannot stretch out his hand at all for vengeance (cf. Exod 20:13–17; 21:24; Matt 5:21–48). It will not require tithes of him who consecrates all his possessions to God, leaving father and mother and all his kindred, and following the Word of God. And there will be no command to remain idle for one day of rest, to him who perpetually keeps sabbath, that is to say, who in the temple of God, which is man's body, does service to God, and in every hour works righteousness. "For I desire mercy," he says, "and not sacrifice; and the knowledge of God more than burnt offerings" (Hos 6:6). But "the wicked that sacrifices to me a calf is as if he should kill a dog; and that offers fine flour, as though he offered swine's blood" (Isa 66:3). But "whosoever shall call on the name of the Lord shall be saved" (Joel 3:5; Rom 10:13). And there is "no other name" of the Lord "given under heaven by which men are saved" (Acts 4:12), except that of God, which is Jesus Christ the Son of God, to which also the demons, the evil spirits, and all those who have apostatized are subject (cf. Mark 1:27).

97. By the invocation of the name of Jesus Christ, crucified under Pontius Pilate, there is a separation and division among mankind; and wherever any of those who believe in him shall invoke and call upon him and do his will, he is near and present, fulfilling the requests of those who call upon him with a pure heart. Through receiving salvation, we continually give thanks to God, who by his great, inscrutable, and unsearchable wisdom delivered us, and proclaimed the salvation from heaven—namely, the visible coming of our Lord, that is, his living as man to which we could not attain by ourselves. "For the things which are impossible with men are possible with God" (Luke 18:27). For this reason also Jeremiah says concerning wisdom, "Who has gone up into heaven, and taken her, and brought her down from the clouds? Who has gone over the sea, found her, and will bring her fine gold? No one has found

her way, and no one has comprehended her path. But the one who knows all things knows her by his understanding. He who prepares the earth forevermore has filled it with four-footed beasts. He who sends forth the light and it goes; he called it, and it obeyed him with fear; and the stars shined in their watches and were glad. He called them, and they said, 'Here we are.' They shined with gladness toward the one who made them. This is our God. No other is to be considered equal to him. He has found out every way by knowledge and has given it to Jacob his servant and to Israel whom he loves. Afterward, he appeared on earth and spoke with men. This is the book of the commandments of God and of the law which endures forever. All those who hold it fast are appointed to life, but those who leave it shall die."[15]

Now by "Jacob" and "Israel" he means the Son of God, who received power from the Father over our life. After having received this, he brought it down to us who were far off from him, when he "appeared on earth and spoke with men," mingling and mixing the Spirit of God the Father with the creature formed by God, that man might be "after the image and likeness of God."

98. This, beloved, is the preaching of the truth, the manner of our redemption, and the way of life, which the prophets proclaimed, Christ established, and the apostles delivered. This is also what the church in all the world hands on to her children. We must keep this with all certainty, being pleasing to God through good works and a sound mind.

99. Neither should anyone imagine God the Father to be anyone other than our creator, as the heretics imagine. For they despise the God who is, and make gods of that which is not. They fashion a Father of their own above our creator and imagine that they have discovered for themselves something greater than the truth. For all these are impious and blasphemers against their creator and against the Father, as we have shown in the *Exposure and Overthrow of Knowledge Falsely So-called*.[16] Others reject the advent of the Son of God and the economy of his incarnation, which is the summing up of mankind. As we have shown you briefly, this is what the apostles delivered and the prophets foretold. The ones who reject this should be reckoned among those who lack faith. Still others do not receive the gifts of the Holy Spirit and cast away from themselves the prophetic grace, the water through which man bears the fruit of life unto God. These are those of whom Isaiah speaks, "For they shall be ... as an oak that is stripped of leaves, and as a garden that has no water" (Isa 1:30). Because these cannot bear any fruit, they are in no way serviceable to God.

---

15 This quotation is from *Baruch* 3.29–4.1.
16 This title is likely a reference to Books 1–2 of *Against Heresies*.

100. So then, with respect to the three points of our seal, error has strayed widely from the truth. For either they reject the Father, or they do not accept the Son and speak against the economy of his incarnation; or else they do not receive the Spirit, that is, they reject prophecy. If we truly desire to be well-pleasing to God and to attain the redemption that is from him, we must be especially cautious of all such error and shun their ways.

4

The Gospel according to the Scriptures

Selections from Book 3 of *Against Heresies*

Overview

Building on the critical work of Books 1–2 of *Against Heresies*, in Book 3 Irenaeus gives a constructive account of the claims of the gospel based on the writings of the prophets and apostles. In contrast to the heretics, the apostles preached one God who created the world and one Christ who redeemed humanity. The four Gospels and the writings of the apostles correctly understand the prophetic Scriptures and represent the true teachings of Christ. Teachings that reject the Old Testament or deny the reality of the incarnation are false. The God presented in the Scriptures is one and rules over all things with both justice and mercy.

The Purpose of Book 3

3.0.1 My very dear friend, you have indeed requested that I should bring to light the Valentinian doctrines which their devout followers imagine are concealed; that I should exhibit their diversity and compose a treatise in refutation of them. I have therefore undertaken to exhibit both their doctrines and successions—showing that they spring from Simon, the father of all heretics—and to set forth arguments against them all. For this reason, since the conviction of these men and their exposure is in many points but one work, I have sent certain books to you. The first of which comprises the opinions of all these men and exhibits their customs and the character of their behavior. In the second, again, their perverse teachings are cast down and overthrown, and, such as they really are, laid bare and open to view. But in this, the third book, I shall present proofs from the Scriptures, so that I may come behind in nothing of what you have requested. Yes, that over and above what you were expecting, you may receive from me the means of combating and vanquishing those who are spreading any kind of falsehood. For, the love of God, being rich and ungrudging, confers upon the suppliant more than he can ask from it. Call to mind then, the things which I have stated in the two preceding books, and, taking these in connection with them, you shall have from me a comprehensive refutation of all the heretics; and faithfully and strenuously shall you resist them in defense of the only true and life-giving faith, which the church has received from the apostles and imparted to her sons. For the Lord of all gave to his apostles the power of the gospel, through whom also we have known the truth, that is, the doctrine of the Son of God; to whom also did the Lord declare, "He that hears you, hears me; and he that despises you, despises me, and him that sent me" (Luke 10:16).

The Soundness of the Apostolic Preaching and the Apostolic Writings

3.1.1 We have learned the plan of our salvation from no others than those through whom the gospel has come down to us. They proclaimed this gospel at one time in public, and at a later period they handed it down to us in the Scriptures to be the ground and pillar of our faith by the will of God (cf. 1 Tim 3:15). For it is unlawful to assert that they preached before they possessed "perfect knowledge," as some even venture to say, boasting themselves as improvers of the apostles. For, after our Lord rose from the dead, the apostles were invested with power from on high when the Holy Spirit came down upon them, were filled from all his gifts, and had perfect knowledge. They departed to the ends of the earth, preaching the glad tidings of the good things sent from God to us and proclaiming the peace of heaven to men. All of them indeed possessed the gospel of God equally and individually. Matthew also issued a written Gospel among the Hebrews in their own dialect, while Peter and Paul were preaching at Rome and laying the foundations of the church. After their departure, Mark, the disciple and interpreter of Peter, also handed down to us in writing what had been preached by Peter. Luke also, the companion of Paul, recorded in a book the gospel preached by him. Afterwards, John himself, the disciple of the Lord who had also leaned upon his breast, published a Gospel during his residence at Ephesus in Asia.

3.1.2 These have all declared to us that there is one God, creator of heaven and earth, announced by the Law and the Prophets; and one Christ the Son of God. If anyone does not agree to these truths, he despises the companions of the Lord. More than that, he despises Christ himself the Lord; yes, he despises the Father also, and stands self-condemned, resisting and opposing his own salvation, as is the case with all heretics.

3.2.1 When, however, they are proven wrong from the Scriptures, they turn around and accuse these same Scriptures, as if they were not correct nor authoritative, and assert that they are ambiguous and that the truth cannot be extracted from them by those who are ignorant of tradition. For they allege that the truth was not delivered by means of written documents, but by a "living voice" (*viva voce*). For this reason Paul also declared, "But we speak wisdom among those that are perfect, but not the wisdom of this world" (1 Cor 2:6). And this wisdom each one of them indeed alleges to be the fiction of his own inventing; so that, according to their idea, the truth properly resides at one time in Valentinus, at another in Marcion, at another in Cerinthus, then afterwards in Basilides, or has even been indifferently located in any other opponent who could speak nothing pertaining to salvation. For every one of these men is not ashamed to preach himself, depraving the system of truth and being altogether of a perverse disposition.

3.2.2 But, again, when we refer them to that tradition which originates from the apostles, and which is preserved by means of the succession of presbyters in the churches, they object to tradition, saying that they themselves are wiser not merely than the presbyters, but even than the apostles, because they have discovered the unadulterated truth. For they maintain that the apostles intermingled the things of the law with the words of the savior; and that not the apostles alone, but even the Lord himself spoke as at one time from the Demiurge, at another from the intermediate place, and yet again from the Pleroma, but that they themselves, without doubt, without corruption, and with purity, have knowledge of the hidden mystery. This is, indeed, to blaspheme their creator in a most disrespectful manner! It comes to this, therefore, that these men consent neither to Scripture nor to tradition.

3.2.3 These are the kinds of adversaries that we are dealing with, my very dear friend, endeavoring like slippery serpents to escape at all points. For this reason, they must be opposed at all points, if perhaps, by cutting off their retreat, we may succeed in turning them back to the truth. For, though it is not an easy thing for a soul under the influence of error to repent, yet on the other hand, it is not altogether impossible to escape from error when the truth is brought alongside it.

The Connection of the Churches to the Apostolic Preaching

3.3.1 Therefore, it is within the power of all in every church who may wish to see the truth to contemplate clearly the tradition of the apostles that has been manifested throughout the whole world. We are in a position to account for those who were instituted as bishops in the churches by the apostles and to demonstrate the succession of these men down to our own times. These are those who neither taught nor knew of anything like what these heretics rave about. For if the apostles had known hidden mysteries which they were in the habit of imparting to "the perfect" apart from and privately from the rest, they would have delivered them especially to those to whom they were also committing the churches themselves. For they desired that these men should be perfect and blameless in all things, whom they were also leaving behind as their successors, delivering up their own place of government to these men. If they fulfilled their functions honestly, these men would be a great benefit to the church, but if they should fall away, it would be the direst calamity.

3.3.2 Since, however, it would be very tedious to account for the successions of all the churches in such a volume as this, we do put to confusion all those who assemble in unauthorized meetings, in whatever manner, whether by an evil manner of pleasing oneself, by vainglory, or by blindness and perverse opinion. We do this, I say, by specifying that tradition derived from the apostles, of the very great, the very ancient, and universally known church founded and organized at Rome by the two most glorious apostles, Peter and Paul. We also do this by pointing out the faith preached to men which comes down to our time by means of the successions of the bishops. For it is a matter of necessity that every church should agree with this church on account of its pre-eminent authority, that is, the faithful everywhere, inasmuch as the tradition of the apostles has been preserved continuously by those faithful men who exist everywhere.[1]

3.3.3 Having founded and built up the church, the blessed apostles then committed the office of the episcopate into the hands of Linus. Paul mentions this Linus in the epistles to Timothy. To him succeeded Anacletus; and after him, in the third place from the apostles, Clement was allotted the rank of bishop. This man, as he had seen and spoken to the blessed apostles, might be said to have the preaching of the apostles still echoing in his ears and their traditions before his eyes. Nor was he alone in this, for there were many still remaining who had received instructions from the apostles. In the time of this Clement, after a sizeable conflict had occurred among the brothers at

---

[1] The editors of the ANF note the difficulty of translating the phrase "its pre-eminent authority" and discuss the history of interpretation on the role of the church at Rome in early Christianity (415n3).

Corinth, the church in Rome dispatched a most powerful letter to the Corinthians. In it, they exhorted them to peace, renewing their faith and declaring the tradition which they had lately received from the apostles. They also proclaimed the one God, omnipotent, the maker of heaven and earth, the creator of man, who brought on the flood, and called Abraham, who led the people from the land of Egypt, spoke with Moses, set forth the law, sent the prophets, and who has prepared fire for the devil and his angels. From this document, whoever chooses to do so may learn that he, the Father of our Lord Jesus Christ, was preached by the churches and may also understand the apostolic tradition of the church. These things can be discerned because this epistle is of an older date than these men who are now propagating falsehood and who conjure into existence another god beyond the creator and the maker of all existing things. To this Clement there succeeded Evaristus. Alexander followed Evaristus; then, sixth from the apostles, Sixtus was appointed; after him, Telesphorus, who was gloriously martyred; then Hyginus; after him, Pius; then after him, Anicetus. Soter having succeeded Anicetus, Eleutherius does now, in the twelfth place from the apostles, hold the inheritance of the episcopate. In this order and by this succession, the ecclesiastical tradition from the apostles and the preaching of the truth have come down to us. And this is most abundant proof that there is one and the same vivifying faith, which has been preserved in the church from the apostles until now and handed down in truth.

3.3.4 But Polycarp was also not only instructed by apostles and spoke with many who had seen Christ but was also appointed bishop of the church in Smyrna by apostles in Asia. I also saw Polycarp in my early youth, for he tarried on earth a very long time. When he was a very old man, he departed this life by gloriously and most nobly suffering martyrdom, having always taught the things which he had learned from the apostles, and which the church has handed down, and which alone are true. All the churches in Asia testify to these things as well as those men who have succeeded Polycarp down to the present time. Polycarp was a man who was of much greater weight and a more steadfast witness of truth than Valentinus, Marcion, and the rest of the heretics. Coming to Rome in the time of Anicetus, it was he who caused many to turn away from the previously mentioned heretics to the church of God. He proclaimed that he had received this one and sole truth from the apostles, namely, that which is handed down by the church. There are also those who heard from Polycarp that John, the disciple of the Lord, went to bathe at Ephesus and after perceiving that Cerinthus was within, rushed out of the bathhouse without bathing and exclaimed, "Let us fly, lest even the bathhouse fall down, because Cerinthus, the enemy of the truth, is within." Polycarp himself met Marcion on one occasion. Marcion asked, "Do you know me?" and Polycarp replied, "I do know you, the first-born of Satan." Such was the horror which the apostles and their disciples had against holding even verbal communication with any corrupters of the truth. As Paul also says, "After the first and second admonition, reject a man that is a heretic; knowing that such a person sins and is subverted, being condemned himself" (Titus 3:10). Polycarp also wrote a very powerful epistle to the Philippians. Anyone who is anxious about their salvation and chooses to read it can learn the character of their faith and the preaching of the truth. The church in Ephesus is also a true witness of the tradition of the apostles. Paul founded this church, and John remained among them permanently until the times of Trajan.

3.4.1. Therefore, since we have such proofs, it is not necessary to seek the truth among others which it is easy to obtain from the church. Like a rich man depositing his money in a bank, the apostles most abundantly put into the hands of the church all things pertaining to the truth. Any person that wants to can thus draw from the church the water of life (cf. Rev 22:17). For she is the entrance to life. All others are thieves and robbers. On this account we are bound to avoid these others, to pursue the teachings associated with the church with the utmost diligence, and to lay hold of the tradition of the truth. For how does the case stand? Suppose a dispute arises about some important question among us. Should we not have recourse to the most ancient churches with which the apostles had constant dealings and learn from them what is certain and clear in regard to the present question? For how should it be if the apostles themselves had not left us writings? Would it not be necessary, in that case, to follow the course of the tradition which they handed down to those to whom they committed the churches?

3.4.2 Many of those barbarian nations who believe in Christ have taken this course. Having had salvation written in their hearts without paper or ink by the Spirit, they carefully preserve the ancient tradition and believe in one God, the creator of heaven and earth, and all things therein, by means of Christ Jesus, the Son of God. Because of his surpassing love toward his creation, he condescended to be born of the virgin, he himself uniting man through himself to God. Having suffered under Pontius Pilate, and rising again, and having been received up in splendor, he shall come in glory as the savior of those who are saved and the judge of those who are judged. He will also send into eternal fire those who transform the truth and despise his Father and his advent. Those who have believed this faith in the absence of written documents are barbarians in relation to our language, but in relation to our doctrine, manner, and tenor of life, they are very wise indeed because of faith. They please God and order their conversations in all righteousness, purity, and wisdom. If anyone were to preach the inventions of the heretics to these men in their own language, they would at once stop their ears and flee as far off as possible. They would not be willing even to listen to the blasphemous address. Thus, by means of that ancient tradition of the apostles, they do not allow their mind to conceive anything of the doctrines suggested by the pretentious language of these teachers, among whom neither church nor doctrine has ever been established.

3.4.3 For, prior to Valentinus, those who follow Valentinus had no existence. Nor did those from Marcion exist before Marcion. In short, none of those malignant-minded people mentioned above had any being before the existence of the initiators and inventors of their perversity. For Valentinus came to Rome in the time of Hyginus, flourished under Pius, and remained until Anicetus. Cerdon, too, Marcion's predecessor, himself arrived in the time of Hyginus, who was the ninth bishop. Coming frequently into the church and making public confession, he thus remained, one time teaching in secret and then again making public confession. But at last, having been denounced for corrupt teaching, he was excommunicated from the assembly of the brothers. Marcion, then, succeeding him, flourished under Anicetus, who held the tenth place of the episcopate. But the rest, who are called Gnostics, take rise from Menander, Simon's disciple, as I have shown. Each one of them appeared to be both the father and the high priest of that doctrine into which he has been initiated. But all these (the Marcosians) broke out into their apostasy much later, even during the intermediate period of the church.

The Truth of the Apostolic Preaching about God's Being

3.5.1 Therefore, since the tradition from the apostles does exist in the church in this way and is permanent among us, let us return to the scriptural proof furnished by those apostles who also wrote the Gospel, in which they recorded the doctrine regarding God, pointing out that our Lord Jesus Christ is the truth and that no lie is in him (John 14:6). As David also says, prophesying his birth from a virgin and the resurrection from the dead, "Truth has sprung out of the earth" (Ps 85:2). Being disciples of the truth, the apostles are likewise above all falsehood. A lie has no fellowship with the truth, just as darkness has none with light, but the presence of the one shuts out that of the other. Our Lord, therefore, being the truth, did not speak lies. He would never have acknowledged one whom he knew to have taken origin from a defect as God, even the God of all, the supreme king, too, and his own Father. He would never have acknowledged an imperfect being as a perfect one, an animal one as spiritual, him who was without the Pleroma as him who was within it. Neither did his disciples make mention of any other god, nor name any other lord, except him who truly was the God and Lord of all. This is necessary to affirm because these most vain sophists claim that the apostles framed their doctrine with hypocrisy according to the capacity of their hearers and gave answers after the opinions of their questioners—making up blind things for the blind, according to their blindness; for the dull according to their dullness; for those in error according to their error. And to those who imagined that the Demiurge alone was God, they preached him. But to those who are capable of comprehending the unnamable Father, they declared the unspeakable mystery through parables and enigmas. They thus allege that the Lord and the apostles exercised the office of teacher not to further the cause of truth, but even in hypocrisy, and as each individual was able to receive it!

3.5.2 Such a line of conduct belongs not to those who heal or who give life, but to those who bring on diseases and increase ignorance. Truer than these men also is the law that pronounces a curse on those who would send a blind man astray on his path. For the apostles, who were commissioned to search out the wanderers, and to be for sight to those who could not see, and medicine to the weak, certainly did not address them in accordance with their opinion at the time, but according to revealed truth. For no persons of any kind would act properly, if they should advise blind men who were just about to fall over a cliff to continue their most dangerous path as if it were the right one and as if they might go on in safety. Or what medical man, anxious to heal a sick person, would prescribe in accordance with the patient's whims and not according to the requisite medicine? But that the Lord came as the physician of the sick, he himself declares saying, "Those who are whole do not need not a physician, but rather those that are sick; I came not to call the righteous, but sinners to repentance" (Luke 5:31–32). How then shall the sick be strengthened, or how shall sinners come to repentance? Is it by persevering in the very same courses? Or, on the contrary, is it by undergoing a great change and reversal of their former mode of living, by which they have brought upon themselves no slight amount of sickness and many sins? But ignorance, the mother of all these, is driven out by knowledge. For this reason, the Lord used to impart knowledge to his disciples, by which it was also his practice to heal those who were suffering, and to keep back sinners from sin. He therefore did not address them in accordance with their pristine notions, nor did he reply to them in harmony with the opinion of his questioners, but according to the doctrine leading to salvation, without hypocrisy or respect of person.

3.5.3 This is also made clear from the words of the Lord, who truly revealed the Son of God to those of the circumcision. He had been foretold as the Christ by the prophets. That is, he set himself forth, who had restored freedom to men and bestowed on them the inheritance of incorruption. And again, the apostles taught the gentiles that they should leave vain stocks and stones, which they imagined to be gods, and worship the true God who had created and made the whole human family, and, by means of his creation, nourished, increased, strengthened, and preserved them in being. They also taught that they might look for his Son Jesus Christ, who redeemed us from apostasy with his own blood, so that we should also be a sanctified people—who shall also descend from heaven in his Father's power and pass judgment upon all, and who shall freely give the good things of God to those who have kept his commandments. Appearing in these last times as the chief cornerstone, he has gathered into one and united those that were far off and those that were near; that is, the circumcision and the uncircumcision, enlarging Japheth, and placing him in the dwelling of Shem (Eph 2:17; Gen 9:27).

The Truth of the Apostolic Preaching about God the Son

3.6.1 Therefore neither would the Lord, nor the Holy Spirit, nor the apostles, have ever definitely and absolutely named as God him who was not God, unless he were truly God. Nor would they have named any one in his own person Lord, except God the Father ruling over all, and his Son who has received dominion from his Father over all creation, as this passage has it: "The Lord said to my Lord, 'Sit at my right hand, until I make your enemies your footstool'" (Ps 110:1). Here the Scripture presents to us the Father addressing the Son, that is, he who gave him the inheritance of the heathen and subjected to him all his enemies. Since, therefore, the Father is truly Lord, and the Son truly Lord, the Holy Spirit has fittingly designated them by the title of Lord. And again, referring to the destruction of the people of Sodom, the Scripture says, "Then the Lord rained upon Sodom and upon Gomorrah fire and brimstone from the Lord out of heaven" (Gen 19:24). For it here points out that the Son, who had also been talking with Abraham, had received power to judge the people of Sodom for their wickedness. And this following text declares the same truth: "Your throne, O God, is for ever and ever; the scepter of your kingdom is an upright scepter. You have loved righteousness, and hated iniquity; therefore God, your God, has anointed you" (Ps 45:6). For the Spirit designates both of them by the name of God—both him who is anointed as Son, and him who anoints, that is, the Father. And again, "God stood in the congregation of the gods, he judges among the gods" (Ps 82:1). He here refers to the Father and the Son, and those who have received the adoption; but these are the church. For she is the synagogue of God, which God—that is, the Son himself—has gathered by himself. Of whom he again speaks, "The God of gods, the Lord has spoken, and has called the earth" (Ps 50:1). Who is meant by God? He of whom he has said, "God shall come openly, our God, and shall not keep silence" (Ps 50:3). That is, the Son, who came manifested to men who said, "I have openly appeared to those who do not seek me" (Isa 65:1). But of what gods does he speak? Of those to whom he says, "I have said, you are gods, and all sons of the Most High" (Ps 82:6). To those, no doubt, who have received the grace of the "adoption, by which we cry, Abba Father" (Rom 8:15).

3.6.2 For this reason, as I have already stated, no other is named as God, or is called Lord, except him who is God and Lord of all, who also said to Moses, "I am that I am. And thus shall you say to the children of Israel; he who is, has sent me to you" (Exod 3:14). Also named as God is the Son, Jesus Christ our Lord, who makes those that believe in his name the sons of God. And again, when the Son speaks to Moses, he says, "I have come down to deliver this people" (Exod 3:8). For it is he who descended and ascended for the salvation of men. Therefore, God has been declared through the Son, who is in the Father, and has the Father in himself—He who is, the Father bearing witness to the Son, and the Son announcing the Father. As also Isaiah says, "I too am witness," he declares, "says the Lord God, and the Son whom I have chosen, that you may know, and believe, and understand that I am" (Isa 43:10).

3.6.3 When, however, the Scripture terms them gods which are no gods, it does not, as I have already remarked, declare them as gods in every sense, but with a certain addition and signification. In this way, they are shown to be no gods at all. As with David, "The gods of the heathen are idols of demons" (Ps 96:5); and, "You shall not follow other gods" (Ps 81:9). For in that he says "the gods of the heathen"—but the heathen are ignorant of the true God—and calls them "other gods," he bars their claim to be looked upon as gods at all. But as to what they are in their own person, he speaks concerning them; "for they are," he says, "the idols of demons." And Isaiah, "Let them be confounded, all who blaspheme God, and carve useless things" (Isa 44:9). He removes them from the category of gods, but he makes use of the word alone, for this purpose, that we may know of whom he speaks. Jeremiah also says the same, "The gods that have not made the heavens and earth, let them perish from the earth which is under the heaven" (Jer 10:11). For, from the fact of his having added their destruction, he shows them to be no gods at all. Elijah, too, when all Israel was assembled at Mount Carmel, wishing to turn them from idolatry, says to them, "How long will you halt between two opinions? If the Lord is God, follow him" (1 Kgs 18:21). And again, at the burnt offering, he thus addresses the idolatrous priests, "You shall call upon the name of your gods, and I will call on the name of the Lord my God; and the Lord that will listen by fire, he is God." Now, from the fact of the prophet having said these words, he proves that these gods which were reputed so among those men, are no gods at all. He directed them to that God upon whom he believed, and who was truly God. Accordingly, he exclaimed, "Lord God of Abraham, God of Isaac, and God of Jacob, hear me today, and let all this people know that you are the God of Israel" (1 Kgs 18:36).

3.6.4 For this reason, I also call upon you, Lord God of Abraham, Isaac, and Jacob, who are the Father of our Lord Jesus Christ, the God who, through the abundance of your mercy, have had favor toward us, that we should know you, who have made heaven and earth, who rules over all, who is the only and the true God, above whom there is none other God; by our Lord Jesus Christ and the governing power of the Holy Spirit, grant that every reader of this book come to know you, that you are God alone, to be strengthened in you, and to avoid every heretical, godless, and impious doctrine.

3.6.5 The apostle Paul has also made a distinction between those that were not gods and him who is God. As he says, "For though you have served them which are no gods; you now know God, or rather, are known by God" (Gal 4:8–9). And again, speaking of the antichrist, he says, "who opposes and exalts himself above all that is called God, or that is worshipped" (2 Thess 2:4). Here he points out those who are called gods by people who do not know God, that is, idols. For the Father of all is called God, and is so; and the antichrist shall be lifted up, not above him, but above those which are indeed called gods, but are not. And Paul himself says that this is true: "We know that an idol is nothing, and that there is no other God but one. For though there are those that are called gods, whether in heaven or in earth; yet to us there is but one God, the Father, of whom are all things, and we through him; and one Lord Jesus Christ, by whom are all things, and we by him" (1 Cor 8:4). For he has made a distinction, and separated those which are indeed called gods, but which are none, from the one God the Father, from whom are all things, and, he has confessed in the most decided manner in his own person, one Lord Jesus Christ. But in this clause, "whether in heaven or in earth," he does not speak of the formers of the world, as these teachers expound it; but his meaning is similar to that of Moses, when he says, "You shall not make for yourself any image for

God, of whatsoever things that are in heaven above, whatsoever in the earth beneath, and whatsoever in the waters under the earth" (Deut 5:8). And he thus explains what is meant by the things in heaven. "Lest when," he says, "looking toward heaven, and observing the sun, and the moon, and the stars, and all the ornament of heaven, falling into error, you should adore and serve them" (Deut 4:9). And Moses himself, being a man of God, was indeed given as a god before Pharaoh (Exod 7:1). But he is not properly named Lord nor is he called God by the prophets but is spoken of by the Spirit as "Moses, the faithful minister and servant of God," which also he was (Heb 3:5; Num 12:7).

The Gospels Proclaim the Same God Revealed by the Prophets

3.9.1 This, therefore, having been clearly demonstrated here (and it shall yet be so still more clearly), that neither the prophets, nor the apostles, nor the Lord Christ in his own person, acknowledged any other lord or god, but the God and Lord supreme: the prophets and the apostles confessing the Father and the Son; but naming no other as god, and confessing no other as lord; and the Lord himself handing down to his disciples, that he, the Father, is the only God and Lord, who alone is God and ruler of all—it is essential for us to follow their testimonies to this effect if we are indeed their disciples. For Matthew the apostle knew that the one who had given the promise to Abraham that he would make his seed as numerous as the stars of heaven was one and the same God as him who has called us to the knowledge of himself through his Son Christ Jesus. This one God calls us away from the worship of stones so that those who were not a people might be made a people, and she who was not beloved might become the beloved. Matthew thus declares that when John was preparing the way for Christ, he spoke to those who were boasting of their relationship to Abraham according to the flesh. But these same ones had their mind tinged and stuffed with all manner of evil. John preached about the kind of repentance that might call them back from their evil doings. He therefore said, "O generation of vipers, who has warned you to flee from the wrath to come? Bring forth therefore fruit fit for repentance. And do not think to say within yourselves, We have Abraham as our father; for I say to you that God is able to raise up children of Abraham from these stones" (Matt 3:7). He preached to them, therefore, about repentance from wickedness, but he did not declare to them another god besides him who made the promise to Abraham. He was the forerunner of Christ. Matthew again says of him, and Luke likewise, "For this is he who was spoken of from the Lord by the prophet, the voice of one crying in the wilderness, Prepare the way of the Lord, make straight the paths of our God. Every valley shall be filled, and every mountain and hill brought low; and the crooked shall be made straight, and the rough into smooth ways; and all flesh shall see the salvation of God" (Matt 3:3). There is therefore one and the same God, the Father of our Lord, who also promised through the prophets that he would send his forerunner. And he caused his salvation—that is, his Word—to be made visible to all flesh. The Word himself became incarnate so that in all things their king might become manifest. For it is necessary that those who are judged actually see the judge and know the one from whom they receive judgment. It is also proper that those who follow on to glory should know him who bestows upon them the gift of glory.

3.9.2 Then again Matthew, when speaking of the angel, says, "The angel of the Lord appeared to Joseph in his sleep" (Matt 1:20). Of what Lord he himself interprets, "That it may be fulfilled which was spoken of the Lord by the prophet, Out of Egypt have I called my son" (Matt 2:15). "Behold, a virgin shall conceive, and shall bring forth a son, and they shall call his name Emmanuel; which is, being interpreted, God with us" (Matt 1:23). David likewise speaks of him who, from the virgin, is Emmanuel, "Do not turn away the face of your anointed. The Lord has sworn a truth to David, and will not turn from him. I will set upon your throne one from the fruit of your body" (Ps 132:11). And again, "In Judea God is known; his place has been made in peace, and his dwelling in Zion" (Ps 76:1). Therefore, there is one and the same God, who was proclaimed by the prophets and announced by the Gospel; and his Son, who was of the fruit of David's body, that is, of the virgin of the house of David, and Emmanuel; whose star also Balaam thus prophesied, "A star shall come out of Jacob, and a leader shall rise in Israel" (Num 24:17). But Matthew says that the Magi, coming from the east, exclaimed "For we have seen his star in the east, and have come to worship him" (Matt 2:2); and that, having been led by the star into the house of Jacob to Emmanuel, they showed by these gifts which they offered who it was that was worshipped: myrrh, because it was he who should die and be buried for the mortal human race; gold, because he was a king, "of whose kingdom is no end (Luke 1:33); and frankincense, because he was God, who also "was made known in Judea" (Ps 76:1), and was "declared to those who sought him not" (Isa 65:1).

3.9.3 And then, speaking of his baptism, Matthew says, "The heavens were opened, and he saw the Spirit of God, as a dove, coming upon him; and behold, a voice from heaven saying, This is my beloved Son, in whom I am well pleased" (Matt 3:16). For Christ did not at that time descend upon Jesus, neither was Christ one and Jesus another; but the Word of God—who is the savior of all, and the ruler of heaven and earth, who is Jesus, as I have already pointed out, who also took on human flesh, and was anointed by the Spirit from the Father—was made Jesus Christ. As Isaiah also says, "There shall come forth a rod from the root of Jesse, and a flower shall rise from his root; and the Spirit of God shall rest upon him; the spirit of wisdom and understanding, the spirit of counsel and might, the spirit of knowledge and piety, and the spirit of the fear of God, shall fill him. He shall not judge according to glory, nor reprove after the manner of speech; but he shall dispense judgment to the humble man, and reprove the haughty ones of the earth" (Isa 11:1). And again Isaiah, pointing out beforehand his anointing, and the reason why he was anointed, himself says, "The Spirit of God is upon me, because he has anointed me; he has sent me to preach the gospel to the lowly, to heal the brokenhearted, to proclaim liberty to the captives, and sight to the blind; to announce the favorable year of the Lord, and the day of vengeance; to comfort all that mourn" (Isa 61:1). For inasmuch as the Word of God was man from the root of Jesse and son of Abraham, in this respect did the Spirit of God rest upon him and anoint him to preach the gospel to the lowly. But inasmuch as he was God, he did not judge according to glory nor reprove after the manner of speech. For "he did not need anyone to testify to him about man, for he himself knew what was in man" (John 2:25). For he called all men that mourn; and granting forgiveness to those who had been led into captivity by their sins, he freed them from their chains, of whom Solomon says, "Every one shall be bound with the cords of his own sins" (Prov 5:22). Accordingly, the Spirit of God descended upon him so that we might receive from the abundance of his anointing and be saved. This is the Spirit of him who had promised by the prophets that he would anoint him. Such, then, is the witness of Matthew.

3.10.1 Luke also, the follower and disciple of the apostles, referring to Zacharias and Elisabeth, from whom, according to promise, John was born, says, "And they were both righteous before God, walking in all the commandments and ordinances of the Lord blameless" (Luke 1:6). And again, speaking of Zacharias, "And it came to pass, that while he executed the priest's office before God in the order of his course, according to the custom of the priest's office, his lot was to burn incense"; and he came to sacrifice, "entering into the temple of the Lord" (Luke 1:8). Whose angel Gabriel, also, who stands prominently in the presence of the Lord, simply, absolutely, and decidedly confessed in his own person as God and Lord, him who had chosen Jerusalem, and had instituted the priestly office. For he knew of none other above him; since, if he had been in possession of the knowledge of any other more perfect God and Lord besides him, he surely would never—as I have already shown—have confessed him, whom he knew to be the fruit of a defect, as absolutely and altogether God and Lord. And then, speaking of John, he thus says, "For he shall be great in the sight of the Lord, and he shall turn many of the children of Israel to the Lord their God. And he shall go before him in the spirit and power of Elijah, to make ready a people prepared for the Lord" (Luke 1:15). For whom, then, did he prepare the people, and in the sight of what Lord was he made great? Truly of him who said that John had something even "more than a prophet," and that "among those born of women none is greater than John the Baptist" (Matt 11:9–11). John also made the people ready for the Lord's advent, warning his fellow servants and preaching to them repentance so that they might receive forgiveness from the Lord when he should be present, having been converted to him, from whom they had been alienated because of sins and transgressions. As David also says, "The alienated are sinners from the womb; they go astray as soon as they are born" (Ps 58:3). And it was on account of this that he, turning them to their Lord, prepared, in the spirit and power of Elijah, a perfect people for the Lord.

3.10.2 And again, speaking in reference to the angel, he says, "But at that time the angel Gabriel was sent from God, who also said to the virgin, Fear not, Mary; for you have found favor with God" (Luke 1:26). And he says concerning the Lord, "He shall be great, and shall be called the Son of the Most High; and the Lord God shall give unto him the throne of his father David; and he shall reign over the house of Jacob forever; and of his kingdom there shall be no end" (Luke 1:32–33). For who else is there who can reign without interruption over the house of Jacob forever, except Jesus Christ our Lord, the Son of the Most High God, who promised by the Law and the Prophets that he would make his salvation visible to all flesh; so that he would become the Son of Man for this purpose, that man also might become the Son of God? And Mary, exulting because of this, cried out, prophesying on behalf of the church, "My soul magnifies the Lord, and my spirit has rejoiced in God my savior. For he has taken up his child Israel, in remembrance of his mercy, as he spoke to our fathers, Abraham, and his seed forever" (Luke 1:46–47). By these and similar passages, the Gospel points out that it was God who spoke to the fathers; that it was he who, by Moses, instituted the legal dispensation, by which giving of the law we know that he spoke to the fathers. This same God, after his great goodness, poured his compassion upon us, through which compassion "the Day-spring from on high has looked upon us, and appeared to those who sat in darkness and the shadow of death, and has guided our feet into the way of peace" (Luke 1:78). As Zachariah also, recovering from not being able to speak which he had suffered on account of unbelief, having been filled with a new spirit, blessed God in a new manner. For all things had entered into a new phase, the Word arranging after a new manner the advent in the flesh, that he might win back to God that human nature which had departed from God. Therefore men were taught to worship God after a new fashion, but not another god, because in truth there is but "one God, who justifies the circumcision by faith, and the uncircumcision through faith" (Rom 3:30). But Zachariah prophesying, exclaimed, "Blessed be the Lord God of Israel; for he has visited and redeemed his people, and has raised up an horn of salvation for us in the house of his servant David; as he spoke by the mouth of his holy prophets, which have been since the world begun; salvation from our enemies, and from the hand of all that hate us; to perform the mercy promised to our fathers, and to remember his holy covenant, the oath which he swore to our father Abraham, that he would grant unto us, that we, being delivered out of the hand of our enemies, might serve him without fear, in holiness and righteousness before him, all our days" (Luke 1:68). Then he says to John, "And you, child, shall be called the prophet of the highest; for you shall go before the face of the Lord to prepare his ways; to give knowledge of salvation to his people, for the remission of their sins" (Luke 1:76). For this is the knowledge of salvation which they lacked, that of the Son of God, which John made known, saying, "Behold the Lamb of God, who takes away the sin of the world. This is he of whom I said, After me comes a man who was made before me; because he was prior to me; and of his fulness have all we received" (John 1:29; 1:15–16).

This, therefore, was the knowledge of salvation. But it did not consist in another god, nor another Father, nor Bythus, nor the Pleroma of thirty Aeons, nor the Mother of the lower Ogdoad. Rather, the knowledge of salvation was the knowledge of the Son of God who is both called and actually is, salvation, savior, and the one who sustains our well-being. Salvation, indeed, as follows, "I have waited for your salvation, O Lord" (Gen 49:18). And then again, savior, "Behold my God, my savior, I will put my trust in him" (Isa 12:2). But as bringing salvation, thus, "God has made known his salvation in the sight of the heathen" (Ps 98:2). For he is indeed savior, being the Son and Word of God. He is also the one who sustains our well-being, since he is Spirit. For he says, "The Spirit of our countenance, Christ the Lord" (Lam 4:20 LXX). But as for salvation being embodied, for "the Word was made flesh, and dwelt among us" (John 1:14). This knowledge of salvation, therefore, John imparted to those repenting and believing in the Lamb of God who takes away the sin of the world.

3.10.3 And the angel of the Lord, he says, appeared to the shepherds, proclaiming joy to them, "For there is born in the house of David, a savior, who is Christ the Lord. Then a multitude of the heavenly host appeared, praising God, and saying, Glory in the highest to God, and on earth peace, to men of good will" (Luke 2:11). The falsely-called Gnostics say that these angels came from the ogdoad, and made manifest the descent of the superior Christ. But they are again in error, when saying that the Christ and savior from above was not born, but that also, after the baptism of the dispensational Jesus, he, the Christ of the Pleroma, descended upon him as a dove. Therefore, according to these men, the angels of the ogdoad lied, when they said, "For unto you is born this day a savior, who is Christ the Lord, in the city of David." For by their account neither Christ nor the savior was born at that time. But it was he, the dispensational Jesus, who is from the framer of the world, the Demiurge, and upon whom, after his baptism, that is, after the lapse of thirty years, they maintain the savior from above descended. But why did the angels add, "in the city of David," if they did not proclaim the glad tidings of the fulfillment of God's promise made to David, that from the fruit of his body there should be an eternal king? For the framer Demiurge of the entire universe made promise to David, as David himself declares, "My help is from God, who made heaven and earth" (Ps 124:8); and again, "In his hand are the ends of the earth, and the heights of the mountains are his. For the sea is his, and he made it himself; and his hands founded the dry land. Come, let us worship and fall down before him, and weep in the presence of the Lord who made us; for he is the Lord our God" (Ps 95:4). The Holy Spirit evidently thus declares by David to those hearing him, that there shall be those who despise him who formed us, and who is God alone. For this reason, he also uttered the foregoing words, meaning to say, "See that you do not err; besides or above him there is no other God, to whom you should rather stretch out your hands, thus rendering us pious and grateful toward him who made, established, and still nourishes us." What, then, shall happen to those who have been the authors of so much blasphemy against their creator? This identical truth was also what the angels proclaimed. For when they exclaim, "Glory to God in the highest, and on earth peace," they have glorified with these words him who is the creator of the highest, that is, of super-celestial things, and the founder of everything on earth; who has sent to his own handiwork, that is, to men, the blessing of his salvation from heaven. For this reason, he adds, "The shepherds returned, glorifying God for all that they had heard and seen, as it was told to them" (Luke 2:20). For the Israelite shepherds did not glorify another god, but him who had been announced by the Law and the Prophets, the maker of all things, whom also the angels glorified. But if the angels who were from the ogdoad were accustomed to glorify any other, different from him whom the shepherds adored, these angels from the ogdoad brought to them error and not truth.

3.10.4 And still further Luke says in reference to the Lord, "When the days of purification were accomplished, they brought him up to Jerusalem, to present him before the Lord, as it is written in the law of the Lord, that every male opening the womb shall be called holy to the Lord; and that they should offer a sacrifice, as it is said in the law of the Lord, a pair of turtle-doves, or two young pigeons" (Luke 2:22); in his own person most clearly calling him Lord, who appointed the legal dispensation. But "Simeon," he also says, "blessed God, and said, Lord, let your servant now depart in peace; for my eyes have seen your salvation, which you have prepared before the face of all people; a light for the revelation of the gentiles, and the glory of your people Israel" (Luke 2:29). And "Anna" also, "the prophetess," he says, in like manner glorified God when she saw Christ, "and spoke of him to all who were looking for the redemption of Jerusalem" (Luke 2:38). Now by all these statements, one God is shown forth, revealing to men the new dispensation of liberty, the covenant, through the new advent of his Son.

3.10.5 For this reason also Mark, the interpreter and follower of Peter, thus commences his Gospel narrative, "The beginning of the Gospel of Jesus Christ, the Son of God; as it is written in the prophets, Behold, I send my messenger before your face, which shall prepare your way. The voice of one crying in the wilderness, Prepare the way of the Lord, make the paths straight before our God" (Mark 1:2). The commencement of the Gospel quotes plainly the words of the holy prophets, and points him out at once, whom they confessed as God and Lord; him, the Father of our Lord Jesus Christ, who had also made promise to him, that he would send his messenger before his face, who was John, crying in the wilderness, in "the spirit and power of Elijah" (Luke 1:17), "Prepare the way of the Lord, make straight paths before our God" (Mark 1:2). For the prophets did not announce one and another god, but one and the same; under various aspects, however, and many titles. For the Father is varied and rich in attributes, as I have already shown in the book preceding this (cf. *Haer.* 2.35.3). I shall show the same truth from the prophets themselves in the further course of this work. Also, toward the conclusion of his Gospel, Mark says, "So then, after the Lord Jesus had spoken to them, he was received up into heaven, and sits at the right hand of God" (Mark 16:19); confirming what had been spoken by the prophet, "The Lord said to my Lord, Sit at my right hand, until I make your foes your footstool" (Ps 110:1). Thus God and the Father are truly one and the same; he who was announced by the prophets, and handed down by the true gospel; whom we Christians worship and love with the whole heart, as the maker of heaven and earth, and of everything this world contains.

3.11.1 John, the disciple of the Lord, preaches this faith and seeks by the proclamation of the gospel to remove that error which had been disseminated among men by Cerinthus and a long time previously by those termed Nicolaitans and which was an offset of that "knowledge" falsely so called. In this preaching, John sought to confound them and persuade them that there is but one God, who made all things by his Word; and not, as they allege, that the creator was one, but the Father of the Lord another; and that the son of the creator was indeed one, but the Christ from above another, who also continued impassible, descending upon Jesus, the son of the creator, and flew back again into his Pleroma; and that Monogenes was the beginning, but Logos was the true son of Monogenes; and that this creation to which we belong was not made by the primary God, but by some power lying far below him, and shut off from communion with the things invisible and ineffable. The disciple of the Lord therefore desiring to put an end to all such doctrines and to establish the rule of truth in the church, that there is one almighty God, who made all things by his Word, both visible and invisible; showing at the same time, that by the Word, through whom God made the creation, he also bestowed salvation on the men included in the creation; thus commenced his teaching in the Gospel, "In the beginning was the Word, and the Word was with God, and the Word was God. The same was in the beginning with God. All things were made by him, and without him nothing was made. What was made was life in him, and the life was the light of men. And the light shines in darkness, and the darkness does not comprehend it" (John 1:1–4). "All things," he says, "were made by him"; therefore in "all things" this creation of ours is included, for we cannot concede to these men that the words "all things" are spoken in reference to those within their Pleroma. For if their Pleroma does indeed contain these, this creation, as being such, is not outside, as I have demonstrated in the preceding book (cf. *Haer.* 2.1). But if they are outside the Pleroma, which indeed appeared impossible, in that case it follows that their Pleroma cannot be "all things." Therefore, this vast creation is not outside the Pleroma.

3.11.2 John himself, however, puts this matter beyond all controversy for our part when he says, "He was in this world, and the world was made by him, and the world did not know him. He came unto his own, and his own people did not receive him" (John 1:10–11). But according to Marcion, and those like him, neither was the world made by him; nor did he come to his own things, but to those of another. And, according to certain of the Gnostics, this world was made by angels, and not by the Word of God. But according to the followers of Valentinus, the world was not made by him, but by the Demiurge. For he, Soter, caused such similitudes to be made after the pattern of things above, as they allege; but the Demiurge accomplished the work of creation. For they say that he, the Lord and creator of the plan of creation, by whom they hold that this world was made, was produced from the Mother; while the Gospel affirms plainly that by the Word, which was in the beginning with God, all things were made, which Word, he says, "was made flesh, and dwelt among us" (John 1:14).

3.11.3 But, according to these men, neither was the Word made flesh, nor Christ, nor the savior, who was produced from the joint contributions of all the Aeons. For they will have it, that the Word and Christ never came into this world; that the savior, too, never became incarnate, nor suffered, but that he descended like a dove upon the dispensational Jesus; and that, as soon as he had declared the unknown Father, he did again ascend into the Pleroma. Some, however, make the assertion, that this dispensational Jesus did become incarnate, and suffered, whom they represent as having passed through Mary just as water through a tube; but others allege him to be the son of the Demiurge, upon whom the dispensational Jesus descended; while others, again, say that Jesus was born from Joseph and Mary, and that the Christ from above descended upon him, being without flesh, and impassible. But according to the opinion of not one of the heretics was the Word of God made flesh. For if anyone carefully examines the systems of them all, he will find that the Word of God is brought in by all of them as not having become incarnate and impassible, as is also the Christ from above. Others consider him to have been manifested as a transfigured man; but they maintain him to have been neither born nor to have become incarnate; while others hold that he did not assume a human form at all, but that, as a dove, he descended upon that Jesus who was born from Mary. Therefore, the Lord's disciple, pointing them all out as false witnesses, says, "And the Word was made flesh, and dwelt among us."

3.11.4 And that we may not have to ask, Of what God was the Word made flesh? he himself previously teaches us, saying, "There was a man sent from God, whose name was John. The same came as a witness, that he might bear witness of that light. He was not that light, but came that he might testify of the light" (John 1:6). By what God, then, was John, the forerunner, who testifies of the light, sent into the world? Truly it was by him, of whom Gabriel is the angel, who also announced the glad tidings of his birth; that God who also had promised by the prophets that he would send his messenger before the face of his Son, who should prepare his way, that is, that he should bear witness of that light in the spirit and power of Elijah (Mal 3:1; Luke 1:17). But, again, of what God was Elijah the servant and the prophet? Of him who made heaven and earth, as he does himself confess. John, therefore, having been sent by the founder and maker of this world, how could he testify of that light which came down from things unspeakable and invisible? For all the heretics have decided that the Demiurge was ignorant of that power above him, whose witness and herald John is found to be. For this reason, the Lord said that he deemed him "more than a prophet" (Matt 11:9; Luke 7:26). For all the other prophets preached the advent of the paternal light, and desired to be worthy of seeing him whom they preached; but John both announced the advent beforehand, in a like manner as did the others, and actually saw him when he came, and pointed him out, and persuaded many to believe in him, so that he himself held the place of both prophet and apostle. For this is to be more than a prophet, because, "first apostles, secondarily prophets" (1 Cor 12:28); but all things from one and the same God himself.

3.11.5 That wine, which was produced by God in a vineyard, and which was first consumed, was good. None of those who drank of it found fault with it; and the Lord partook of it also (John 2:3). But that wine was better which the Word made from water, in the moment, and simply for the use of those who had been called to the marriage. For although the Lord had the power to supply wine to those feasting, independently of any created substance, and to fill with food those who were hungry, he did not adopt this course; but, taking the loaves which the earth had produced, and giving thanks, and on the other occasion making water into wine, he satisfied those who were reclining at table, and gave drink to those who had been invited to the marriage; showing that the God who made the earth, and commanded it to bring forth fruit, who established the waters, and brought forth the fountains, was he who in these last times bestowed upon mankind, by his Son, the blessing of food and the favor of drink; the incomprehensible acting thus by means of the comprehensible, and the invisible by the visible; since there is none beyond him, but he exists in the bosom of the Father.

3.11.6 For "no man," he says, "has seen God at any time," unless "the only-begotten Son of God, which is in the bosom of the Father, he has declared him" (John 1:18). For he, the Son who is in his bosom, declares to all the Father who is invisible. For this reason, they know him to whom the Son reveals him; and again, the Father, by means of the Son, gives knowledge of his Son to those who love him. By whom also Nathanael, being taught, recognized him, he to whom also the Lord bore witness, that he was "an Israelite indeed, in whom was no guile" (John 1:47). The Israelite recognized his king, therefore he cried out to him, "Rabbi, You are the Son of God, You are the king of Israel." By whom also Peter, having been taught, recognized Christ as the Son of the living God, when God said, "Behold my dearly beloved Son, in whom I am well pleased; I will put my Spirit upon him, and he shall show judgment to the gentiles. He shall not strive, nor cry; neither shall any man hear his voice in the streets. A bruised reed he shall not break, and smoking flax he shall not quench, until he sends forth judgment into contention; and in his name shall the gentiles trust" (John 1:49; Matt 12:17–21; Isa 42:1–3).

The Shape and Theological Function of the Fourfold Gospel

3.11.7 Such, then, are the first principles of the gospel: that there is one God, the maker of this universe; he who was also announced by the prophets, and who by Moses set forth the dispensation of the law—principles which proclaim the Father of our Lord Jesus Christ and ignore any other God or Father except him. So firm is the ground upon which these Gospels rest, that the very heretics themselves bear witness to them, and, starting from these documents, each one of them endeavors to establish his own peculiar doctrine. For the Ebionites, who use Matthew's Gospel only, are proven wrong out of this very same, making false suppositions with regard to the Lord. But Marcion, mutilating that according to Luke, is proved to be a blasphemer of the only existing God from those passages which he still retains. Those, again, who separate Jesus from Christ, alleging that Christ remained impassible but that it was Jesus who suffered, preferring the Gospel by Mark, if they read it with a love of truth, may have their errors rectified. Those, moreover, who follow Valentinus, making copious use of that according to John, to illustrate their conjectures, shall be proved to be totally in error by means of this very Gospel, as I have shown in the first book. Since, then, our opponents bear testimony to us, and make use of these documents, our proof derived from them is firm and true.

3.11.8 It is not possible that the Gospels can be either more or fewer in number than they are. For, since there are four zones of the world in which we live, and four principal winds, while the church is scattered throughout all the world, and the "pillar and ground" of the church is the gospel and the spirit of life; it is fitting that she should have four pillars, breathing out immortality on every side and giving new life to men.[2] From this

---

[2] The phrase "four principal winds" might also be translated as "four catholic spirits" (τέσσαρα καθολικὰ πνεύματα). The phrase "pillars of truth" is drawn from 1 Tim 3:15.

fact, it is evident that the Word, the skilled craftsman of all, he that sits upon the cherubim and contains all things, and he who was manifested to men, has given us the gospel under four aspects but bound together by one Spirit. As David also says, when addressing his manifestation, "You that sits between the cherubim, shine forth" (Ps 80:1). For the cherubim, too, were four-faced, and their faces were images of the economy of the Son of God. For, as the Scripture says, "The first living creature was like a lion" (Rev 4:7), symbolizing his effectual working, his leadership, and royal power; the second living creature was like a calf, signifying his sacrificial and priestly order; but "the third had, as it were, the face as of a man," an evident description of his advent as a human being; "the fourth was like a flying eagle," pointing out the gift of the Spirit hovering with his wings over the church. And therefore the Gospels are in accord with these things, among which Christ Jesus is seated. For that according to John relates his original, effectual, and glorious generation from the Father, thus declaring, "In the beginning was the Word, and the Word was with God, and the Word was God" (John 1:1). Also, "all things were made by him, and without him nothing was made." For this reason, too, is that Gospel full of all confidence, for such is his person. But that according to Luke, taking up his priestly character, commenced with Zachariah the priest offering sacrifice to God. For now was made ready the fatted calf, about to be offered as sacrifice for the finding again of the younger son. Matthew, again, relates his generation as a man, saying, "The book of the generation of Jesus Christ, the son of David, the son of Abraham"; and also, "The birth of Jesus Christ took place in this way" (Matt 1:1, 18). This, then, is the Gospel of his humanity; for which reason it is, too, that the character of a humble and meek man is kept up through the whole Gospel. Mark, on the other hand, commences with a reference to the prophetic spirit coming down from on high to men, saying, "The beginning of the gospel of Jesus Christ, as it is written in Isaiah the prophet," pointing to the winged aspect of the Gospel; and on this account he made a concise and cursory narrative, for such is the prophetic character. And the Word of God himself used to speak with the patriarchs who came before Moses, in accordance with his divinity and glory; but for those under the law he instituted a priestly and liturgical service. Afterwards, being made man for us, he sent the gift of the celestial Spirit over all the earth, protecting us with his wings. Such, then, as was the course followed by the Son of God, so also was the form of the living creatures; and such as was the form of the living creatures, so also was the character of the gospel. For the living creatures have a fourfold form, and the gospel has a fourfold form, as is also the course followed by the Lord. For this reason, there were four principal covenants given to the human race: one, prior to the flood, under Adam; the second, that after the flood, under Noah; the third, the giving of the law, under Moses; the fourth, that which renovates man, and sums up all things in itself by means of the gospel, raising and bearing men upon its wings into the heavenly kingdom.[3]

3.11.9 These things being so, all who destroy the form of the gospel are vain, unlearned, and also audacious. I mean those who represent the aspects of the gospel as being either more in number than previously mentioned, or, on the other hand, fewer. The former class do so, that they may seem to have discovered more than is of the truth; the latter, that they may set the dispensations of God aside. For Marcion, rejecting the entire gospel, yes rather, cutting himself off from the gospel, boasts that he has part in the blessings of the gospel. Others, again the Montanists, that they may consider as nothing the gift of the Spirit, which in the latter times has been by the good pleasure of the Father poured out upon the human race, do not admit that aspect of the evangelical dispensation presented by John's Gospel, in which the Lord promised that he would send the Paraclete (John 14:6); but set aside at once both the gospel and the prophetic Spirit. Wretched men! who wish to be pseudo-prophets, indeed, but who set aside the gift of prophecy from the church; acting like those . . . who, on account of such hypocrisy, hold themselves aloof from the communion of the brothers. We must conclude, moreover, that these men, the Montanists, cannot recognize the apostle Paul either. For, in his epistle to the Corinthians, he speaks expressly of prophetic gifts, and recognizes men and women prophesying in the church (1 Cor 11:4–5). Sinning, therefore, in all these particulars, against the Spirit of God, they fall into the unpardonable sin (Matt 12:31). But those who are from Valentinus, being, on the other hand, altogether reckless, while they put forth their own compositions, boast that they possess more Gospels than there really are. Indeed, they have arrived at such a pitch of audacity as to entitle their comparatively recent writing "the Gospel of Truth," though it agrees in nothing with the Gospels of the apostles, so that they have really no gospel which is not full of blasphemy. For if what they have published is the gospel of truth, and yet is totally unlike those which have been handed down to us from the apostles, any who please may learn, as is shown from the Scriptures themselves, that that which has been handed down from the apostles can no longer be reckoned the gospel of truth.

---

3 The phrase "four principal" covenants could also be understood as "four catholic" (καθολικά) covenants.

But that these Gospels alone are true and reliable and admit neither an increase nor reduction of the previously mentioned number, I have proved by so many and such arguments. For, since God made all things in due proportion and adaptation, it was fitting also that the outward aspect of the gospel should be well-arranged and harmonized. The opinion of those men, therefore, who handed the gospel down to us, having been investigated from their very fountainheads, let us proceed also to the remaining apostles, and inquire into their doctrine with regard to God; then, in due course we shall listen to the very words of the Lord.

The Unified Preaching of the Apostles among the Early Churches

3.12.4 For this reason, too, when the chief priests were assembled, Peter, full of boldness, said to them, "You rulers of the people, and elders of Israel, if today we are examined by you regarding the good deed done to the helpless man, by what means he has been made whole; be it known to you all, and to all the people of Israel, that by the name of Jesus Christ of Nazareth, whom you crucified, whom God raised from the dead, even by him does this man stand here before you whole. This is the stone which was considered as nothing by you builders, which has become the chief cornerstone. Neither is there salvation in any other; for there is no other name under heaven, which is given to men, by which we must be saved" (Acts 4:8). Thus the apostles did not change God, but preached to the people that the Christ was Jesus the crucified one, whom the same God that had sent the prophets, being God himself, raised up, and gave salvation to men in him.

3.12.5 They were confounded, therefore, both by this instance of healing ("for the man was over forty years old on whom this miracle of healing took place"), and by the doctrine of the apostles and by the exposition of the prophets, when the chief priests had sent away Peter and John. Then Peter and John returned to the rest of their fellow apostles and disciples of the Lord, that is, to the church, and related what had occurred and how courageously they had acted in the name of Jesus. The whole church, it is then said, "when they had heard that, lifted up their voice to God with one accord, and said, Lord, You are God, who has made heaven and earth and the sea and all that is in them; who, through the Holy Spirit, by the mouth of our father David, your servant, has said, Why did the heathen rage, and the people imagine vain things? The kings of the earth stood up, and the rulers were gathered together against the Lord, and against his Christ. For truly, in this city, against your holy Son Jesus, whom you have anointed, both Herod and Pontius Pilate, with the gentiles, and the people of Israel, were gathered together, to do whatsoever your hand and your counsel determined before to be done" (Acts 4:24). These are the voices of the church from which every church has its origin. These are the voices of the metropolis of the citizens of the new covenant. These are the voices of the apostles. These are voices of the disciples of the Lord, the truly perfect, who, after the ascension of the Lord, were perfected by the Spirit. They called upon the God who made heaven and earth and the sea, who was announced by the prophets, and Jesus Christ his Son whom God anointed and who knew no other God. For at that time and place there was neither Valentinus, nor Marcion, nor the rest of these subverters of the truth and their adherents. For this reason God, the maker of all things, heard them. For it is said, "The place was shaken where they were assembled together; and they were all filled with the Holy Spirit, and they spoke the word of God with boldness" to everyone that was willing to believe (Acts 4:31). "And with great power," it is added, "gave the apostles witness of the resurrection of the Lord Jesus" (Acts 4:33), saying to them, "The God of our fathers raised up Jesus, whom you seized and killed, hanging him upon a beam of wood; God has raised him up by his right hand to be a prince and savior, to give repentance to Israel, and forgiveness of sins. And we are in this witnesses of these words; as also is the Holy Spirit, whom God has given to them that believe in him" (Acts 5:30). "And daily," it is said, "in the temple, and from house to house, they did not cease teaching and preaching Christ Jesus," the Son of God (Acts 5:42). For this was the knowledge of salvation which renders those who acknowledge his Son's advent perfect toward God.

The God of the Jews is the God of the Gentiles

3.12.7 From the words of Peter, therefore, which he addressed in Caesarea to Cornelius the centurion, and those gentiles with him, to whom the word of God was first preached, we can understand what the apostles used to preach, the nature of their preaching, and their idea with regard to God.... He thus clearly indicates that he whom Cornelius had previously feared as God, of whom he had heard through the Law and the Prophets, for whose sake also he used to give alms, is, in truth, God.... The apostles, therefore, preached the Son of God, of whom men were ignorant; and his advent, to those who had already been instructed about God; but they did not bring in another god. For if Peter had known any such thing, he would have preached freely to the gentiles that the God of the Jews was indeed one, but the God of the Christians another. And all of them, doubtless, being awestruck because of the vision of the angel, would have believed whatever he told them. But it is evident from Peter's words that he did indeed still retain the God who was already known to them. But he also bore witness to them that Jesus Christ was the Son of God, the judge of quick and dead, into whom he also commanded them to be baptized for the remission of sins. And not this alone, but he witnessed that Jesus was himself the Son of God, who also, having been anointed with the Holy Spirit, is called Jesus Christ. And he is the same being that was born of Mary, as the testimony of Peter implies. Can it really be, that Peter was not at that time as yet in possession of the perfect knowledge which these men discovered afterwards? According to them, therefore, Peter was imperfect, and the rest of the apostles were imperfect. So it would be fitting that they, coming to life again, should become disciples of these men in order that they too might be made perfect. But this is truly ridiculous. These men, in fact, are proved not to be disciples of the apostles, but of their own wicked notions. To this cause also are due the various opinions which exist among them, inasmuch as each one adopted error just as he was capable of embracing it. But the church throughout all the world, having its origin firm from the apostles, perseveres in one and the same opinion with regard to God and his Son.

[...]

3.12.12 Ignorance of the Scriptures and of the dispensation of God has brought all these things upon them. And in the course of this work, I shall touch upon the cause of the difference of the covenants on the one hand, and, on the other hand, of their unity and harmony.

3.12.13 But that both the apostles and their disciples thus taught as the church preaches, and that teaching in this way they were then perfected, for this reason also they were called away to that which is perfect—Stephen, teaching these truths, when he was yet on earth, saw the glory of God, and Jesus on his right hand, and exclaimed, "Behold, I see the heavens opened, and the Son of Man standing at the right hand of God" (Acts 7:56). He said these words, and then he was stoned. In this way, he fulfilled the perfect doctrine, copying in every respect the leader of martyrdom. He also prayed for those who were slaying him in these words, "Lord, lay not this sin to their charge." They were thus perfected who knew one and the same God, who from beginning to end was present with mankind in the various dispensations. As the prophet Hosea declares, "I have filled up visions, and used similitudes by the hands of the prophets" (Hos 12:10). Those, therefore, who delivered up their souls to death for Christ's gospel—how could they have spoken to men in accordance with old established opinion? If this had been the course adopted by them, they should not have suffered. But inasmuch as they did preach things contrary to those persons who did not assent to the truth, for that reason they suffered. It is evident, therefore, that they did not relinquish the truth, but with all boldness preached to the Jews and Greeks. To the Jews, indeed, they proclaimed that the Jesus who was crucified by them was the Son of God, the judge of quick and dead, and that he has received from his Father an eternal kingdom in Israel, as I have pointed out. But to the Greeks they preached one God, who made all things, and Jesus Christ his Son.

Paul Preaches the Same Message as the Apostles

3.15.1 But again, we allege the same against those who do not recognize Paul as an apostle. We think that they should either reject the other words of the gospel which we have come to know through Luke alone, and not make use of them; or else, if they do receive all these, they must necessarily admit also that testimony concerning Paul, when he (Luke) tells us that the Lord spoke at first to him from heaven, "Saul, Saul, why do you persecute me? I am Jesus Christ, whom you persecute." And then to Ananias, saying regarding him, "Go your way; for he is my chosen vessel to bear my name among the gentiles, and kings, and the children of Israel. For I will show him, from this time, how great are the things that he must suffer for my name's sake" (Acts 12:8; 26:15; 9:15–16). Those, therefore, who do not accept him as a teacher, who was chosen by God for this purpose that he might boldly bear his name as being sent to the previously mentioned nations, do despise the election of God and separate themselves from the company of the apostles. For neither can they contend that Paul was no apostle, when he was chosen for this purpose; nor can they prove Luke guilty of falsehood, when he proclaims the truth to us with all diligence. It may be, indeed, that it was with this view that God set forth very many gospel truths, through Luke's instrumentality, which all should esteem it necessary to use, in order that all persons, following his subsequent testimony, which treats upon the acts and the doctrine of the apostles, and holding the unadulterated rule of truth, may be saved. His testimony, therefore, is true, and the doctrine of the apostles is open and steadfast, holding nothing in reserve. They also did not teach one set of doctrines in private and another in public.

3.15.2. For this is the deceptive strategy of false persons, evil seducers, and hypocrites, as they act who are from Valentinus. These men speak to the multitude about those who belong to the church, whom they themselves term "vulgar" and "ecclesiastic." By these words they entrap the more simple and entice them, imitating our phraseology so that the ones being deceived might listen to them more frequently; and then these are asked regarding us, how it is that when they hold doctrines similar to ours, we keep ourselves aloof from their company without cause. They also ask how it is that when they say the same things and hold the same doctrine, we call them heretics. When they have by means of questions thus overthrown the faith of any and rendered them compliant hearers of their own, they describe to them in private the unspeakable mystery of their Pleroma. But they are altogether deceived who imagine that they may learn from the scriptural texts adduced by heretics that doctrine which their words plausibly teach. For error is plausible and bears a resemblance to the truth, but must be disguised; while truth is without disguise, and therefore has been entrusted to children. And if any one of their listeners indeed demand explanations or start objections to them, they affirm that he is one not capable of receiving the truth, and not having the seed from above derived from their Mother. They thus really give him no reply but simply declare that he is of the intermediate regions, that is, belongs to animal natures. But if any one does yield himself up to them like a little sheep and follows out their practice and their "redemption," such a one is puffed up to such an extent that he thinks he is neither in heaven nor on earth, but that he has passed within the Pleroma; and having already embraced his angel, he walks with a strutting gait and a condescending countenance, possessing all the pompous air of a rooster. There are those among them who assert that that man who comes from above ought to follow a good course of conduct. For this reason they also pretend a gravity of demeanor with a certain haughtiness. The majority, however, having become scoffers also, as if already perfect and living without regard to appearances even in contempt of that which is good, call themselves "the spiritual" and allege that they have already become acquainted with that place of refreshing which is within their Pleroma.

3.15.3. But let us return to the same line of argument we have pursued up to this point. For when it has been manifestly declared, that they who were the preachers of the truth and the apostles of liberty called no one else God or named him Lord except the only true God the Father, and his Word, who has the preeminence in all things; it shall then be clearly proved that the apostles confessed as the Lord God him who was the creator of heaven and earth, who also spoke with Moses, gave to him the dispensation of the law, and who called the fathers; and that they knew no other. The opinion of the apostles, therefore, and of those who learned from their words concerning God (i.e., Mark and Luke) has been made manifest.

What Was Lost in Adam is Gained in Christ

3.18.1 As it has been clearly demonstrated, the Word who existed in the beginning with God, by whom all things were made, who was also always present with mankind, was in these last days united to his own workmanship according to the time appointed by the Father, inasmuch as he became a man liable to suffering. It therefore follows that every objection is set aside of those who say, "If our Lord was born at that time, Christ had therefore no previous existence." For I have shown that the Son of God did not then begin to exist but was with the Father from the beginning. When he became incarnate and was made man, he commenced afresh the long line of human beings. He thus furnished us with salvation in a brief, comprehensive manner such that what we had lost in Adam we might recover in Christ Jesus—namely, to be according to the image and likeness of God.

3.18.2 For as it was not possible that the man who had once for all been conquered, and who had been destroyed through disobedience could reform himself and obtain the prize of victory; and as it was also impossible that he could attain to salvation who had fallen under the power of sin, the Son effected both these things. He was able to do them both because he was the Word of God who descended from the Father and became incarnate, stooping low, even to death, and consummated the arranged plan of our salvation. Paul exhorts us to believe in him without hesitation, saying, "Who shall ascend into heaven? that is to bring down Christ; or who shall descend into the deep? that is to liberate Christ again from the dead" (Rom 10:6–7). Then he continues, "If you shall confess with your mouth the Lord Jesus, and shall believe in your heart that God has raised him from the dead, you shall be saved" (Rom 10:9). And he renders the reason why the Son of God did these things, saying, "For to this end Christ both lived and died, and lived again, that he might rule over the living and the dead" (Rom 14:9). And again, writing to the Corinthians, he declares, "But we preach Christ Jesus crucified," and adds, "the cup of blessing which we bless, is it not the communion of the blood of Christ?" (1 Cor 1:23; 10:16).

[...]

3.18.6. This likewise also answers the case of those who maintain that he suffered only in appearance. For if he did not truly suffer, no thanks to him, since there was no suffering at all; and when we shall actually begin to suffer, he will seem to be leading us astray, exhorting us to endure affliction and to turn the other cheek, if he did not himself before us in reality suffer the same. And as he misled them by seeming to them what he was not, so he also misled us by exhorting us to endure what he did not endure himself. In that case, we shall be even above the master, because we suffer and sustain what our master never bore or endured. But as our Lord is alone truly master, so the Son of God is truly good and patient, the Word of God the Father having been made the Son of Man. For he fought and conquered; for he was man contending for the fathers, and through obedience doing away with disobedience completely. For he bound the strong man, set free the weak, and endowed his own handiwork with salvation by destroying sin. For he is a most holy and merciful Lord and loves the human race.

3.18.7 Therefore, as I have already said, he caused man (i.e., human nature) to cling to and become one with God. For unless man had overcome the enemy of man, the enemy would not have been legitimately vanquished. And again, unless it had been God who had freely given salvation, we could never have possessed it securely. And unless man had been joined to God, he could never have become a partaker of incorruptibility. For it was incumbent upon the mediator between God and men, by his relationship to both, to bring both to friendship and concord and present man to God, while he revealed God to man. For, in what way could we be partaken of the adoption of sons, unless we had received from him through the Son that fellowship which refers to himself, unless his Word, having been made flesh, had entered into communion with us? For this reason also he passed through every stage of life, restoring to all communion with God. Those, therefore, who assert that he appeared allegedly, and was neither born in the flesh nor truly made man, are as yet under the old condemnation, holding out patronage to sin. For, by their showing, death has not been vanquished, which "reigned from Adam to Moses, even over them that had not sinned after the likeness of Adam's transgression" (Rom 5:14). But the law coming, which was given by Moses, and testifying of sin that it is a sinner, truly took away death's kingdom, showing that he was no king, but a robber and it revealed him as a murderer. It laid, however, a weighty burden upon man who had sin in himself, showing that he was liable to death. For as the law was spiritual, it merely made sin to stand out in relief, but did not destroy it. For sin had no dominion over the spirit, but over man. For it was fitting for him who was to destroy sin and redeem man under the power of death, that he should himself be made that very same thing which he was, that is, man; who had been drawn by sin into bondage, but was held by death, so that sin should be destroyed by man, and man should go forth from death. For as by the disobedience of the one man who was originally molded from virgin soil, the many were made sinners, and forfeited life; so was it necessary that, by the obedience of one man, who was originally born from a virgin, many should be justified and receive salvation (Rom 5:19). Thus, then, was the Word of God made man, as also Moses says, "God, true are his works" (Deut 32:4). But if, not having been made flesh, he merely appeared as if in the flesh, his work was not a true one. But what he did appear, that he also was. God recapitulated in himself the ancient formation of man, that he might kill sin, deprive death of its power, and give life to man. Therefore, his works are true.

The Reality of the Son's Incarnation

3.19.1 But again, those who assert that he was simply a mere man, begotten by Joseph, remaining in the bondage of the old disobedience, are in a state of death having been not as yet joined to the Word of God the Father, nor receiving liberty through the Son, as he does himself declare, "If the Son shall make you free, you shall be free indeed" (John 8:36). But, being ignorant of him who from the virgin is Emmanuel, they are deprived of his gift, which is eternal life; and not receiving the incorruptible Word, they remain in mortal flesh and are debtors to death, not obtaining the antidote of life. To whom the Word says, mentioning his own gift of grace, "I said, You are all the sons of the Most High, and gods; but you shall die like men" (Ps 82:6–7). He speaks undoubtedly these words to those who have not received the gift of adoption but who despise the incarnation of the pure generation of the Word of God, defraud human nature of promotion into God, and prove themselves ungrateful to the Word of God, who became flesh for them. For it was for this end that the Word of God was made man, and he who was the Son of God became the Son of Man, that man, having been taken into the Word and receiving the adoption, might become the son of God. For by no other means could we have attained to incorruptibility and immortality unless we had been united to incorruptibility and immortality. But how could we be joined to incorruptibility and immortality, unless, first, incorruptibility and immortality had become that which we also are, so that the corruptible might be swallowed up by incorruptibility, and the mortal by immortality, that we might receive the adoption of sons?

3.19.2 For this reason it is said, "Who shall declare his generation?" (Isa 53:8), since "He is a man, and who shall recognize him?" (Jer 17:9). But he to whom the Father which is in heaven has revealed him, knows him, so that he understands that he who "was not born either by the will of the flesh, or by the will of man," is the Son of Man, this is Christ, the Son of the living God (Matt 16:16; John 1:13). For I have shown from the Scriptures that none of the sons of Adam is as to everything and absolutely called God or named Lord. But that he is himself in his own right, beyond all men who ever lived, God and Lord and king eternal and the incarnate Word, proclaimed by all the prophets, the apostles, and by the Spirit himself, may be seen by all who have attained to even a small portion of the truth. Now, the Scriptures would not have testified these things of him, if, like others, he had been a mere man. But that he had beyond all others in himself that preeminent birth which is from the most high Father, and also experienced that preeminent generation which is from the virgin, the divine Scriptures in both respects testify of him. Also, that he was a man without pleasing appearance and liable to suffering (Isa 53:2); that he sat upon the foal of a donkey (Zech 9:9); that he received for drink, vinegar and gall (Ps 69:2); that he was despised among the people and humbled himself even to death and that he is the holy Lord, the wonderful, the counsellor, the beautiful in appearance, and the mighty God (Isa 9:6), coming on the clouds as the judge of all men (Dan 7:13)—all these things did the Scriptures prophesy of him.

3.19.3 For as he became man in order to undergo temptation, so also was he the Word that he might be glorified; the Word remaining at rest, that he might be capable of being tempted, dishonored, crucified, and of suffering death; but the human nature being swallowed up (by the Word), when he conquered, endured without yielding, performed acts of kindness, rose again, and was received up into heaven.[4] He therefore, the Son of God, our Lord, being the Word of the Father, and the son of man, since he had a generation as to his human nature from Mary—who was descended from mankind, and who was herself a human being—was made the Son of Man. For this reason also the Lord himself gave us a sign which man did not ask for in the depth below and in the height above, because he never expected that a virgin could conceive, or that it was possible that one remaining a virgin could bring forth a son, and that what was thus born should be "God with us," and descend to those things which are of the earth beneath, seeking the sheep which had perished, which was indeed his own peculiar handiwork, and ascend to the height above, offering and commending to his Father that human nature which had been found, making in his own person the first fruits of the resurrection of man. As the head rose from the dead, so also when the time is fulfilled of that condemnation which existed by reason of disobedience the remaining part of the body—namely, the body of every man who is found in

---

4 The phrase "the Word remaining at rest" (or "remaining quiescent") translates the Latin words *requiescente quidem Verbo*. The phrase "but the human nature being swallowed up" translates the Latin words *absorpto autem homine*.

life—will arise, blended together and strengthened through means of joints and bands by the increase of God, each of the members having its own proper and fit position in the body (Eph 4:16). For there are many mansions in the Father's house, inasmuch as there are also many members in the body (John 14:2).

The Weakness of False Teaching and the Gift of Sound Doctrine

3.24.1 In this way, all these men have been exposed, who introduce impious doctrines regarding our maker and framer who also formed this world and above whom there is no other God. Those who teach falsehoods regarding the substance of our Lord and the economy which he fulfilled for the sake of his own creature man have been overthrown by their own arguments. But it has, on the other hand, been shown that the preaching of the church is everywhere consistent and continues in an even course and receives testimony from the prophets, the apostles, and all the disciples—as I have proved—through those in the beginning, the middle, and the end, and through the entire economy of God, and that well-grounded system which tends to man's salvation, namely, our faith. Having received this faith from the church, we preserve it. By the Spirit of God, this faith always renews its youth as if it were some precious deposit in an excellent vessel which also causes the vessel itself containing it to renew its youth also. For this gift of God has been entrusted to the church, as breath was to the first created man, for this purpose, that all the members who receive it might be brought to life. The means of communion with Christ has been distributed throughout it, that is, the Holy Spirit, the earnest of incorruption, the means of confirming our faith, and the ladder of ascent to God. "For in the church," it is said, "God has set apostles, prophets, teachers" (1 Cor 12:28), and all the other means through which the Spirit works; of which all those are not partakers who do not join themselves to the church but defraud themselves of life through their perverse opinions and infamous behavior. For where the church is, there is the Spirit of God. And where the Spirit of God is, there is the church, and every kind of grace. But the Spirit is truth. Those, therefore, who do not partake of him are neither nourished into life from the mother's breasts nor do they enjoy that most unclouded fountain which issues from the body of Christ. But they rather dig for themselves broken cisterns out of earthly trenches and drink putrid water out of the mire, fleeing from the faith of the church for fear that they be convicted. They also reject the Spirit so that they might not be instructed.

3.24.2 Alienated in this way from the truth, they deservedly wallow in all error, tossed to and fro by it, thinking differently in regard to the same things at different times and never attaining to a well-grounded knowledge. They are more anxious to be sophists of words than disciples of the truth. For they have not been founded upon the one rock, but upon the sand, which has in itself a multitude of stones. For this reason they also imagine many gods, and they always have the excuse of searching after truth but never succeed in finding it for they are blind. For they blaspheme the creator, the one who is truly God and who furnishes power to find the truth. They imagine that they have discovered another god beyond God, or another Pleroma, or another dispensation. For this reason also the light which is from God does not illumine them, because they have dishonored and despised God, holding him of small account, because, through his love and infinite kindness, he has come within reach of human knowledge. This knowledge, however, does not relate to his greatness or to his essence—for that no man has measured or handled—but after this sort: that we should know that he who made and formed and breathed in them the breath of life and nourishes us by means of the creation establishes all things by his Word and binds them together by his Wisdom. This is he who is the only true God. But they dream of a non-existent being above him, that they may be regarded as having found out the great God whom nobody can recognize. . . . That is to say they discover the god of Epicurus, who does nothing either for himself or others. That is, he exercises no providence at all.

The Sovereign God is Both Good and Just

3.25.1 God does, however, exercise a providence over all things, and therefore he also gives counsel. And when giving counsel, he is present with those who attend to moral discipline. It follows then of course, that the things which are watched over and governed should be acquainted with their ruler. These things are also not irrational or vain, but they have understanding derived from the providence of God. And for this reason some of the gentiles, who were less addicted to sensual allurements and luxurious desires and were not led away to such a degree of superstition with regard to idols were only slightly moved by his providence but were nevertheless convinced that they should call the maker of this universe the Father, who exercises a providence over all things and arranges the affairs of our world.

3.25.2 Again, that they might remove the rebuking and judicial power from the Father, reckoning that as unworthy of God and thinking that they had discovered a God both without anger and merely good, they have alleged that one God judges, but that another saves, unconsciously taking away the intelligence and justice of both deities. For if the judicial one is not also good, to bestow favors upon the deserving and to direct reproofs against those requiring them, he will appear neither a just nor a wise judge. On the other hand, the good God, if he is merely good, and not one who tests those upon whom he shall send his goodness, will be out of the range of justice and goodness; and his goodness will seem imperfect, as not saving all; for it should do so, if it is not accompanied by judgment.

3.25.3 Marcion himself, therefore, in fact puts an end to deity on both sides by dividing God into two, maintaining one to be good and the other judicial. For he that is the judicial one, if he is not good, he is not God. This is because he from whom goodness is absent is no God at all. And again, he who is good, if he has no judicial power, suffers the same loss as the former, by being deprived of his character of deity. And how can they call the Father of all wise if they do not assign to him a judicial faculty? For if he is wise, he is also one who tests others. But the judicial power belongs to him who tests, and justice follows the judicial faculty that it may reach a just conclusion. Justice calls forth judgment, and judgment, when it is executed with justice, will pass on to wisdom. Therefore, the Father's wisdom will surpass all human and angelic wisdom because he is Lord and judge and the just one and ruler over all. For he is good and merciful and patient and saves the ones he should. Goodness also does not desert him in the exercise of justice, nor is his wisdom lessened. For he saves those whom he should save and judges those worthy of judgment. He also does not show himself unmercifully just, for his goodness, no doubt, goes on before and takes precedence.

Praying with Hope for the Heretic

3.25.7 We do indeed pray that these men may not remain in the pit which they themselves have dug, but separate themselves from a mother of this nature and depart from Bythus and stand away from the void and relinquish the shadow. We also pray that they might be converted to the church of God and be lawfully begotten, and that Christ may be formed in them, and that they may know the framer and maker of this universe, the only true God and Lord of all. We pray for these things on their behalf, loving them better than they seem to love themselves. For our love, inasmuch as it is true, is healing for them, if they will but receive it. It may be compared to a severe remedy which carves out the proud and decaying flesh of a wound; for it puts an end to their pride and haughtiness. For this reason it shall not weary us to endeavor with all our might to stretch out our hand to them.

Over and above what has already been stated, I have deferred to the following book to present the words of the Lord. My hope is that by convincing some among them through means of the very instruction of Christ, I may succeed in persuading them to abandon such error and to cease from blaspheming their creator, who is both God alone and the Father of our Lord Jesus Christ. Amen.

5

The Testimony of Christ and His Apostles

Selections from Books 4–5 of *Against Heresies*

Overview

In Books 4–5 of *Against Heresies*, Irenaeus continues to establish that there is one God who is creator of all things and the Father of Jesus Christ. Irenaeus focuses in these books on the parables and speeches of Jesus in the Gospels and also on the letters of Paul. The way Jesus and the apostles speak of God demonstrates a fundamental unity across redemptive history. From the creation of the world to the giving of the law, to the incarnation of Christ, to the establishment of the church in the Spirit, to the reality of final judgment, the same God is at work. Of this one God, Irenaeus insists, the prophets spoke, Jesus proclaimed, and the apostles preached. Irenaeus brings his work to a conclusion in Book 5 with a reflection on the reality of the incarnation and the hope of the resurrection of the body.

The Purpose of Book 4

4.0.1 My very dear friend, by transmitting to you this fourth book of the work which is entitled *The Detection and Refutation of False Knowledge*, as I have promised, I shall add weight to what I have already advanced by means of the words of the Lord; so that you also, as you have requested, may obtain from me the means of refuting all the heretics everywhere, and not permit them, beaten back at all points, to launch out further into the depth of error nor to be drowned in the sea of ignorance; but that by redirecting them into the haven of the truth you may cause them to attain their salvation.

4.0.2 However, the one who would undertake their conversion must possess an accurate knowledge of their systems or schemes of doctrine. For it is impossible for anyone to heal the sick if he has no knowledge of the disease of the patients. This was the reason that my predecessors—much superior men to myself, too—were unable to refute the Valentinians satisfactorily, because they were ignorant of their system. I have with all care delivered this kind of knowledge to you in the first book in which I have also shown that their doctrine is a recapitulation of all the heretics. For this reason also, in the second, we have had, as in a mirror, a sight of their entire disorientation. For they who oppose these men by the right method thereby oppose all who are of an evil mind. They who overthrow them do in fact overthrow every kind of heresy.

4.0.3 For their system is blasphemous above all others since they claim that the maker and framer, who is one God, as I have shown, was produced from a defect or apostasy. They also utter blasphemy against our Lord by cutting off and dividing Jesus from Christ, and Christ from the savior, and again the savior from the Word, and the Word from the only begotten. And since they allege that the creator originated from a defect or apostasy, so they have also taught that Christ and the Holy Spirit were emitted on account of this defect and that the savior was a product of those Aeons who were produced from a defect. There is therefore nothing but blasphemy to be found among them. In the preceding book, then, the ideas of the apostles concerning all these points have been presented, to the effect that not only did they "who from the beginning were eye-witnesses and ministers of the word" of truth hold no such opinions, but that they also preached to us to shun these doctrines, foreseeing by the Spirit those weak-minded persons who should be led astray (Luke 1:2; 2 Tim 2:23).

4.0.4 For as the serpent beguiled Eve by promising her what he did not have himself, so also do these men, by pretending to possess superior knowledge and to be acquainted with ineffable mysteries and by promising that admittance which they speak of as taking place within the Pleroma, plunge those that believe them into death and render them apostates from him who made them. And at that time, indeed, the apostate angel, having brought about the disobedience of mankind by means of the serpent, imagined that he escaped the notice of the Lord. For this reason God assigned him the form and name of a serpent. But now, since the last times have come upon us, evil is spread abroad among men which not only renders them apostates but by many schemes the devil raises up blasphemers against the creator, namely, by means of all the heretics already mentioned. For all these, although they issue forth from diverse regions and spread different opinions, nevertheless concur in the same blasphemous design, wounding men unto death by teaching blasphemy against God our maker and supporter and detracting from the salvation of man. Now man is a mixed organization of soul and flesh, who was formed after the likeness of God and molded by his hands, that is, by the Son and Holy Spirit, to whom also he said, "Let us make man" (Gen 1:26). This, then, is the aim of him who envies our life, to render men disbelievers in their own salvation and blasphemous against God the creator. For whatever all the heretics may have advanced with the utmost solemnity, they come to this at last, that they blaspheme the creator and disallow the salvation of God's workmanship, which the flesh truly is. On behalf of which I have proved, in a variety of ways, that the Son of God accomplished the whole economy of mercy and have shown that there is none other called God by the Scriptures except the Father of all, and the Son, and those who possess the adoption.

There Is No Other God than the One Proclaimed by the Scriptures

4.1.1 Since, therefore, this is sure and steadfast, that no other God or Lord was announced by the Spirit, except him who rules over all as God, together with his Word and those who receive the Spirit of adoption, that is, those who believe in the one and true God, and in Jesus Christ the Son of God. Likewise, the apostles themselves termed no one else as God or named no other as Lord. More importantly, our Lord truly acted likewise by commanding us to confess no one as Father except him who is in the heavens and who is the one God and the one Father. On the contrary, the heretics maintain that the being whom they have themselves invented is by nature both God and Father. These things that these deceivers and most perverse sophists advance are thus clearly shown to be false.

4.1.2 If the Lord had known many fathers and many gods, he would not have taught his disciples to know only one God and to call him alone Father. To whom is this not clear? But he did distinguish those who are merely termed gods by word from him who is truly God, that they should not err as to his doctrine nor understand one in mistake for another. And if he indeed taught us to call one being Father and God, while he does from time to time himself confess other fathers and gods in the same sense, then he will appear to demand a different course from his disciples than what he follows himself. Such conduct, however, does not characterize the good teacher but rather a misleading and unjust one. If he is not alone God and Father, the apostles, too, according to these men's showing are proved to be transgressors of the commandment, since they confess the creator as God and Lord and Father, as I have shown. Jesus, therefore, will be to them the author and teacher of such transgression, inasmuch as he commanded that one being should be called

Father, thus imposing upon them the necessity of confessing the creator as their Father, as has been pointed out.

4.2.1 Moses, therefore, making a recapitulation of the whole law which he had received from the creator, thus speaks in Deuteronomy, "Give ear, O you heavens, and I will speak; and hear, O earth, the words of my mouth" (Deut 32:1). Again, David saying that his help came from the Lord, asserts, "My help is from the Lord, who made heaven and earth" (Ps 124:8). And Isaiah confesses that words were uttered by God, who made heaven and earth, and governs them. He says, "Hear, O heavens; and give ear, O earth; for the Lord has spoken" (Isa 1:2). And again, "Thus says the Lord God, who made the heaven, and stretched it out; who established the earth, and the things in it; and who gives breath to the people upon it, and spirit to them who walk therein" (Isa 42:5).

4.2.2 Again, our Lord Jesus Christ confesses this same being as his Father, where he says, "I confess to you, O Father, Lord of heaven and earth" (Matt 11:25; Luke 10:21). What Father will those men have us to understand by these words, those who are most perverse sophists of pandora? Whether shall it be Bythus, whom they have fabled of themselves; or their mother; or the only begotten? Or shall it be he whom the Marcionites or the others have invented as god whom I indeed have amply demonstrated to be no god at all? Or shall it be, as is really the case, the maker of heaven and earth, whom also the prophets proclaimed, whom Christ, too, confesses as his Father, whom also the law announces, saying, "Hear, O Israel; The Lord your God is one God?" (Deut 6:4).

4.2.3 But since the writings of Moses are the words of Christ, he does himself declare to the Jews, as John has recorded in the Gospel, "If you had believed Moses, you would have believed me; for he wrote of me. But if you do not believe his writings, neither will you believe my words" (John 5:46–47). He thus indicates in the clearest manner that the writings of Moses are his words. If, then, this be the case with regard to Moses, so also beyond a doubt, the words of the other prophets are his words, as I have pointed out. And again, the Lord himself exhibits Abraham as having said to the rich man with reference to all those who were still alive, "If they do not obey Moses and the prophets, neither will they believe him if anyone were to rise from the dead and go to them" (Luke 16:31).

4.2.4 Now, he has not merely related to us a story respecting a poor man and a rich one; but he has taught us, in the first place, that no one should lead a luxurious life, nor, living in worldly pleasures and perpetual feastings, should be the slave of his lusts and forget God. "For there was," he says, "a rich man, who was clothed in purple and fine linen, and delighted himself with splendid feasts" (Luke 16:19).

The Testimony of Christ and His Apostles

4.2.5 Of such persons, too, the Spirit has spoken by Isaiah, "They drink wine with the accompaniment of harps, and tablets, and psalteries, and flutes; but they do not regard the works of God, neither do they consider the work of his hands" (Isa 5:12). Therefore, so that we might not incur the same punishment as these men, the Lord reveals to us their end; showing at the same time that if they obeyed Moses and the prophets, they would believe in him whom these had preached, the Son of God, who rose from the dead and bestows life upon us. And he shows that all are from one essence, that is, Abraham, and Moses, and the prophets, and also the Lord himself, who rose from the dead, in whom many believe who are of the circumcision, who also hear Moses and the prophets announcing the coming of the Son of God. But those who scoff at the truth assert that these men were from another essence, and they do not know the first begotten from the dead. They understand Christ to be a distinct being who continued as if he were impassible, and Jesus, who suffered, as being altogether separate from him.

4.2.6 For they do not receive from the Father the knowledge of the Son; neither do they learn who the Father is from the Son, who teaches clearly and without parables him who truly is God. He says, "Do not Swear at all; neither by heaven, for it is God's throne; nor by the earth, for it is his footstool; neither by Jerusalem, for it is the city of the great king" (Matt 5:34). For these words are evidently spoken with reference to the creator, as also Isaiah says, "Heaven is my throne, the earth is my footstool" (Isa 66:1). And besides this being there is no other God. Otherwise he would not be termed by the Lord either "God" or "the great king." For a being who can be so described admits neither of any other being compared with nor set above him. For he who has any superior over him, and is under the power of another, this being never can be called either "God" or "the great king."

4.2.7 But neither will these men be able to maintain that such words were uttered in an ironic manner, since it is proved to them by the words themselves that they were in earnest. For he who uttered them was truth, and truly vindicated his own house by driving out of it the changers of money who were buying and selling, saying unto them, "It is written, my house shall be called the house of prayer; but you have made it a den of thieves" (Matt 21:13). And what reason did he have for doing and saying this and vindicating his house if he preached another god? But he did so, that he might point out the transgressors of his Father's law. For he neither brought any accusation against the house nor blamed the law which he had come to fulfill. Rather, he reproved those who were putting his house to an improper use and those who were transgressing the law. And therefore the scribes and Pharisees, too, who from the times of the law had begun to despise God, did not receive his Word, that is, they did not believe on Christ. Of these Isaiah says, "Your princes are rebellious, companions of thieves, loving gifts, following after rewards, not judging the fatherless, and negligent of the cause of the widows" (Isa 1:23). And Jeremiah, in like manner, "They," he says, "who rule my people did not know me; they are senseless and imprudent children; they are wise to do evil, but to do good they have no knowledge" (Jer 4:22).

4.2.8 But as many as feared God and were anxious about his law, these ran to Christ and were all saved. For he said to his disciples, "Go to the sheep of the house of Israel, which have perished" (Matt 5:6). And many more Samaritans, it is said, when the Lord had tarried among them for two days "believed because of his words, and said to the woman, now we believe, not because of your saying, for we ourselves have heard him and know that this man is truly the savior of the world" (John 4:41). And Paul likewise declares, "And so all Israel shall be saved" (Rom 11:26). But he has also said that the law was our teacher to bring us to Christ Jesus (Gal 3:24). Let them not therefore ascribe to the law the unbelief of certain among them. For the law never hindered them from believing in the Son of God. Rather, it even exhorted them to do so, saying that men can be saved in no other way from the old wound of the serpent than by believing in him who, in the likeness of sinful flesh, is lifted up from the earth upon the tree of martyrdom and draws all things to himself and gives new life to the dead (Num 21:8; John 3:14; 12:32).

God is Above All and Will Endure Forever

4.3.1 Again, as to their malicious assertion that if heaven is indeed the throne of God and earth his footstool, and if it is declared that the heaven and earth shall pass away, then when these pass away the God who sits above must also pass away, and therefore he cannot be the God who is over all. In the first place, they are ignorant about what the expression means, that heaven is his throne and earth his footstool. For they do not know what God is, but they imagine that he sits after the fashion of a man and is contained within bounds but does not contain. And they are also unacquainted with the meaning of the passing away of the heaven and earth. But Paul was not ignorant of it when he declared, "For the figure of this world passes away" (1 Cor 7:31). In the next place, David explains their question, for he says that when the fashion of this world passes away, not only shall God remain, but his servants also, expressing himself in this way in Psalm 101: "In the beginning, you, O Lord, have founded the earth, and the heavens are the works of your hands. They shall perish, but you shall endure, and all shall wax old as a garment; and as a garment you shall change them, and they shall be changed; but you are the same, and your years shall not fail. The children of your servants shall continue, and their seed shall be established for ever" (Ps 102:25–28; LXX: 101:25–28). David points out plainly here what things they are that pass away and who it is that endures forever—God, together with his servants. And in like manner Isaiah says, "Lift up your eyes to the heavens, and look upon the earth beneath; for the heaven has been set together as smoke, and the earth shall wax old like a garment, and they who dwell therein shall die in like manner. But my salvation shall be forever, and my righteousness shall not pass away" (Isa 51:6).

The Old Covenant and Its Institution Are Fulfilled in the New Covenant

4.4.1 Further, also, concerning Jerusalem and the Lord, they venture to assert that if it had been "the city of the great king," it would not have been deserted (Matt 5:35). This is just as if anyone should say that if straw were a creation of God, it would never part company with the wheat; and that the vine twigs, if made by God, would never be lopped away and deprived of the clusters. But as these vine twigs have not been originally made for their own sake, but for that of the fruit growing upon them, which being come to maturity and taken away, they are left behind, and those which do not bear fruit are lopped off altogether; so also was it with Jerusalem, which had in herself borne the yoke of bondage—under which man was reduced, who in former times was not subject to God when death was reigning, and being subdued, became a fit subject for liberty—when the fruit of liberty had come, and reached maturity, and been reaped and stored in the barn, and when those which had the power to produce fruit had been carried away from her (i.e., from Jerusalem) and scattered throughout all the world. Even as Isaiah says, "The children of Jacob shall strike root, and Israel shall flourish, and the whole world shall be filled with his fruit" (Isa 27:6). The fruit, therefore, having been sown throughout all the world, Jerusalem was deservedly forsaken, and those things which had formerly brought forth fruit abundantly were taken away; for from these, according to the flesh, Christ and the apostles were enabled to bring forth fruit. But now these are no longer useful for bringing forth fruit. For all things which have a beginning in time must of course have an end in time also.

4.4.2 Since, then, the law originated with Moses, it terminated with John as a necessary consequence. Christ had come to fulfill it. For this reason "the law and the prophets were" with them "until John" (Luke 16:16). And therefore

Jerusalem, taking its commencement from David, and fulfilling its own times, must have an end of legislation when the new covenant was revealed. For God does all things by measure and in order. Nothing is unmeasured with him because nothing is out of order. He who said that the unmeasurable Father was himself subjected to measure in the Son spoke well. For the Son is the measure of the Father, since he also comprehends him. But that the administration of the Jews was temporary, Isaiah says, "And the daughter of Zion shall be left as a cottage in a vineyard, and as a lodge in a garden of cucumbers" (Isa 1:8). And when shall these things be left behind? Is it not when the fruit shall be taken away, and the leaves alone shall be left, which now have no power to produce fruit?

4.4.3 But why do we speak of Jerusalem, since, indeed, the fashion of the whole world must also pass away when the time of its disappearance has come, in order that the fruit may indeed be gathered into the storehouse, but the chaff left behind may be consumed by fire? "For the day of the Lord comes as a burning furnace, and all sinners shall be stubble, they who do evil things, and the day shall burn them up" (Mal 4:1). Now, who this Lord is that brings such a day about, John the Baptist points out when he says of Christ, "He shall baptize you with the Holy Spirit and with fire, having his fan in his hand to cleanse his threshing floor; and he will gather his fruit into the storehouse, but the chaff he will burn up with unquenchable fire" (Matt 3:11). For he who makes the chaff and he who makes the wheat are not different persons, but one and the same, who judges them, that is, separates them. But the wheat and the chaff, being inanimate and irrational, have been made such by nature. But man, being endowed with reason, and in this respect similar to God, having been made free in his will and with power over himself, is himself the cause to himself, that sometimes he becomes wheat and sometimes chaff. For this reason also he shall be justly condemned, because, having been created a rational being, he lost the true rationality, and living irrationally, opposed the righteousness of God, giving himself over to every earthly spirit and serving all lusts. As the prophet says, "Man, being in honor, did not understand; he was assimilated to senseless beasts and made like them" (Ps 49:12).

The God Who Promises Is the Same as the God Who Fulfills

4.5.1 God, therefore, is one and the same, who rolls up the heaven as a book and renews the face of the earth; who made the things of time for man, so that coming to maturity in them, he may produce the fruit of immortality; and who, through his kindness also bestows upon him eternal things, "that in the ages to come he may show the exceeding riches of his grace" (Eph 2:7); who was announced by the Law and the Prophets, whom Christ confessed as his Father. Now he is the creator, and it is he who is God over all, as Isaiah says, "I am witness, says the Lord God, and my servant whom I have chosen, that you may know, and believe, and understand that I am. Before me there was no other God, neither shall be after me. I am God, and besides me there is no savior. I have proclaimed, and I have saved" (Isa 43:10–12). And again, "I myself am the first God, and I am above things to come." For neither in an ambiguous nor arrogant nor boastful manner does he say these things; but since it was impossible, without God, to come to a knowledge of God, he teaches men through his Word to know God. To those, therefore, who are ignorant of these matters, and on this account imagine that they have discovered another Father, justly does one say, "You do err, not knowing the Scriptures, nor the power of God" (Matt 22:29).

4.5.2 For our Lord and master, in the answer which he gave to the Sadducees who say that there is no resurrection and who therefore dishonor God and lower the credit of the law, both indicated a resurrection and also revealed God, saying to them, "You err, not knowing the Scriptures, nor the power of God." "For, concerning the resurrection of the dead," he says, "have you not read that which was spoken by God, saying, I am the God of Abraham, the God of Isaac, and the God of Jacob?" (Matt 22:29). And he added, "He is not the God of the dead, but of the living; for all live to him." By these arguments he unquestionably made it clear that he who spoke to Moses out of the bush and declared himself to be the God of the fathers, he is the God of the living. For who is the God of the living unless he who is God and above whom there is no other god? Whom also Daniel the prophet, when Cyrus king of the Persians said to him, "Why do you not worship Bel?" proclaimed, saying, "Because I do not worship idols made with hands, but the living God, who established the heaven and the earth and has dominion over all flesh." Again he said, "I will adore the Lord my God, because he is the living God."[1] He, then, who was adored by the prophets as the living God, he is the God of the living; and his Word is he who also spoke to Moses, who also put the Sadducees to silence, who also bestowed the gift of resurrection, thus revealing both truths to those who are blind, that is, the resurrection and God in his true character. For if he is not the God of the dead but of the living, yet was called the God of the fathers who were sleeping, they do undoubtably live to God and have not passed out of existence since they are children of the resurrection. But our Lord is himself the resurrection, as he himself declares, "I

---

1 This quotation is from the apocryphal book, *Bel and the Dragon*, 4–5.

am the resurrection and the life" (John 11:25). But the fathers are his children. For it is said by the prophet, "Instead of your fathers, your children have been made to you" (Ps 45:16). Christ himself, therefore, together with the Father, is the God of the living, who spoke to Moses and who was also manifested to the fathers.

4.5.3 And teaching this very thing, he said to the Jews, "Your father Abraham rejoiced that he should see my day; and he saw it, and was glad" (John 8:56). What is intended? "Abraham believed God, and it was imputed unto him for righteousness" (Rom 4:3). In the first place, he believed that he was the maker of heaven and earth, the only God; and in the next place, that he would make his seed as the stars of heaven. This is what is meant by Paul when he says, "as lights in the world" (Phil 2:15). Righteously, therefore, having left his earthly kindred, he followed the Word of God, walking as a pilgrim with the Word, that he might afterwards have his abode with the Word.

4.5.4 Righteously also the apostles, being of the race of Abraham, left the ship and their father, and followed the Word. Righteously also do we, possessing the same faith as Abraham, and taking up the cross as Isaac did the wood, follow him. For in Abraham, man had learned beforehand and had been accustomed to follow the Word of God. For Abraham, according to his faith, followed the command of the Word of God and with a ready mind delivered up as a sacrifice to God his only begotten and beloved son, in order that God also might be pleased to offer up, for all his seed, his own beloved and only begotten Son as a sacrifice for our redemption.

4.5.5 Since, therefore, Abraham was a prophet and saw in the Spirit the day of the Lord's coming and the dispensation of his suffering, through whom both he himself and all who trust in God by following the example of his faith should be saved, he rejoiced exceedingly. The Lord, therefore, was not unknown to Abraham, whose day he desired to see. Neither was the Lord's Father, for Abraham had learned from the Word of the Lord and believed him. For this reason it was credited to him by the Lord as righteousness. For faith toward God justifies a man. Therefore he said, "I will stretch forth my hand to the most high God, who made the heaven and the earth" (Gen 14:22). Those holding perverse opinions, however, endeavor to overthrow all these truths because of one passage which they certainly do not understand correctly.

The One Creator is the God and Father of Jesus Christ

4.6.1. For the Lord, revealing himself to his disciples that he himself is the Word who imparts knowledge of the Father, and reproving the Jews who imagined that they had the knowledge of God while they nevertheless rejected his Word through whom God is made known, declared, "No man knows the Son but the Father; neither does any man know the Father except the Son and anyone to whom the Son has willed to reveal him" (Matt 6:27; Luke 10:22). Thus has Matthew set it down, and Luke in like manner, and Mark the very same; for John omits this passage. They, however, who would be wiser than the apostles, write the verse in the following manner: "No man knew the Father, but the Son; nor the Son, but the Father, and he to whom the Son has willed to reveal him"; and they explain it as if the true God were known to none prior to our Lord's advent; and that God who was announced by the prophets, they allege not to be the Father of Christ.

4.6.2 But if Christ only then began to have existence when he came into the world as man, and if the Father remembered only in the times of Tiberius Caesar to provide for the wants of men, and his Word was shown to have not always coexisted with his creatures; it may be remarked that neither then was it necessary that another god should be proclaimed, but rather that the reasons for so great carelessness and neglect on his part should be made the subject of investigation. For it is fitting that no such question should arise and gather such strength that it would indeed both change God and destroy our faith in that creator who supports us by means of his creation. For as we do direct our faith toward the Son, so also should we possess a firm and immoveable love toward the Father. In his book against Marcion, Justin says rightly, "I would not have believed the Lord himself, if he had announced any other than he who is our framer, maker, and nourisher. But because the only begotten Son came to us from the one God who both made this world and formed us and contains and administers all things, summing up his own handiwork in himself, my faith toward him is steadfast, and my love to the Father immoveable, God bestowing both upon us."

4.6.3 For no one can know the Father, unless through the Word of God, that is, unless by the Son revealing him. Neither can he have knowledge of the Son unless through the good pleasure of the Father. But the Son performs the good pleasure of the Father. For the Father sends and the Son is sent and comes. And his Word knows that his Father is, as far as regards us, invisible and infinite. Since he cannot be declared by anyone else, he himself declares him to us. On the other hand, it is the Father alone who knows his own Word. Our Lord has declared both these truths. For this reason, the Son reveals the knowledge of the Father through his own manifestation. For the manifestation of the Son is the knowledge of the Father. For all things are manifested through the Word. In order, therefore, that we might know that the Son who came is he who imparts to those believing on him a knowledge of the Father, he said to his disciples, "No man knows the Son but the Father, nor the Father but the Son, and those to whomever the Son shall reveal him" (Matt 6:27; Luke 10:22). He thus sets forth himself and the Father as he really is so that we may not receive any other Father except him who is revealed by the Son.

The Unknown God Is Revealed in and by the Son

4.6.4 But this Father is the maker of heaven and earth, as is shown from his words; and not he, the false father, who has been invented by Marcion, or by Valentinus, or by Basilides, or by Carpocrates, or by Simon, or by the rest of the "Gnostics," falsely so called. For none of these was the Son of God. Rather, Christ Jesus our Lord was, against whom they set their teaching in opposition and have the daring to preach an unknown God. But they ought to hear this against themselves: How is it that he is unknown, who is known by them? for, whatever is known even by a few is not unknown. But the Lord did not say that both the Father and the Son could not be known at all, for in that case his advent would have been unnecessary. For why did he come to this place? Was it that he should say to us, "Never mind seeking after God; for he is unknown, and you shall not find him," as also the disciples of Valentinus falsely declare that Christ said to their Aeons? But this is indeed vain. For the Lord taught us that no man is capable of knowing God, unless he be taught of God; that is, that God cannot be known without God; but that this is the express will of the Father, that God should be known. For they shall know him, to whomsoever the Son has revealed him.

4.6.5 And for this purpose the Father revealed the Son, that through his instrumentality he might be manifested to all and might receive those righteous ones who believe in him into incorruption and everlasting enjoyment. Now, to believe in him is to do his will. But those who do not believe and who consequently avoid his light, he shall righteously shut out into the darkness which they have chosen for themselves. The Father therefore has revealed himself to all by making his Word visible to all. Conversely, the Word has declared to all the Father and the Son since he has become visible to all. Therefore the righteous judgment of God shall fall upon all who, like others, have seen, but have not, like others, believed.

4.6.6 For by means of the creation itself, the Word reveals God the creator. By means of the world he declares the Lord to be the maker of the world. By means of the formation of man, the skilled craftsman who formed him. By the Son, that Father who begat the Son. These things do indeed address all men in the same manner, but all do not in the same way believe them. But by the Law and the Prophets the Word preached both himself and the Father alike to all. And all the people heard him alike, but all did not alike believe. Through the Word himself who had been made visible and palpable, the Father was shown forth although all did not equally believe in him. However, all saw the Father in the Son, for the Father is the invisible of the Son, but the Son the visible of the Father. For this reason, all spoke with Christ when he was present upon earth, and they named him God. Yes, even the demons exclaimed on beholding the Son, "We know who you are, the Holy One of God" (Mark 1:24). And the devil looking at him and tempting him said, "If you are the Son of God" (Matt 4:3; Luke 4:3). All thus indeed saw and spoke of the Son and the Father, but all did not believe in them.

4.6.7 For it was fitting that the truth should receive testimony from all and should become a means of judgment for the salvation indeed of those who believe, but for the condemnation of those who do not believe. This was so that all should be fairly judged and that the faith in the Father and Son should be approved by all, that is, that it should be established by all as the one means of salvation, receiving testimony from all, both from those belonging to it, since they are its friends, and by those having no connection with it, though they are its enemies. For that evidence is true and cannot be denied, which elicits striking testimonies on its behalf even from its adversaries. These adversaries are initially convinced with respect to the matter at hand by their own plain contemplation of it, and by bearing testimony to it, as well as by declaring it. But after a while they break forth into enmity and become accusers of that which they had initially approved. They then desire that their own previously given testimony should not be regarded as true. He, therefore, who was known was not a different being from him who declared, "No man knows the Father," but one and the same, the Father making all things subject to him; while he received testimony from all that he was very man and that he was very God, from the Father, from the Spirit, from angels, from the creation itself, from men, from apostate spirits and demons, from the enemy, and last of all, from death itself. But the Son, administering all things for the Father, works from the beginning even to the end, and without him no man can attain the knowledge of God. For the Son is the knowledge of the Father; but the knowledge of the Son is in the Father and has been revealed through the Son. This was the reason why the Lord declared, "No man knows the Son, but the Father; nor the Father, except the Son, and those to whomsoever the Son shall reveal him" (Matt 11:27; Luke 10:22). For "shall reveal" was not said with reference to the future alone, as if only then the Word had begun to manifest the Father when he was born of Mary, but it applies indifferently throughout all time. For the Son, being present with his own handiwork from the beginning, reveals the Father to all: to whom he wills, and when he wills, and as the Father wills. For this reason, then, in all things and through all things, there is one God, the Father, and one Word, and one Son, and one Spirit, and one salvation to all who believe in him.

The Revelation of the Son is From the Beginning

4.7.1 Therefore Abraham also, knowing the Father through the Word, who made heaven and earth, confessed him to be God. Having learned by an announcement made to him that the Son of God would be a man among men and by whose advent his seed should be as the stars of heaven, he desired to see that day, so that he might himself also embrace Christ. Seeing it through the spirit of prophecy, he rejoiced. For this reason Simeon also, one of his descendants, carried out fully the rejoicing of the patriarch, and said, "Lord, let now your servant depart in peace. For my eyes have seen your salvation, which you have prepared before the face of all people; a light for the revelation of the gentiles, and the glory of the people Israel" (Luke 2:29). And the angels, in like manner, announced tidings of great joy to the shepherds who were keeping watch by night. Moreover, Mary said, "My soul magnifies the Lord, and my spirit has rejoiced in God my salvation," the rejoicing of Abraham descending upon those who sprang from him, namely, those who were watching and who beheld Christ and believed in him; while, on the other hand, there was a reciprocal rejoicing which passed backwards from the children to Abraham, who did also desire to see the day of Christ's coming. Rightly, then, did our Lord bear witness to him, saying, "Your father Abraham rejoiced to see my day; and he saw it, and was glad."

4.7.2 For not on Abraham's account alone did he say these things but also that he might point out how all who have known God from the beginning and have foretold the advent of Christ have received the revelation from the Son himself; who also in the last times was made visible and passible, and spoke with the human race, that he might from the stones raise up children unto Abraham, and fulfill the promise which God had given him, and that he might make his seed as the stars of heaven, as John the Baptist says, "For God is able from these stones to raise up children unto Abraham" (Matt 3:9). Now, Jesus did this by drawing us away from the religion of stones and by bringing us over from hard and fruitless contemplation and establishing in us a faith like to Abraham. As Paul also testifies, saying that we are children of Abraham because of the similarity of our faith and the promise of inheritance (Rom 4:12).

4.7.3 He is therefore one and the same God who called Abraham and gave him the promise. He is also the creator who through Christ prepares lights in the world, namely, those who believe from among the gentiles. And he says, "You are the light of the world" (Matt 5:14), that is, as the stars of heaven. Therefore, I have rightly shown him to be known by no man unless he is made known by the Son and anyone to whom the Son shall reveal him. But the Son reveals the Father to whomever he wills that he should be known. And no man can know God without the goodwill of the Father or the agency of the Son. For this reason, the Lord said to his disciples, "I am the way, the truth, and the life and no man comes to the Father except by me. If you had known me, you would have known my Father also; and from this time on you have both known him and have seen him" (John 14:6–7). From these words it is evident that he is known by the Son, that is, by the Word.

4.7.4 Therefore the Jews have departed from God by not receiving his Word but imagining that they could know the Father apart by himself without the Word, that is, without the Son. They are ignorant of that God who spoke in human shape to Abraham, and again to Moses, saying, "I have surely seen the affliction of my people in Egypt, and I have come down to deliver them" (Exod 3:7–8). For the Son, who is the Word of God, arranged these things beforehand from the beginning, the Father being in no want of angels, in order that he might call the creation into being and form man, for whom also the creation was made. He also does not stand in need of any instrumentality for the framing of created things or for the ordering of those things which had reference to man. At the same time, he has a vast and unspeakable number of servants. For his offspring and his likeness minister to him in every respect; that is, the Son and the Holy Spirit, the Word and Wisdom; whom all the angels serve and to whom they are subject. Vain, therefore, are those who introduce another unknown Father because of that declaration, "No man knows the Father, but the Son."

The Same God Establishes Both the Old and New Covenants

4.9.1 All things therefore are of one and the same substance, that is, from one and the same God. As also the Lord says to the disciples, "Therefore every scribe, which is instructed unto the kingdom of heaven, is like a man that is a householder, who brings forth out of his treasure things new and old" (Matt

13:52). He did not teach that he who brought forth the old was one, and he that brought forth the new, another. But rather that they were one and the same. For the Lord is the good man of the house who rules the entire house of his Father; and who delivers a law suited both for slaves and those who are as yet undisciplined. And he gives fitting precepts to those who are free and have been justified by faith, as well as throws his own inheritance open to those who are sons. And he called his disciples "scribes" and "teachers of the kingdom of heaven," of whom also he elsewhere says to the Jews, "Behold, I send unto you wise men, and scribes, and teachers; and some of them you shall kill, and persecute from city to city" (Matt 23:34). Now, without contradiction, he means by those things which are brought forth from the treasure new and old, the two covenants. The old is that giving of the law which took place formerly, and he points out as the new, that manner of life required by the gospel. Of this covenant David says, "Sing unto the Lord a new song" (Ps 96:1); and Isaiah, "Sing unto the Lord a new hymn. His beginning, his name is glorified from the height of the earth; they declare his powers in the islands" (Isa 42:10); and Jeremiah says, "Behold, I will make a new covenant, not as I made with your fathers" in Mount Horeb (Jer 31:31). But one and the same householder produced both covenants, the Word of God, our Lord Jesus Christ, who spoke with both Abraham and Moses, and who has restored us anew to liberty, and has multiplied that grace which is from himself.

4.9.2 He declares, "For in this place is one greater than the temple" (Matt 12:6). But the words greater and less are not applied to those things which have nothing in common between themselves, and are of an opposite nature, and mutually repugnant. Rather, these terms are used in the case of those of the same substance, and which possess properties in common, but merely differ in number and size. For example, water from water, and light from light, and grace from grace. Greater, therefore, is that legislation which has been given for the purpose of freedom than that given for the purpose of bondage. It has therefore been diffused throughout the whole world and not only one nation. For one and the same Lord, who is greater than the temple, greater than Solomon, and greater than Jonah, confers gifts upon men, that is, his own presence, and the resurrection from the dead. He does not change God nor proclaim another Father. The Father he proclaims is the very same one who always has more to measure out to those of his household. As their love toward God increases, he also bestows more and greater gifts. As the Lord also said to his disciples, "You shall see greater things than these" (John 1:50). And Paul declares, "Not that I have already attained, or that I am justified, or have already been made perfect. For we know in part, and we prophesy in part; but when that which is perfect has come, the things which are in part shall be done away with" (drawn from Phil 3:12; 1 Cor 4:4; 1 Cor 13:9–10). As, therefore, when that which is perfect is come, we shall not see another Father but him whom we now desire to see. For "blessed are the pure in heart; for they shall see God" (Matt 5:8). We will also not look for another Christ and Son of God other than him who was born of the virgin Mary, who also suffered, in whom too we trust, and whom we love. As Isaiah says, "And they shall say in that day, Behold our Lord God, in whom we have trusted, and we have rejoiced in our salvation" (Isa 25:9). Peter also says in his epistle, "Though you have not seen him, you love him. Though you do not see him now, you have believed in him and shall rejoice with unspeakable joy" (1 Pet 1:8). Neither do we receive another Holy Spirit besides him who is with us and who cries, "Abba, Father" (Rom 8:15). And we shall increase in the very same things as now, and shall make progress, so that no longer through a glass, or by means of enigmas, but we will enjoy the gifts of God face to face—so also now, receiving more than the temple and more than Solomon, that is, the advent of the Son of God, we have not been taught another god besides the framer and the maker of all, who has been pointed out to us from the beginning. We have also not been taught another Christ, the Son of God, besides him who was foretold by the prophets.

4.9.3 For the new covenant having been known and preached by the prophets, he who was to carry it out according to the good pleasure of the Father was also preached, having been revealed to men as God pleased; that they might always make progress through believing in him, and by means of the successive covenants, should gradually attain to perfect salvation. For there is one salvation and one God, but the precepts which form the man are numerous, and the steps which lead man to God are not a few. Though he is but a man, it is allowable for an earthly and temporal king to grant to his subjects greater advantages at times. Would this not be lawful for God, since he is ever the same and is always willing to confer a greater degree of grace upon the human race and to honor continually those who please him with many gifts? But if this is to make progress, namely, to find out another Father besides him who was preached from the beginning; and again, besides him who is imagined to have been discovered in the second place, to find out a third other; then the progress of this man will consist in his also proceeding from a third to a fourth; and from this, again, to another and another; and thus he who thinks that he is always making progress of such a kind, will never rest in one God. For, being driven away from him who truly is God, and being turned backwards, he shall be forever seeking yet shall never discover God. Rather, he will continually swim in an abyss without limits, unless, being converted by repentance, he returns to the place from which he had been cast out, confessing one God, the Father, the creator, and believing in him who was declared by the Law and the Prophets, who was borne witness to by Christ, as he did himself declare to those who were accusing his disciples of not observing the tradition of the elders, "Why do you make void the law of God by reason of your tradition? For God said, Honor your father and mother; and, whoever curses father or mother, let him die the death" (Matt 15:3–4). And again, he says to them a second time, "And you have made void the word of God by reason of your tradition." In this Christ confesses in the plainest manner that the Father and God is the same one who said in the law, "Honor your father and mother; that it may be well with you" (Exod 20:12, LXX). For the true God confessed the commandment of the law as the word of God, and also called no one else God besides his own Father.

Christ's Advent Foretold by Moses

4.10.1 For this reason also John appropriately relates that the Lord said to the Jews, "You search the Scriptures, in which you think you have eternal life; these are they which testify of me. And you are not willing to come to me, that you may have life" (John 5:39–40). How therefore did the Scriptures testify of him unless they were from one and the same Father, instructing men beforehand as to the advent of his Son, and foretelling the salvation brought in by him? "For if you had believed Moses, you would also have believed me; for he wrote of me." He says this, no doubt, because the Son of God is implanted everywhere throughout his writings. At one time, indeed, speaking with Abraham, when about to eat with him; at another time with Noah, giving to him the dimensions of the ark; at another; inquiring after Adam; at another, bringing down judgment upon the people of Sodom; and again, when he becomes visible, and directs Jacob on his journey, and speaks with Moses from the bush. It would be endless to recount the occasions upon which the Son of God is shown forth by Moses. Of the day of his passion, too, he was not ignorant but foretold him, after a figurative manner, by the name given to the Passover. At that very festival, which had been proclaimed such a long time previously by Moses, our Lord suffered, thus fulfilling the Passover. He did not describe the day only, but also the place, the time of day at which the sufferings ceased, and the sign of the setting of the sun, saying, "You may not sacrifice the Passover within any other of your cities which the Lord God gives you; but in the place which the Lord your God shall choose that his name be called on there, you shall sacrifice the Passover in the evening, toward the setting of the sun" (Deut 16:5–6).

4.10.2 And already he had also declared his advent, saying, "There will not fail to be a ruler in Judah, nor a leader from his loins, until the one to whom it belongs comes, and he is the hope of the nations; binding his foal to the vine, and his donkey's colt to the creeping ivy. He shall wash his robe in wine, and his upper garment in the blood of the grape; his eyes shall be more joyous than wine, and his teeth whiter than milk" (Gen 49:10–12). For, let those who have the reputation of investigating everything inquire at what time a prince and leader failed to be in Judah, and who is the hope of the nations, who also is the vine, what was the donkey's colt referred to as his, what the clothing, and what the eyes, what the teeth, and what the wine, and thus let them investigate every one of the details mentioned. They will find that there was none other announced than our Lord, Christ Jesus. For this reason Moses, when chiding the ingratitude of the people, said, "You infatuated and unwise people, do you thus repay the Lord?" (Deut 32:6). And again, he indicates that he who from the beginning founded and created them, the Word, who also redeems and gives life to us in the last times, is shown as hanging on the tree, and they will not believe in him. For he says, "And your life shall be hanging before your eyes, and you will not believe your life" (Deut 28:66). And again, "Has not this same one, your Father, owned you, and made you, and created you?" (Deut 32:6).

Humans Are Granted Knowledge of God by God Alone

4.11.1 But that it was not only the prophets and many righteous men, who, foreseeing through the Holy Spirit his advent, prayed that they might attain to that period in which they should see their Lord face to face, and hear his words, the Lord has made manifest when he says to his disciples, "Many prophets and righteous men have desired to see those things which you see, and have not seen them; and to hear those things which you hear, and have not heard them" (Matt 13:17). In what way, then, did they desire both to hear and to see unless they had foreknowledge of his future advent? But how could they have foreknown it unless they had previously received foreknowledge from himself? And how do the Scriptures testify of him unless all things had ever been revealed and shown to believers by one and the same God through the Word; he at one time conferring with his creature and at another propounding his law; at one time, again, reproving, at another exhorting and then setting free his servant and adopting him as a son; and, at the proper time, bestowing an incorruptible inheritance for the purpose of bringing man to perfection? For he formed him for growth and increase, as the Scripture says, "Increase and multiply" (Gen 1:28).

4.11.2 And in this respect God differs from man, that God indeed makes, but man is made; and truly, he who makes is always the same; but that which is made must receive both beginning, and middle, addition, and increase. And God does indeed create after a skillful manner, while with regard to man, he is skillfully created. God is also truly perfect in all things, himself equal and similar to himself, as he is all light, and all mind, and all substance, and the fount of all good. But man receives advancement and increase toward God. For as God is always the same, so also man, when found in God, shall always go on toward God. For neither does God at any time cease to confer benefits upon or to enrich man; nor does man ever cease from receiving the benefits and being enriched by God. For the receptacle of his goodness and the instrument of his glorification is the man who is grateful to him that made him; and again, the receptacle of his just judgment is the ungrateful man, who both despises his maker and is not subject to his Word; who has promised that he will give very much to those always bringing forth fruit, and more and more to those who have the Lord's money. "Well done," he says, "good and faithful servant; because you have been faithful in little, I will appoint you over many things; enter into the joy of your Lord" (Matt 25:21). The Lord himself thus promises very much.

4.11.3 As, therefore, he has promised to give very much to those who now bring forth fruit, according to the gift of his grace, but not according to the changeableness of "knowledge," for the Lord remains the same, and the same Father is revealed. In this way, the one and the same Lord granted by means of his advent a greater gift of grace to those of a later period than what he had granted to those under the Old Testament dispensation. For they indeed used to hear, by means of his servants, that the king would come, and they rejoiced to a certain extent insofar as they hoped for his coming. But those who have beheld him actually present and have obtained freedom and been made partakers of his gifts possess a greater amount of grace and a higher degree of exultation. They are able to rejoice because of the king's arrival. As also David says, "My soul shall rejoice in the Lord; it shall be glad in his salvation" (Ps 35:9). For this cause, upon his entrance into Jerusalem, all those who were in the way recognized David their king in his sorrow of soul and spread their garments for him and adorned the way with green branches, crying out with great joy and gladness, "Hosanna to the Son of David; blessed is he that comes in the name of the Lord; hosanna in the highest" (Matt 21:8).

But to the envious wicked stewards who circumvented those under them and ruled over those that had no great intelligence, and for this reason were unwilling that the king should come, and who said to him, "Do you hear what these say?" the Lord replied, "Have you never read, out of the mouths of babies and infants have you perfected praise?" (Matt 21:16). He thus pointed out that what had been declared by David concerning the Son of God was accomplished in his own person. He also indicated that they were indeed ignorant of the meaning of the Scripture and the dispensation of God and declared that it was he himself who was announced by the prophets as the Christ, whose name is praised in all the earth, and who perfects praise to his Father from the mouth of babies and infants. For this reason also his glory has been raised above the heavens.

4.11.4 If, therefore, the selfsame person is present who was announced by the prophets, our Lord Jesus Christ, and if his advent has brought in a fuller measure of grace and greater gifts to those who have received him, it is plain that the Father is also himself the same who was proclaimed by the prophets, and that the Son, on his coming, did not spread the knowledge of another Father, but of the same one who was preached from the beginning. From whom also he has brought down freedom to those who serve him in a lawful manner and with a willing mind and with all their heart.

Now there are also scoffers and those who are not subject to God and who follow outward purifications for the praise of men. These kinds of observances had been given previously as a type of future things, the law typifying as it were certain things in a shadow and delineating eternal things by temporal things, celestial ones by terrestrial ones. There are also those who pretend that they themselves observe more than what has been prescribed. In this way, they act as if they prefer their own zeal to God himself, while within they are full of hypocrisy, covetousness, and all wickedness. To those such as these, he has assigned everlasting perdition by cutting them off from life.

The Author of the Law and the Gospel Is the Same

4.12.1 For the tradition of the elders themselves, which they pretended to observe from the law, was contrary to the law given by Moses. For this reason also Isaiah declares, "Your dealers mix the wine with water" (Isa 1:22), showing that the elders were in the habit of mingling a watered-down tradition with the simple command of God. That is, they set up a spurious law and one contrary to the true law. The Lord also made this plain when he said to them, "Why do you transgress the commandment of God for the sake of your tradition?" (Matt 15:3). For not only by actual transgression did they set the law of God aside as nothing, mingling the wine with water; but they also set up their own law in opposition to it, which is termed, even to the present day, the pharisaical. In this law they suppress certain things, add others, and interpret others, again, as they think proper, which their teachers use, each one in particular. Desiring to uphold these traditions, they were unwilling to be subject to the law of God which prepares them for the coming of Christ. But they even blamed the Lord for healing on the Sabbath-days, which the law did not prohibit as I have already observed. For they themselves, in one sense, performed acts of healing upon the Sabbath day when they circumcised a man on that day. But they did not blame themselves for transgressing the command of God through tradition and the previously mentioned pharisaical law and for not keeping the commandment of the law which is the love of God.

4.12.2 But that this is the first and greatest commandment and that the next has respect to love toward our neighbor, the Lord has taught when he says that the entire Law and the Prophets hang upon these two commandments. Moreover, he did not himself bring down from heaven any other commandment greater than this one but renewed this very same one to his disciples, when he commanded them to love God with all their heart and others as themselves. But if he had descended from another Father, he never would have made use of the first and greatest commandment of the law. He would undoubtedly have rather endeavored by all means to bring down a greater one than this from the perfect Father so that he would not have to make use of that which had been given by the God of the law. And Paul in like manner declares, "Love is the fulfilling of the law" (Rom 13:10). He declares that when all other things have been destroyed, there shall remain "faith, hope, and love; but the greatest of all is love" (1 Cor 13:13). Apart from the love of God, neither knowledge avails anything, nor the understanding of mysteries, nor faith, nor prophecy, but without love all are hollow and vain. Moreover, love makes man perfect. He who loves God is perfect, both in this world and in that which is to come. For we never cease from loving God; but in proportion as we continue to contemplate him, so much the more do we love him.

4.12.3 Both in the law and the gospel, the first and greatest commandment is to love the Lord God with the whole heart and then there follows a commandment similar to it, to love one's neighbor as one's self. The author of the law and the gospel is shown to be one and the same. For the precepts of an absolutely perfect life, since they are the same in each testament, have pointed out to us the same God, who certainly has promulgated particular laws adapted for each; but the more prominent and the greatest commandments, without which salvation cannot be attained, he has exhorted us to observe the same in both.

4.12.4 The Lord, too, does not do away with this God when he shows that the law was not derived from another god, expressing himself as follows to those who were being instructed by him to the multitude and to his disciples, "The scribes and Pharisees sit in Moses' seat. Everything that they bid you to observe, observe and do those things; but do not imitate their works; for they say, and do not. For they bind heavy burdens and lay them upon men's shoulders but they themselves will not so much as move them with a finger" (Matt 23:2–4). He therefore did not throw blame upon that law which was given by Moses when he exhorted it to be observed, Jerusalem being as yet in safety, but he did throw blame upon those persons because they repeated indeed the words of the law yet were without love. For this reason they were held to be unrighteous with respect to God and with respect to their neighbors. As also Isaiah says, "This people honors me with their lips, but their heart is far from me; nevertheless in vain do they worship me, teaching the doctrines and the commandments of men" (Isa 29:13). He does not call the law given by Moses commandments of men, but the traditions of the elders themselves which they had invented. By upholding these traditions, they made the law of God of no effect and were on this account also not subject to his Word. For this is what Paul says concerning these men, "For they, being ignorant of God's righteousness and going about to establish their own righteousness have not submitted themselves to the righteousness of God. For Christ is the end of the law for righteousness to everyone that believes" (Rom 10:3–4). And how is Christ the end of the law, if he is not also the final cause of it? For he who has brought in the end has himself also brought about the beginning. It is also he who himself says to Moses, "I have surely seen the affliction of my people which is in Egypt, and I have come down to deliver them" (Exod 3:7–8). It was customary from the beginning for the Word of God to ascend and descend for the purpose of saving those who were in affliction.

4.12.5 Now, that the law did beforehand teach mankind the necessity of following Christ, he himself makes manifest when he replied as follows to him who asked him what he should do that he might inherit eternal life, "If you will enter into life, keep the commandments" (Matt 19:17–18). But upon the other asking "Which?" again the Lord replies, "Do not commit adultery, do not kill, do not steal, do not bear false witness, honor father and mother, and you shall love your neighbor as yourself." By saying this, he set the precepts of the law as the entrance into life as an ascending series before those who wished to follow him. What he then said to one, he said to all. But when the former said, "All these have I done" (and most likely he had not kept them, for in that case the Lord would not have said to him, "Keep the commandments"), the Lord, exposing his covetousness, said to him, "If you will be perfect, go, sell all that you have and distribute to the poor; and come, follow me," promising the portion belonging to the apostles to those who would act in this way. And he did not preach to his followers another god the father besides him who was proclaimed by the law from the beginning; nor another son; nor the mother, the enthymesis of the Aeon, who existed in suffering and apostasy; nor the Pleroma of the thirty Aeons, which has been proved vain, and incapable of being believed in; nor that fable invented by the other heretics. But he taught that they should obey the commandments which God commanded from the beginning and that they should do away with their former covetousness by good works and follow after Christ. But that possessions distributed to the poor do annul former covetousness, Zacchaeus made evident when he said, "Behold, half of my goods I give to the poor; and if I have defrauded anyone, I will restore fourfold" (Luke 19:8).

The One God Is above All Created Things

4.19.1 Now the gifts, offerings, and all the sacrifices, these the people received in a figure, as was shown to Moses in the mount from one and the same God whose name is now glorified in the church among all nations. But it is proper that those earthly things, indeed, which are spread all around us, should be types of the celestial, being both, however, created by the same God. For in no other way could he assimilate an image of spiritual things to suit our comprehension. But to allege that those things which are super-celestial and spiritual, and, as far as we are concerned, invisible and ineffable, are in their turn the types of celestial things and of another Pleroma, and to say that God is the image of another Father is to play the part both of wanderers from the truth and of absolutely foolish and stupid persons. For, as I have repeatedly shown, such persons will find it necessary to be continually finding out types of types, and images of images, and will never be able to fix their minds on one and the true God. For their imaginations range beyond God, having in their hearts surpassed the master himself. Indeed in their own minds, they are elated and exalted above him, but in reality they are turning away from the true God.

4.19.2 To these persons one may with justice say, as Scripture itself suggests, to what distance above God do you lift up your imaginations, you rashly elated men? You have heard "that the heavens are meted out in the palm of his hand" (Isa 40:12). Tell me the measure and recount the endless multitude of cubits, explain to me the fullness, the breadth, the length, the height, the beginning and end of the measurement—things which the heart of man does not understand, neither does it comprehend them. For the heavenly treasuries are indeed great. God cannot be measured in the heart, and he is incomprehensible in the mind; he who holds the earth in the hollow of his hand. Who perceives the measure of his right hand? Who knows his finger? Or who understands his hand—that hand which measures immensity; that hand which, by its own measure, spreads out the measure of the heavens, and which comprises in its hollow the earth with the abysses; which contains in itself the breadth, and length, and the deep below, and the height above of the whole creation; which is seen, which is heard and understood, and which is invisible? And for this reason God is "above all principality, and power, and dominion, and every name that is named," of all things which have been created and established (Eph 1:21). It is he who fills the heavens and views the abysses, who is also present with every one of us. For he says, "Am I a God at hand, and not a God afar off? If any man is hidden in secret places, shall I not see him?" (Jer 23:23). For his hand lays hold of all things and it is that which illumines the heavens and lightens also the things which are under the heavens and tries the reins and the hearts. His hand is also present in hidden things and in our secret thoughts and openly nourishes and preserves us.

4.19.3 But if man does not comprehend the fullness and the greatness of his hand, how shall anyone be able to understand or know in his heart so great a God? Yet, as if they had now measured and thoroughly investigated him and explored him on every side, they feign that beyond him there exists another Pleroma of Aeons, and another Father; certainly not looking up to celestial things, but truly descending into a profound abyss of madness; maintaining that their Father extends only to the border of those things which are beyond the Pleroma, but that, on the other hand, the Demiurge does not reach so far as the Pleroma; and thus they represent neither of them as being perfect and comprehending all things. For the former will be defective in regard to the whole world formed outside of the Pleroma, and the latter in respect of that ideal world which was formed within the Pleroma; and therefore neither of these can be the God of all. But that no one can fully declare the goodness of God from the things made by him is a point evident to all. And that his greatness is not defective but contains all things and extends even to us, and is with us, everyone will confess who entertains worthy conceptions of God.

God Was Never Without His Word and His Wisdom

4.20.1 With regard to his greatness, therefore, it is not possible to know God, for it is impossible that the Father can be measured; but with regard to his love (for it is this which leads us to God by his Word), when we obey him, we always learn that there is so great a God, and that it is he who by himself has established, selected, adorned, and contains all things; and among the all things, both ourselves and this our world. We also then were made along with those things which are contained by him. And this is he of whom the Scripture says, "And God formed man, taking clay of the earth, and breathed into his face the breath of life" (Gen 2:7). It was not angels, therefore, who made us nor who formed us, neither had angels power to make an image of God nor anyone else except the Word of the Lord, nor any power remotely distant from the Father of all things. For God did not stand in need of these beings in order to accomplish what he had himself determined with himself beforehand should be done, as if he did not possess his own hands. For with him were always present the Word and Wisdom, the Son and the Spirit, by whom and in whom, freely and spontaneously, he made all things, to whom he also speaks, saying, "Let us make man after our image and likeness" (Gen 1:26); he taking from himself the substance of the creatures formed, the pattern of things made, and the type of all the adornments in the world.

4.20.2 Truly, then, the Scripture declared, which says, "First of all believe that there is one God, who has established all things, and completed them, and having caused that from what had no being, all things should come into existence," he who contains all things and is himself contained by no one.[2] Rightly also has Malachi said among the prophets, "Is it not one God who has established us? Have we not all one Father?" (Mal 2:10). In accordance with this, too, does the apostle say, "There is one God, the Father, who is above all, and in us all" (Eph 4:6). Likewise does the Lord also say, "All things are delivered to me by my Father," manifestly by him who made all things; for he did not deliver to him the things of another, but his own (Matt 12:27). But in all things it is implied that nothing has been kept back from him, and for this reason the same person is the judge of the living and the dead, "having the key of David; he shall open and no man shall shut; he shall shut and no man shall open" (Rev 3:7). For no one was able, either in heaven or on earth or under the earth to open the book of the Father or to behold him, with the exception of the lamb who was slain and who redeemed us with his own blood, receiving power over all things from the same God who made all things by the

---

2 This quotation is from Shepherd of Hermas, *Mand.* 1.1.

Word, and adorned them by his Wisdom, when "the Word was made flesh," that even as the Word of God had the sovereignty in the heavens, so also might he have the sovereignty in earth, inasmuch as he was a righteous man, "who did no sin, neither was there found guile in his mouth" (1 Pet 2:23); and that he might have the preeminence over those things which are under the earth, he himself being made "the first begotten of the dead" (Col 1:18); and that all things, as I have already said, might behold their king; and that the paternal light might meet with and rest upon the flesh of our Lord, and come to us from his resplendent flesh, and that thus man might attain to immortality, having been invested with the paternal light.

4.20.3 I have also largely demonstrated that the Word, namely the Son, was always with the Father. That Wisdom also, which is the Spirit, was present with him prior to all creation, he declares by Solomon, "God by Wisdom founded the earth, and by understanding he has established the heaven. By his knowledge the depths burst forth, and the clouds dropped down the dew" (Prov 3:19–20). And again, "The Lord created me the beginning of his ways in his work; he set me up from everlasting, in the beginning, before he made the earth, before he established the depths, and before the fountains of waters gushed forth; before the mountains were made strong, and before all the hills, he brought me forth" (Prov 8:22–25). And again, "When he prepared the heaven, I was with him, and when he established the fountains of the deep; when he made the foundations of the earth strong, I was with him preparing them. I was he in whom he rejoiced, and throughout all time I was daily glad before his face, when he rejoiced at the completion of the world and was delighted in the sons of men" (Prov 8:27–31).

4.20.4 There is therefore one God, who by the Word and Wisdom created and arranged all things. But this is the creator who has granted this world to the human race, and who, with regard to his greatness, is indeed unknown to all who have been made by him (for no man has searched out his height, either among the ancients who have gone to their rest, or any of those who are now alive). But with regard to his love, he is always known through him by whose means he ordained all things. Now this is his Word, our Lord Jesus Christ, who in the last times was made a man among men that he might join the end to the beginning, that is, man to God. For this reason the prophets, receiving the prophetic gift from the same Word, announced his advent according to the flesh by which the blending and communion of God and man took place according to the good pleasure of the Father, the Word of God foretelling from the beginning that God should be seen by men and speak with them upon earth, should confer with them, and should be present with his own creation, saving it, and becoming capable of being perceived by it, and freeing us from the hands of all that hate us, that is, from every spirit of wickedness; and causing us to serve him in holiness and righteousness all our days, in order that man, having embraced the Spirit of God, might pass into the glory of the Father.

4.20.5 The prophets set forth these things in a prophetic manner. They did not, as some allege, proclaim that he who was seen by the prophets was a different God, the Father of all being invisible. Yet this is what those heretics declare, who are altogether ignorant of the nature of prophecy. For prophecy is a prediction of future things, that is, a setting forth beforehand of those things which shall be afterwards. The prophets, then, indicated beforehand that God should be seen by men. As the Lord also says, "Blessed are the pure in heart, for they shall see God" (Matt 5:8). But with respect to his greatness and his wonderful glory, "no man shall see God and live," for the Father is incomprehensible (Exod 33:20). But with regard to his love, kindness, and his infinite power, even this he grants to those who love him, that is, to see God. This is something that the prophets also predicted. "For those things that are impossible with men, are possible with God" (Luke 18:27). For man does not see God by his own powers. Rather, when God pleases he is seen by men, by whom he wills, and when he wills, and as he wills. For God is powerful in all things, having been seen at that time indeed, prophetically through the Spirit, and seen too, adoptively through the son. He shall also be seen paternally in the kingdom of heaven, the Spirit truly preparing man in the Son of God, and the Son leading him to the Father, while the Father, too, confers upon him incorruption for eternal life which comes to everyone from the fact that he has seen God. For as those who see the light are within the light and partake of its brilliancy; even so, those who see God are in God and receive his splendor. But his splendor gives life to them. Those, therefore, who see God, receive life. And for this reason, he, although beyond comprehension, boundless, and invisible, rendered himself visible, comprehensible, and within the capacity of those who believe, that he might give new life to those who receive and behold him through faith. For as his greatness is past finding out, so also his goodness is beyond expression. He bestows life upon those who see him through this same greatness and goodness. It is not possible to live apart from life, and the means of life is found in fellowship with God; but fellowship with God is to know God and to enjoy his goodness.

4.20.6 Men therefore shall see God, that they may live, being made immortal by that sight, and attaining even unto God. As I have already said, this reality was declared figuratively by the prophets, that God should be seen by men who bear his Spirit in them and always wait patiently for his coming. As Moses also says in Deuteronomy, "We shall see in that day that God will talk to man, and he shall live" (Deut 5:24). For some of these men used to see the prophetic Spirit and his active influences poured forth for all kinds of gifts. Others, again, beheld the advent of the Lord and that dispensation which obtained from the beginning by which he accomplished the will of the Father with regard to things both celestial and terrestrial. Still others beheld paternal glories adapted to the times, to those who saw and who heard them then, and to all those who were to hear them in subsequent times. In this way, therefore, God was revealed. For God the Father is shown forth through all these operations, with the Spirit indeed working, and the Son ministering, while the Father was approving, and man's salvation was being accomplished. As he also declares through Hosea the prophet, "I," he says, "have multiplied visions and have used similitudes by the ministry of the prophets" (Hos 12:10). But the apostle expounded this very passage when he said, "Now there are diversities of gifts, but the same Spirit; and there are differences of ministries, but the same Lord; and there are diversities of operations, but it is the same God who works all in all. But the manifestation of the Spirit is given to every man to profit all the same" (1 Cor 12:4–7). But as he who works all things in all is God, as to the points of what nature and how great he is, God is invisible and indescribable to all things which have been made by him, but he is by no means unknown; for all things learn through his Word that there is one God the Father who contains all things and who grants existence to all. As is written in the Gospel, "No man has seen God at any time, except the only begotten Son, who is in the bosom of the Father; he has declared him" (John 1:18).

4.20.7 Therefore the Son of the Father declares him from the beginning, inasmuch as he was with the Father from the beginning, who also showed to the human race prophetic visions, diversities of gifts, his own ministries, and the glory of the Father, in regular order and connection, at the fitting time for the benefit of mankind. For where there is a regular succession, there is also fixedness; and where fixedness, there is suitability to the period; and where suitability, there is also utility. And for this reason the Word became the dispenser of the paternal grace for the benefit of men, for whom he made such great dispensations, revealing God indeed to men, but presenting man to God, and preserving at the same time the invisibility of the Father, lest man should at any time become a despiser of God, and that he should always possess something toward which he might advance; but, on the other hand, revealing God to men through many dispensations, lest man, falling away from God altogether, should cease to exist. For the glory of God is a living man, while the life of man consists in beholding God. For if the manifestation of God which is made by means of the creation affords life to all those living in the earth, much more does that revelation of the Father which comes through the Word give life to those who see God.

The Incomprehensible God Is Made Known through Christ's Incarnation

4.20.9. And the Word spoke to Moses, appearing before him, "just as anyone might speak to his friend" (Num 12:8). But Moses desired to see him openly who was speaking with him and was thus addressed, "Stand in the deep place of the rock, and with my hand I will cover you. But when my splendor shall pass by, then you shall see my back, but my face you shall not see; for no man sees my face and lives" (Exod 33:19–22). Two facts are thus signified: that it is impossible for man to see God, and that through the wisdom of God man shall see him in the last times, in the depth of a rock, that is, in his coming as a man. And for this reason the Lord spoke with Moses face to face on the top of a mountain, while Elijah was also present, as the Gospel relates. In this way, he made good in the end the ancient promise.

[…]

4.20.11 If, then, Moses, Elijah, and Ezekiel, who all had many celestial visions, did not see God; and if what they did see were similitudes of the splendor of the Lord and prophecies of things to come, it is manifest that the Father is indeed invisible, of whom also the Lord said, "No man has seen God at any time." But his Word, as he himself willed it and for the benefit of those who beheld, did show the Father's brightness and explained his purposes. . . . He did not appear to those seeing him in one figure or in one character, but according to the reasons and effects aimed at in his dispensations, as it is written in Daniel. For at one time he was seen with those who were around Ananias, Azarias, and Mishael, as present with them in the furnace of fire, in the burning, and preserving them from the effects of fire: "And the appearance of the fourth," it is said, "was like to the Son of God" (Dan 3:26). At another time he is represented as "a stone cut out of the mountain without hands," and as smiting all temporal kingdoms, and as blowing them away, and as himself filling all the earth (Dan 7:13–14). Then, too, is this same individual beheld as the Son of Man coming in the clouds of heaven and drawing near to the Ancient of Days, and receiving from him all power and glory and a kingdom.

"His dominion," it is said, "is an everlasting dominion, and his kingdom shall not perish" (Dan 7:4).

John also, the Lord's disciple, when beholding the priestly and glorious advent of his kingdom, says in the Apocalypse, "I turned to see the voice that spoke with me. And, being turned, I saw seven golden candlesticks; and in the midst of the candlesticks one like the Son of Man, clothed with a garment reaching to the feet, and girded about the chest with a golden sash; and his head and his hairs were white, as white as wool, and as snow; and his eyes were as a flame of fire; and his feet like fine brass, as if he burned in a furnace. And his voice was as the voice of waters; and he had in his right hand seven stars; and out of his mouth went a sharp two-edged sword; and his countenance was as the sun shining in his strength" (Rev 1:12–16). For in these words he sets forth something of the glory which he has received from his Father, as where he makes mention of the head; something in reference to the priestly office also, as in the case of the long garment reaching to the feet.

And this was the reason why Moses vested the high priest after this fashion. Something also alludes to the end of all things, as where he speaks of the fine brass burning in the fire, which denotes the power of faith, and the continuing instant in prayer, because of the consuming fire which is to come at the end of time. But when John could not endure the sight (for he says, "I fell at his feet as dead," that what was written might come to pass, "No man sees God, and shall live"), the Word revived him and reminded him that it was he upon whose bosom he had leaned at supper, when he put the question as to who should betray him. This same one declared, "I am the first and the last, and he who lives, and was dead, and behold I am alive for evermore, and have the keys of death and of hell."

And after these things, seeing the same Lord in a second vision, he says, "For I saw in the midst of the throne, and of the four living creatures, and in the midst of the elders, a Lamb standing as it had been slain, having seven horns, and seven eyes, which are the seven spirits of God, sent forth into all the earth" (Rev 5:6). And again, he says, speaking of this very same lamb, "And behold a white horse; and he that sat upon him was called faithful and true; and in righteousness he judges and makes war. And his eyes were as a flame of fire, and on his head were many crowns; having a name written, that no man knows but himself; and he was girded around with a robe sprinkled with blood; and his name is called the Word of God. And the armies of heaven followed him upon white horses, clothed in pure white linen. And out of his mouth goes a sharp sword, that with it he may smite the nations; and he shall rule them with a rod of iron; and he treads the wine press of the fierceness of the wrath of God almighty. And he has upon his robe and upon his thigh a name written, king of kings and Lord of Lords" (Rev 19:11–17). Thus does the Word of God always preserve the outlines, as it were, of things to come and points out to men the various forms, as it were, of the dispensations of the Father, teaching us the things pertaining to God.

Christ Is the Treasure of the Scriptures

4.26.1 Therefore, if anyone reads the Scriptures with attention, he will find in them an account of Christ and a foreshadowing of the new calling. For Christ is the treasure which was hidden in the field, that is, in this world; for "the field is the world" (Matt 13:38). But the treasure hidden in the Scriptures is Christ, since he was pointed out by means of types and parables. Hence his human nature could not be understood prior to the consummation of those things which had been predicted, that is, the advent of Christ. And therefore it was said to Daniel the prophet, "Shut up the words, and seal the book even to the time of consummation, until many learn, and knowledge be completed. For at that time, when the dispersion shall be accomplished, they shall know all these things" (Dan 12:4, 7). But Jeremiah also says, "In the last days they shall understand these things" (Jer 23:20). For every prophecy, before its fulfillment, is to men full of enigmas and ambiguities. But when the time has arrived and the prediction has come to pass, then the prophecies have a clear and certain exposition. And for this reason, indeed, when at this present time the law is read to the Jews, it is like a fable. For they do not possess the explanation of all things pertaining to the advent of the Son of God which took place in human nature. However, when it is read by the Christians, it is indeed a treasure hidden in a field but one that is brought to light and explained by the cross of Christ. Understood in this way, the law both enriches the understanding of men and shows forth the wisdom of God by declaring his dispensations with regard to man, forming the kingdom of Christ beforehand, preaching by anticipation the inheritance of the holy Jerusalem, and proclaiming beforehand that the man who loves God shall arrive at such excellency so as to even see God and hear his word. And from the hearing of God's discourse, one might be glorified to such an extent that others cannot behold the glory of his countenance. As was said by Daniel, "Those who do understand, shall shine as the brightness of the heavens, and many of the righteous as the stars for ever and ever" (Dan 12:3). Thus, then, I have shown it to be, if anyone reads the Scriptures. For thus it was that the Lord spoke with the disciples after his resurrection from the dead, proving to them from the Scriptures themselves "that Christ must suffer, and enter into his glory, and that forgiveness of sins should be preached in his name throughout all the world" (Luke 24:26, 47). And the disciple will be perfected and rendered like the householder "who brings forth from his treasure things new and old" (Matt 13:52).

Both Testaments Are from One and the Same God

4.32.1 After this fashion also did a presbyter, a disciple of the apostles, reason with respect to the two testaments, proving that both were truly from one and the same God. For he maintained that there was no other God besides him who made and fashioned us, and that the teaching of those men has no foundation who affirm that this world of ours was made either by angels, or by any other power whatsoever, or by another god. For if a man be once moved away from the creator of all things, and if he grant that this creation to which we belong was formed by any other or through any other than the one God, he must of necessity fall into much inconsistency and many contradictions of this sort; to which he will be able to furnish no explanations which can be regarded as either probable or true. And, for this reason, those who introduce other doctrines conceal from us the opinion which they themselves hold respecting God, because they are aware of the untenable and absurd nature of their doctrine and are afraid that if they were vanquished then they might have some difficulty in making good their escape. But if anyone believes in only one God who also made all things by the Word, as Moses likewise says, "God said, Let there be light, and there was light" (Gen 1:3). And as we read in the Gospel, "All things were made by him; and without him was nothing made" (John 1:3). And the apostle Paul says in like manner, "There is one Lord, one faith, one baptism, one God and Father, who is above all, and through all, and in us all," this man will first of all "hold the head, from which the whole body is fitted and held together, and, through means of every joint according to the measure of the service of each individual part, makes increase of the body to the edification of itself in love" (Eph 4:5–6, 16). And then shall every word also seem consistent to him if he for his part diligently read the Scriptures in company with those who are presbyters in the church, among whom is the apostolic doctrine, as I have pointed out.

4.32.2 For all the apostles taught that there were indeed two testaments among the two peoples; but that it was one and the same God who appointed both for the advantage of those men, for whose sakes the testaments were given; who were to believe in God, I have proved in the third book from the very teaching of the apostles; and that the first testament was not given without reason, or to no purpose, or in an accidental sort of manner; but that it subdued those to whom it was given to the service of God, for their benefit, for God needs no service from men, and exhibited a type of heavenly things, inasmuch as man was not yet able to see the things of God through means of immediate vision; and foreshadowed the images of those things which now actually exist in the church, in order that our faith might be firmly established; and contained a prophecy of things to come, in order that man might learn that God has foreknowledge of all things.

[...]

4.33.15 And all those other points which I have shown the prophets to have uttered by means of so long a series of Scriptures, he who is truly spiritual will interpret by pointing out, in regard to every one of the things which have been spoken, to what special point in the dispensation of the Lord is referred, and by thus exhibiting the entire system of the work of the Son of God, knowing always the same God and always acknowledging the same Word of God, although he has but now been manifested to us; acknowledging also at all times the same Spirit of God, although he has been poured out upon us after a new fashion in these last times, knowing that he descends even from the creation of the world to its end upon the human race simply as such, from whom those who believe God and follow his word receive that salvation which flows from him. Those, on the other hand, who depart from him and despise his precepts and by their deeds bring dishonor on him who made them, and by their opinions blaspheme him who nourishes them, heap up against themselves most righteous judgment. The spiritual man therefore sifts and tries them all, but he himself is tried by no man; he neither blasphemes his Father, nor sets aside his dispensations, nor inveighs against the fathers, nor dishonors the prophets by maintaining that they were sent from a different god other than the one he worships, or again, that their prophecies were derived from different sources.

[...]

4.36.5 The Lord, therefore, who has called us everywhere by the apostles is he who called those of old by the prophets, as appears by the words of the Lord; and although they preached to various nations, the prophets were not from one God and the apostles from another; but, proceeding from one and the same, some of them announced the Lord, others preached the Father, and others again foretold the advent of the Son of God, while yet others declared him as already present to those who then were afar off.

Summary of Book 4 and the Purpose of Book 5

41.4 Inasmuch as the words of the Lord are numerous, while they all proclaim one and the same Father, the creator of this world, it was incumbent also upon me, for their own sake, to refute by many arguments those who are involved in many errors, if by any means, when they are refuted by many proofs, they may be converted to the truth and saved. But it is necessary to add to this composition, in what follows, also the doctrine of Paul after the words of the Lord, to examine the opinion of this man and expound the apostle, and to explain whichever passages have received other interpretations from the heretics who have altogether misunderstood what Paul has spoken, and to point out the folly of their mad opinions; and to demonstrate from that same Paul, from whose writings they press questions upon us, that they are indeed utterers of falsehood, but that the apostle was a preacher of the truth, and that he taught all things agreeable to the preaching of the truth; to the effect that it was one God the Father who spoke with Abraham, who gave the law, who sent the prophets beforehand, who in the last times sent his Son and conferred salvation upon his own handiwork—that is, the substance of flesh. Arranging, then, in another book, the rest of the words of the Lord, which he taught concerning the Father, not by parables but by expressions taken in their obvious meaning, and the exposition of the epistles of the blessed apostle, I shall, with God's aid, furnish you with the complete work of the exposure and refutation of knowledge, falsely so called.

5.0.1 In the four preceding books, my very dear friend, which I put forth to you, all the heretics have been exposed and their doctrines brought to light. These men who have devised irreligious opinions have been refuted. I have accomplished this by presenting something from the doctrine peculiar to each of these men, which they have left in their writings, as well as by using arguments of a more general nature and applicable to them all. Then I have pointed out the truth and shown the preaching of the church which the prophets proclaimed, as I have already demonstrated, but which Christ brought to perfection and the apostles have handed down, from whom the church, receiving these truths, and throughout all the world alone preserving them in their integrity, has transmitted them to her sons. Then also, having disposed of all questions which the heretics propose to us and having explained the doctrine of the apostles and clearly set forth many of those things which were said and done by the Lord in parables, I shall endeavor in this the fifth book of the entire work which treats of the exposure and refutation of knowledge falsely so called, to exhibit proofs from the rest of the Lord's doctrine and the apostolic epistles; thus complying with your demand, as you requested of me, since indeed I have been assigned a place in the ministry of the word; and laboring by every means in my power to furnish you with large assistance against the contradictions of the heretics, as also to reclaim the wanderers and convert them to the church of God, to confirm at the same time the minds of the new converts, that they may preserve steadfast the faith which they have received, guarded by the church in its integrity, in order that they might be in no way perverted by those who endeavor to teach them false doctrines and lead them away from the truth. It will be necessary for you, however, and all who may happen to read this writing, to peruse with great attention what I have already said, that you may obtain a knowledge of the subjects against which I am contending. For it is thus that you will both refute them in a legitimate manner and will be prepared to receive the proofs brought forward against them, casting away their doctrines as filth by means of the celestial faith; but following the only true and steadfast teacher, the Word of God, our Lord Jesus Christ, who through his transcendent love became what we are so that he might bring us to be even what he is himself.

The Reality and Revelation of the Incarnation

5.1.1 For in no other way could we have learned the things of God unless our master, existing as the Word, had become man. For no other being had the power of revealing to us the things of the Father except his own proper Word. For what other person "knew the mind of the Lord," or who else "has become his counsellor?" (Rom 11:34). Again, we could have learned in no other way than by seeing our teacher and hearing his voice with our own ears, that, having become imitators of his works as well as doers of his words, we may have communion with him, receiving increase from the perfect one, and from him who is prior to all creation. We—who were but lately created by the only best and good being, by him also who has the gift of immortality having been formed after his likeness . . . and made the first fruits of creation—have received, in the times known beforehand, the blessings of salvation according to the ministry of the Word, who is perfect in all things, as the mighty Word, and very man, who, redeeming us by his own blood in a manner consistent with reason, gave himself as a redemption for those who had been led into captivity. And since the apostasy tyrannized over us unjustly, and, though we were by nature the property of the omnipotent God, alienated us contrary to nature and rendered us its own disciples, the Word of God, powerful in all things and not defective with regard to his own justice righteously turned against that apostasy and redeemed from it his own property. He did not do this by violent means, as the apostasy had obtained dominion over us at the beginning when it insatiably snatched away what was not its own, but by means of persuasion consistent with his character as a God of counsel, who does not use violent means to obtain what he desires. He did this so that neither should justice be infringed upon nor the ancient handiwork of God go to destruction. The Lord has redeemed us through his own blood. He has given his soul for our souls and his flesh for our flesh. He has also poured out the Spirit of the Father for the union and communion of God and man, imparting indeed God to men by means of the Spirit, and, on the other hand, attaching man to God by his own incarnation and bestowing upon us at his coming immortality durably and truly by means of communion with God. Because of all these works of God, all the doctrines of the heretics fall to ruin.

5.1.2 Vain indeed are those who allege that he appeared in mere seeming. For these things were not done in appearance only, but in actual reality. But if he did appear as a man when he was not a man, neither could the Holy Spirit have rested upon him, an occurrence which did actually take place, as the Spirit is invisible; nor, in that case, was there any degree of truth in him, for he was not that which he seemed to be. But I have already remarked that Abraham and the other prophets beheld him after a prophetic manner, foretelling in vision what should come to pass. If, then, such a being has now appeared in outward semblance different from what he was in reality, there has been a certain prophetic vision made to men; and another advent of his must be looked forward to in which he shall be such as he has now been seen in a prophetic manner. And I have proved already that it is the same thing to say that he appeared merely to outward seeming, and to affirm that he received nothing from Mary. For he would not have been one truly possessing flesh and blood by which he redeemed us, unless he had summed up in himself the ancient formation of Adam. Vain therefore are the disciples of Valentinus who put forth this opinion in order that they may exclude the flesh from salvation and cast aside what God has fashioned.

5.1.3 Vain also are the Ebionites, who do not receive by faith into their soul the union of God and man, but who remain in the old leaven of the natural birth, and who do not choose to understand that the Holy Spirit came upon Mary and the power of the most high did overshadow her. For this reason also what was generated is a holy thing, and the Son of the most high God the Father of all, who effected the incarnation of this being and showed forth a new kind of generation; that as by the former generation we inherited death, so by this new generation we might inherit life. Therefore do these men reject the commixture of the heavenly wine and wish it to be water of the world only, not receiving God so as to have union with him, but they remain in that Adam who had been conquered and was expelled from paradise; not considering that as, at the beginning of our formation in Adam, that breath of life which proceeded from God, having been united to what had been fashioned, animated the man, and manifested him as a being endowed with reason; so also, in the times of the end, the Word of the Father and the Spirit of God, having become united with the ancient substance of Adam's formation, rendered man living and perfect, receptive of the perfect Father, in order that as in the natural Adam we all were dead, so in the spiritual we may all be made alive. For never at any time did Adam escape the hands of God, to whom the Father speaking, said, "Let us make man in our image, after our likeness." And for this reason in the last times, not by the will of the flesh, nor by the will of man, but by the good pleasure of the Father, his hands formed a living man, in order that Adam might be created again after the image and likeness of God.

The Resurrection of the Body and the Nature of Resurrected Life

5.13.1 Let our opponents—that is, they who speak against their own salvation—inform us as to this point: The deceased daughter of the high priest; the widow's dead son, who was being carried out to burial near the gate of the city; and Lazarus, who had lain four days in the tomb—in what bodies did they rise again? (Mark 5:22; Luke 7:12; John 9:30). In those same, no doubt, in which they had also died. For if it were not in the very same then certainly those same individuals who had died did not rise again. For the Scripture says, "The Lord took the hand of the dead man, and said to him, young man, I say unto you, Arise. And the dead man sat up, and he commanded that something should be given him to eat; and he delivered him to his mother." Again, he called Lazarus "with a loud voice, saying, Lazarus, come forth; and he that was dead came forth bound with bandages, feet and hands." This was symbolic of that man who had been bound in sins. And therefore the Lord said, "Untie him, and let him depart." As, therefore, those who were healed were made whole in those members which had in times past been afflicted; and the dead rose in the identical bodies, their limbs and bodies receiving health, and that life which was granted by the Lord, who prefigures eternal things by temporal and shows that it is he who is himself able to extend both healing and life to his handiwork, that his words concerning its future resurrection may also be believed; so also at the end, when the Lord utters his voice "by the last trumpet," the dead shall be raised, as he himself declares, "The hour shall come, in which all the dead which are in the tombs shall hear the voice of the Son of Man, and shall come forth; those that have done good to the resurrection of life, and those that have done evil to the resurrection of judgment" (1 Cor 15:52; John 5:28).

5.13.2 Vain, therefore, and truly miserable are those who do not choose to see what is so manifest and clear but shun the light of truth, blinding themselves like the tragic Oedipus. And as those who are not practiced in wrestling, when they contend with others, laying hold with a determined grasp of some part of their opponent's body, really fall by means of that which they grasp, yet when they fall, imagine that they are gaining the victory because they have obstinately kept their hold upon that part which they seized at the outset, and besides falling, become subjects of ridicule; so is it with respect to that favorite expression of the heretics: "Flesh and blood cannot inherit the kingdom of God," while taking two expressions of Paul's, without having perceived the apostle's meaning or examined critically the force of the terms, but keeping fast hold of the mere expressions by themselves, they die in consequence of their influence, overturning as far as in them lies the entire dispensation of God.

5.13.3 For thus they will allege that this passage refers to the flesh strictly so called and not to fleshly works, as I have pointed out, so representing the apostle as contradicting himself. For immediately following in the same epistle, he says conclusively, speaking thus in reference to the flesh, "For this corruptible must put on incorruption, and this mortal must put on immortality. So, when this mortal shall have put on immortality, then shall be brought to pass the saying which is written, Death is swallowed up in victory. O death, where is your sting? O death, where is your victory?" (1 Cor 15:53). Now these words shall be appropriately said at the time when this mortal and corruptible flesh, which is subject to death, which also is pressed down by a certain dominion of death, rising up into life, shall put on incorruption and immortality. For then, indeed, shall death be truly vanquished when that flesh which is held down by it shall go forth from under its dominion. And again, to the Philippians he says, "But our conversation is in heaven, from which place we also look for the savior, the Lord Jesus, who shall transfigure the body of our humiliation conformable to the body of his glory, even as he is able according to the working of his own power" (Phil 3:29). What, then, is this "body of humiliation" which the Lord shall transfigure, so as to be conformed to "the body of his glory?" Plainly it is this body composed of flesh which is indeed humbled when it falls into the earth. Now its transformation takes place thus, that while it is mortal and corruptible it becomes immortal and incorruptible, not after its own proper substance, but after the mighty working of the Lord who is able to invest the mortal with immortality and the corruptible with incorruption. And therefore he says "that mortality may be swallowed up of life. He who has perfected us for this very thing is God, who also has given unto us the earnest of the Spirit" (2 Cor 5:4). He uses these words most manifestly in reference to the flesh; for the soul is not mortal, neither is the spirit. Now, what is mortal shall be swallowed up of life when the flesh is dead no longer but remains living and incorruptible, hymning the praises of God who has perfected us for this very thing. In order, therefore, that we may be perfected for this, aptly does he say to the Corinthians, "Glorify God in your body" (1 Cor 6:20). Now God is he who gives rise to immortality.

5.13.4 That he uses these words with respect to the body of flesh, and to none other, he declares to the Corinthians manifestly, without doubt and free from all ambiguity, "Always bearing about in our body the dying of Jesus, that also the life of Jesus Christ might be manifested in our body. For if we who live are delivered unto death for Jesus' sake, it is that the life of Jesus may also be manifested in our mortal flesh" (2 Cor 4:10). And that the Spirit lays hold on the flesh, he says in the same epistle, "That you are the epistle of Christ, ministered by us, inscribed not with ink, but with the Spirit of the living God, not in tables of stone, but in the fleshly tables of the heart" (2 Cor 3:3). If, therefore, in the present time, fleshly hearts are made partakers of the Spirit, what is there astonishing if, in the resurrection, they receive that life which is granted by the Spirit? Of which resurrection the apostle speaks in the epistle to the Philippians, "Having been made conformable to his death, if by any means I might attain to the resurrection which is from the dead" (Phil 3:11). In what other mortal flesh, therefore, can life be understood as being manifested unless in that substance which is also put to death on account of that confession which is made of God? As he has himself declared, "If, as a man, I have fought with beasts at Ephesus, what advantage is it to me if the dead are not raised? For if the dead are not raised, neither has Christ risen. Now, if Christ has not risen, our preaching is vain, and your faith is vain. In that case, too, we are found false witnesses for God, since we have testified that he raised up Christ, whom upon that supposition he did not raise up. For if the dead are not raised, neither has Christ risen. But if Christ is not risen, your faith is vain, since you are yet in your sins. Therefore those who have fallen asleep in Christ have perished. If in this life only we have hope in Christ, we are more miserable than all men. But now Christ has risen from the dead, the first-fruits of those that sleep; for as by man came death, by man also came the resurrection of the dead" (1 Cor 15:13).

5.13.5 In all these passages, therefore, as I have already said, these men must either allege that the apostle expresses opinions contradicting himself with respect to that statement, "Flesh and blood cannot inherit the kingdom of God" or, on the other hand, they will be forced to make perverse and crooked interpretations of all the passages so as to overturn and alter the sense of the words. For what sensible thing can they say, if they endeavor to interpret otherwise this which he writes, "For this corruptible must put on incorruption, and this mortal put on immortality," and, "That the life of Jesus may be made manifest in our mortal flesh," and all the other passages in which the apostle does manifestly and clearly declare the resurrection and incorruption of the flesh? (1 Cor 15:53; 2 Cor 4:11). And thus shall they be compelled to put a false interpretation upon passages such as these, they who do not choose to understand one correctly.

Reasons Why the Word Became Flesh

5.14.1 And inasmuch as the apostle has not pronounced against the very substance of flesh and blood, that it cannot inherit the kingdom of God, the same apostle has everywhere adopted the term "flesh and blood" with regard to the Lord Jesus Christ, partly indeed to establish his human nature, for he did himself speak of himself as the Son of Man, and partly that he might confirm the salvation of our flesh. For if the flesh were not in a position to be saved, the Word of God would in no way have become flesh. And if the blood of the righteous were not to be inquired after, the Lord would certainly not have had blood in his composition. But inasmuch as blood cries out from the beginning of the world, God said to Cain, when he had slain his brother, "The voice of your brother's blood cries to me" (Gen 4:10). And as their blood will be inquired after, he said to those with Noah, "For your blood of your souls I will require, even from the hand of all beasts." And again, "Whosoever will shed man's blood, it shall be shed for his blood" (Gen 9:5–6). In like manner, too, did the Lord say to those who should afterwards shed his blood, "All righteous blood shall be required which is shed upon the earth, from the blood of righteous Abel to the blood of Zacharias the son of Berechiah, whom you killed between the temple and the altar. Truly I say unto you, all these things shall come upon this generation" (Matt 23:35; Luke 11:50). He thus points out the recapitulation that should take place in his own person of the effusion of blood from the beginning, of all the righteous men and of the prophets, and that by means of himself there should be a requisition of their blood. Now this blood could not be required unless it also had the capability of being saved; nor would the Lord have summed up these things in himself, unless he had himself been made flesh and blood after the way of the original formation of man, saving in his own person at the end that which had in the beginning perished in Adam.

5.14.2 But if the Lord became incarnate for any other order of things and took flesh of any other substance, he has not then summed up human nature in his own person, nor in that case can he be termed flesh. For flesh has been truly made to consist in a transmission of that thing molded originally from the dust. But if it had been necessary for him to draw the material of his body from another substance, the Father would at the beginning have molded the material of flesh from a different substance than from what he actually did. But now the case stands thus, that the Word has saved that which really was created, namely, humanity which had perished, effecting by means of himself that communion which should be held with it and seeking out its salvation. But the thing which had perished possessed flesh and blood. For the Lord, taking dust from the earth, molded man; and it was upon his behalf that all the dispensation of the Lord's advent took place. He had himself, therefore, flesh and blood, recapitulating in himself not a certain other but that original handiwork of the Father, seeking out that thing which had perished. And for this cause the apostle, in the epistle to the Colossians, says, "And though you were formerly alienated and enemies to his knowledge by evil works, yet now you have been reconciled in the body of his flesh, through his death, to present yourselves holy and blameless, and without fault in his sight" (Col 1:21–22). He says, "You have been reconciled in the body of his flesh," because the righteous flesh has reconciled that flesh which was being kept under bondage in sin and brought it into friendship with God.

5.14.3 If, then, anyone allege that in this respect the flesh of the Lord was different from ours, because it indeed did not commit sin, neither was deceit found in his soul, while we on the other hand are sinners, he says what is the fact. But if he pretends that the Lord possessed another substance of flesh, the sayings respecting reconciliation will not agree with that man. For that thing is reconciled which had formerly been in enmity. Now, if the Lord had taken flesh from another substance, he would not by so doing have reconciled that one to God which had become hostile through transgression. But now, by means of communion with himself, the Lord has reconciled man to God the Father, in reconciling us to himself by the body of his own flesh and redeeming us by his own blood, as the apostle says to the Ephesians, "In whom we have redemption through his blood, the remission of sins" (Eph 1:7). And again to the same he says, "You who formerly were far off have been brought near in the blood of Christ" (Eph 2:13). And again, "Abolishing in his flesh the hostilities, even the law of commandments contained in ordinances" (Eph 2:15). And in every epistle the apostle plainly testifies that through the flesh of our Lord and through his blood we have been saved.

The Summing Up of All Things in Christ

5.21.1 He has therefore in his work of recapitulation, summed up all things, both waging war against our enemy and crushing him who had at the beginning led us away as captives in Adam. He also trampled upon his head, as you can perceive in Genesis that God said to the serpent, "And I will put enmity between you and the woman, and between your seed and her seed; he shall bruise your head, and you shall bruise his heel" (Gen 3:15). For from that time, he who should be born of a woman, namely from the virgin, after the likeness of Adam, was preached as one who would one day crush the head of the serpent. In his epistle to the Galatians, the apostle speaks of this seed when he says, "that the law of works was established until the seed should come to whom the promise was made" (Gal 3:19). This fact is exhibited in a still clearer light in the same epistle, where he says, "But when the fullness of time had come, God sent forth his Son, born of a woman" (Gal 4:4). For indeed the enemy would not have been fairly vanquished unless it had been a man born of a woman who conquered him. For it was by means of a woman that he got the advantage over man at first, setting himself up as man's opponent. And therefore does the Lord profess himself to be the Son of Man, comprising in himself that original man out of whom the woman was fashioned, in order that, as our species went down to death through a vanquished man, so we may ascend to life again through a victorious one; and as through a man death received the palm of victory against us, so again by a man we may receive the palm of victory against death.

5.21.2 Now the Lord would not have recapitulated in himself that ancient and primary hostility against the serpent, fulfilling the promise of the creator and performing his command if he had come from another Father. But as he is one and the same, who formed us at the beginning, and sent his Son at the end, the Lord did perform his command, being made of a woman, by both destroying our adversary and perfecting man after the image and likeness of God. And for this reason he did not draw the means of countering him from any other source than from the words of the Law, and made use of the Father's commandment as a help toward the destruction and confusion of the apostate angel. Fasting forty days, like Moses and

Elijah, he afterwards hungered, first, in order that we may perceive that he was a real and substantial man, for it belongs to a man to suffer hunger when fasting; and secondly, that his opponent might have an opportunity of attacking him. For as at the beginning, it was by means of food that the enemy persuaded man, although not suffering hunger, to transgress God's commandments, so in the end he did not succeed in persuading him that hungered to take that food which proceeded from God. For, when tempting him, he said, "If you are the Son of God, command that these stones be made bread" (Matt 4:3). But the Lord repulsed him by the commandment of the law, saying, "It is written, Man does not live by bread alone" (Deut 8:3). As to those words of his enemy, "If you are the Son of God," the Lord made no remark. But by thus acknowledging his human nature he baffled his adversary and exhausted the force of his first attack by means of his Father's word. The corruption of man, therefore, which occurred in paradise by both of our first parents eating was done away with by the Lord's want of food in this world. But he, being thus vanquished by the law, endeavored again to make an assault by himself quoting a commandment of the law. For, bringing him to the highest pinnacle of the temple, he said to him, "If you are the Son of God, cast yourself down. For it is written, That God shall give his angels charge concerning you, and in their hands they shall bear you up, lest you dash your foot against a stone" (Ps 90:11–12 LXX). In doing this, he concealed a falsehood under the guise of Scripture, as is done by all the heretics. For that was indeed written, namely, "That he has given his angels charge concerning him," but "cast yourself down from there" no Scripture said in reference to him. This particular kind of persuasion the devil produced from himself. The Lord therefore refuted him out of the law when he said, "It is written again, you shall not tempt the Lord your God" (Deut 6:16). In doing this, he pointed out by the word contained in the law that which is the duty of man, that he should not tempt God. In regard to himself, since he appeared in human form, he also declared that he would not tempt the Lord his God.

Therefore, the pride of reason which was found in the serpent was put to nothing by the humility which was found in the man Christ. Twice then the devil was conquered from Scripture when he was exposed as advising things contrary to God's commandment and was shown to be the enemy of God by the expression of his thoughts. Having been signally defeated, the serpent, as it were, concentrated his forces by drawing up in order all his available power for falsehood. In the third place, he therefore "showed him all the kingdoms of the world, and the glory of them," saying, as Luke relates, "All these will I give you, for they are delivered to me; and to whom I will, I give them, if you will fall down and worship me" (Luke 4:6–7). The Lord then, exposing him in his true character, says, "Depart, Satan; for it is written, You shall worship the Lord your God, and him only shall you serve" (Matt 4:10). He both revealed him by this name and showed at the same time who he himself was. For the Hebrew word "Satan" signifies an apostate. And thus, vanquishing him for the third time, Christ repelled the serpent away from him finally as one who had been completely conquered through the words of the law. As a result, that infringement of God's commandment which had occurred in Adam was done away with by means of the precept of the law which the Son of Man observed and did not transgress the commandment of God.

5.21.3 Who, then, is this Lord God to whom Christ bears witness, whom no man shall tempt, whom all should worship, and serve him alone? It is, beyond all manner of doubt that God who also gave the law. For these things had been predicted in the law, and by the words of the law the Lord showed that the law does indeed declare the Word of God from the Father; and the apostate angel of God is destroyed by its voice, being exposed in his true colors and vanquished by the Son of Man keeping the commandment of God. For as in the beginning he enticed man to transgress his maker's law and thereby got him into his power; yet his power consists in transgression and apostasy, and with these he bound man to himself; so again, on the other hand, it was necessary that through man himself he should, when conquered, be bound with the same chains with which he had bound man, in order that man, being set free, might return to his Lord, leaving to Satan those bonds by which he himself had been chained, that is, sin. For when Satan is bound, man is set free. This is because "none can enter a strong man's house and spoil his goods, unless he first bind the strong man himself" (Matt 12:29). The Lord therefore exposes him as speaking contrary to the word of that God who made all things and subdues him by means of the commandment. Now the law is the commandment of God. The man proves him to be a fugitive from and a transgressor of the law, an apostate also from God. After the man had done this, the Word bound him securely as a fugitive from himself and made spoil of his goods, namely, those men whom he held in bondage, and whom he unjustly used for his own purposes. And justly indeed is he led captive who had led men unjustly into bondage; while man, who had been led captive in times past, was rescued from the grasp of his possessor according to the tender mercy of God the Father who had compassion on his own handiwork and gave to it salvation, restoring it by means of the Word—that is, by Christ—in order that man might learn by actual proof that he receives incorruptibility not of himself but by the free gift of God.

[...]

5.22.1 Thus then does the Lord plainly show that it was the true Lord and the one God who had been set forth by the law. For him whom the law proclaimed as God, the same did Christ point out as the Father, whom also it is fitting for the disciples of Christ alone to serve.

The Reality of Future Incorruption and Resurrection Life

5.35.2 Now this is what has been said by the apostle, "For the fashion of this world passes away" (1 Cor 7:31). To the same purpose did the Lord also declare, "Heaven and earth shall pass away" (Matt 26:35). When these things, therefore, pass away above the earth, John, the Lord's disciple, says that the new Jerusalem above shall then descend as a bride adorned for her husband; and that this is the tabernacle of God, in which God will dwell with men. Of this Jerusalem the former one is an image—that Jerusalem of the former earth in which the righteous are disciplined beforehand for incorruption and prepared for salvation. And of this tabernacle Moses received the pattern in the mount; and nothing is capable of being allegorized, but all things are steadfast, true, and substantial, having been made by God for righteous men's enjoyment. For as it is truly God who raises up man, so also does man truly rise from the dead, and not allegorically, as I have shown repeatedly. And as he rises actually, so also shall he be actually disciplined beforehand for incorruption and shall go forward and flourish in the times of the kingdom, in order that he may be capable of receiving the glory of the Father. Then, when all things are made new, he shall truly dwell in the city of God. For it is said, "He that sits on the throne said, Behold, I make all things new. And the Lord says, Write all this; for these words are faithful and true. And he said to me, They are done" (Rev 21:5–6). And this is the truth of the matter.

5.36.1 For since there are real men, so there must also be a real establishment, that they vanish not away among non-existent things but progress among those which have an actual existence. For neither is the substance nor the essence of the creation annihilated (for faithful and true is he who has established it), but "the fashion of the world passes away" (1 Cor 8:31). That is, those things among which transgression has occurred, since man has grown old in them. And therefore this present fashion has been formed temporary, God foreknowing all things; as I have pointed out in the preceding book, and have also shown as far as was possible the cause of the creation of this world of temporal things. But when this present fashion of things passes away and man has been renewed and flourishes in an incorruptible state,

The Testimony of Christ and His Apostles

so as to preclude the possibility of becoming old, then there shall be the new heaven and the new earth, in which the new man shall remain continually, always holding fresh converse with God. And since these things shall ever continue without end, Isaiah declares, "For as the new heavens and the new earth which I make continue in my sight, says the Lord, so shall your seed and your name remain" (Isa 66:22). And as the presbyters say, then those who are deemed worthy of an abode in heaven shall go there, others shall enjoy the delights of paradise, and others shall possess the splendor of the city. For the savior shall be seen everywhere according to the worthiness of those who see him.

5.36.2 They say, moreover, that there is this distinction between the habitation of those who produce a hundredfold, that of those who produce sixtyfold, and that of those who produce thirtyfold; for the first will be taken up into the heavens, the second will dwell in paradise, the last will inhabit the city; and that it was on this account that the Lord declared, "In my Father's house are many mansions" (John 14:2). For all things belong to God who supplies all with a suitable dwelling place.... And this is the couch on which the guests shall recline, having been invited to the wedding. The presbyters, the disciples of the apostles, affirm that this is the gradation and arrangement of those who are saved, and that they advance through steps of this nature; also that they ascend through the Spirit to the Son, and through the Son to the Father, and that in due time the Son will yield up his work to the Father, even as it is said by the apostle, "For he must reign till he has put all enemies under his feet. The last enemy that shall be destroyed is death" (1 Cor 15:25–26). For in the times of the kingdom, the righteous man who is upon the earth shall then forget to die. "But when he says, All things shall be subdued unto him, it is manifest that he is excepted who put all things under him. And when all things shall be subdued unto him, then shall the Son also himself be subject unto him who put all things under him, that God may be all in all" (1 Cor 15:27–28).

5.36.3 John, therefore, distinctly foresaw the first "resurrection of the just" and the inheritance in the kingdom of the earth; and what the prophets have prophesied concerning it harmonize with his vision (Luke 14:14). For the Lord also taught these things when he promised that he would have the mixed cup new with his disciples in the kingdom. The apostle, too, has confessed that the creation shall be free from the bondage of corruption, so as to pass into the liberty of the sons of God (Rom 8:21). And in all these things, and by them all, the same God the Father is manifested, who fashioned man and gave promise of the inheritance of the earth to the fathers, who brought this creature forth from bondage at the resurrection of the just, and fulfills the promises for the kingdom of his Son; subsequently bestowing in a paternal manner those things which neither the eye has seen, nor the ear has heard, nor has thought concerning them arisen within the heart of man (1 Cor 2:9; Isa 64:4).

The Salvation Accomplished by the Mission of the Son

5.36.3 For there is one Son who accomplished his Father's will. There is also one human race in which the mysteries of God are brought about, "which the angels desire to look into" (1 Pet 1:12). And they are not able to search out the wisdom of God. By means of this wisdom, his handiwork is brought to perfection, having been confirmed and embodied with his Son. For the Father's will was that his offspring, the first begotten Word, should descend to the creature, that is, to what had been molded, and that it should be contained by him; and, on the other hand, the creature should contain the Word, and ascend to him, passing beyond the angels, and be made after the image and likeness of God.

Further Reading

Behr, John. *Asceticism and Anthropology in Irenaeus and Clement.* Oxford University Press, 2017.
—*Irenaeus of Lyons: Identifying Christianity.* Oxford University Press, 2013.
—*The Way to Nicaea.* Vol. 1 of *The Formation of Christian Theology.* SVS Press, 2001.
Bingham, D. Jeffrey. "Irenaeus of Lyons." Pages 137–153 in D. Jeffrey Bingham, ed. *The Routledge Companion to Early Christian Thought.* Routledge, 2009.
—"Senses of Scripture in the Second Century: Irenaeus, Scripture, and Noncanonical Christian Texts." *The Journal of Religion* 97.1 (January 2017): 26–55.
Blowers, Paul M. "The *Regula Fidei* and the Narrative Character of Early Christian Faith," *Pro Ecclesia* 6 (1997): 199–228.
Brakke, David. *The Gnostics: Myth, Ritual, and Diversity in Early Christianity.* Harvard University Press, 2012.
Briggman, Anthony. *God and Christ in Irenaeus.* Oxford University Press, 2019.
Bushur, James G. *Irenaeus of Lyons and the Mosaic of Christ: Preaching Scripture in the Era of Martyrdom.* Routledge, 2017.
Donovan, Mary Ann. *One Right Reading? A Guide to Irenaeus.* Liturgical Press, 1997.
Ehrman, Bart D. *Lost Christianities: The Battles for Scripture and the Faiths We Never Knew.* Oxford University Press, 2005.
Grant, Robert M. *Irenaeus of Lyons.* Routledge, 2006.
Hill, Charles E. *Who Chose the Gospels? Probing the Great Gospel Conspiracy.* Oxford, 2010.
Köstenberger, Andreas J. and Michael J. Kruger. *The Heresy of Orthodoxy: How Contemporary Culture's Fascination with Diversity has Reshaped our Understanding of Early Christianity.* Crossway, 2010.
Lawson, John. *The Biblical Theology of Saint Irenaeus.* Epworth Press, 1948.
MacDonald, Nathan. "Israel and the Old Testament Story in Irenaeus's Presentation of the Rule of Faith." *Journal of Theological Interpretation* 3.2 (2009): 281–98.
Minns, Denis. *Irenaeus: An Introduction.* T&T Clark, 2010.
Moringiello, Scott D. *The Rhetoric of Faith: Irenaeus and the Structure of the Adversus Haereses.* Catholic University of America Press, 2019.
Osborn, Eric. *Irenaeus of Lyons.* Cambridge University Press, 2005.
Parvis, Sara and Paul Foster, eds. *Irenaeus: Life, Scripture, and Legacy.* Fortress, 2012.
Payton, James R. *Irenaeus on the Christian Faith: A Condensation of Against Heresies.* Pickwick, 2011.
Perkins, Pheme. "Irenaeus and the Gnostics: Rhetoric and Composition in *Adversus Haereses* Book One." *Vigiliae Christianae* 30 (1976): 193–200.
Presley, Stephen. "Biblical Theology and the Unity of Scripture in Irenaeus of Lyons." *Criswell Theological Review* 16.2 (Spring 2019): 3–24.
— "The *Demonstration* of Intertextuality in Irenaeus of Lyons." Pages 195–213 in D. Jeffrey Bingham and Clayton Jefford, ed. *Intertextuality in the Second Century.* Brill, 2016.
—*The Intertextual Reception of Genesis 1–3 in Irenaeus of Lyons.* Brill, 2015.

Seitz, Christopher. *The Character of Christian Scripture: The Significance of a Two-Testament Bible*. Baker, 2011.
Still, Todd D. and David E. Wilhite. *Irenaeus and Paul*. T&T Clark, 2021.
Thomassen, Einar. *The Coherence of "Gnosticism"*. De Gruyter, 2020.
Thomassen, Einar and Christoph Markschies, eds. *Valentinianism: New Studies*. Brill, 2019.
von Balthasar, Hans Urs. *Scandal of the Incarnation: Irenaeus Against the Heresies*. Ignatius Press, 1990.

Works Consulted

The translations listed below show the translations utilized for this volume's selections. These public domain texts were revised, with archaic words, grammar, and syntax updated to reflect contemporary usage. Critical editions and newer translations were also consulted in the updating process where possible.

Translations Used in This Volume

Against Heresies: Roberts and Donaldson (ANF 1)
Demonstration of the Apostolic Preaching: Robinson (London, 1920)
Selections from Eusebius, *Ecclesiastical History*: McGiffert (NPNF, 2nd 1)

Translations and Critical Editions Consulted

Behr, John. *St Irenaeus of Lyons: On the Apostolic Preaching*. SVS, 1997.
Harvey, W. W. *Sancti Irenaei episcopi Lugdunensis libros quinque adversus haereses*. 2 Volumes. Cambridge, 1957.
Keble, J. *Five Books of S. Irenaeus, Against Heresies*. London, 1872.
Smith, J. P. *St. Irenaeus: Proof of the Apostolic Preaching*. Newman, 1952.

Scripture Index

Genesis
1–3   11 n. 29
1:1   40, 63, 63 n. 8
1:3   155
1:26   59, 67, 125, 148
1:28   142
2:5   58
2:7   148
2:8   50
2:9   50
2:16–17   65
2:21–23   51
2:25   51
3:15   165
4:1–2   52
4:10   163
4:25   52
9:1–6   54
9:5–7   68, 163
9:14–15   54
9:25   53, 53 n. 7
9:26   53
9:27   53, 93
12:1   55
14:22   132
15:6   55, 60
17:8   55
18:1–3   63
19:24   63, 93

28:13   64
49:10–11   68, 141
49:18   100

Exodus
3:7–8   137, 145
3:7   64
3:8   94
3:14   46, 94
7:1   96
20:12   140
20:13–17   81
21:24   81
25:40   49
31:18   56
33:19–22   152
33:20   150
34:28   56

Numbers
12:7   96
12:8   152
21:8   128
24:1   69
24:17   97

Deuteronomy
4:9   96
5:8   96

5:24	151	71:17	63 n. 8
6:4	126	72:14	73
6:16	166	76:1	97
8:3	166	80:1	107
16:5–6	141	81:9	94
28:44	80	82:1	94
28:66	76, 141	82:6	94
32:1	126	82:6–7	116
32:4	116	85:2	91
32:6	141	90:11–12	166
32:21	80	95:4	101
32:49–50	58	96:1	138
34:5	58	96:5	94
		98:2	100
1 Kings		102:25–28	129
18:21	95	109:3	63 n. 8
18:36	95	110:1–7	65
		110:1	65, 77, 93, 102
Psalms		124:8	101, 126
1:1	46	132:11	60, 97
2:1–2	75	132:10–12	71
2:7	65, 66	139:39–45	75
3:5	74		
19:4	54, 78	Proverbs	
19:6	77	3:19–20	149
21:4	74	5:22	98
22:14	76	8:22–25	149
22:16	76	8:27–31	149
22:17–18	76		
24:7–8	77	Isaiah	
33:6	48	1:2	126
33:9	39	1:8	130
35:9	142	1:22	143
38:8	73	1:23	128
45:6	65, 93	1:30	82
45:16	132	2:3	78
49:12	130	5:12	127
50:1	94	7:9	47
50:3	94	7:14	67, 69
58:3	99	8:14–15	67
68:17–18	77	9:6	61, 67, 117
69:2	117	10:22–23	78
69:21	76	11:1–10	69, 98

11:2	49	**Jeremiah**	
12:2	100	2:8	80
17:6–8	79	4:22	128
25:9	139	10:11	94
26:19	72	17:9	116
27:6	129	23:20	154
29:13	145	23:23	147
29:18	72	31:31–34	79
35:3–6	72	31:31	138
40:12	147		
42:1–3	106	**Lamentations**	
42:5	126	3:30	73
42:10	138	4:20	73, 100
43:10–12	131		
43:10	94	**Ezekiel**	
43:18–21	79	11:19–20	80
44:9	94		
45:1	65	**Daniel**	
49:5–6	66	3:26	152
50:5–6	59	7:4	153
50:6	73	7:13	117, 152
50:8–9	78	12:3	154
51:6	129	12:4	154
52:7	78	12:7	154
52:13—53:5	72		
53:2	117	**Hosea**	
53:4	72	1:10	80
53:5–6	73	2:23	35, 80
53:7	73	6:6	81
53:8	73, 116	10:6	75
54:1	35, 80	12:10	111, 151
57:1–2	74		
61:1	98	**Joel**	
62:11	71	3:5	81
64:4	170		
65:1	79, 94, 97	**Amos**	
65:2	76	9:11	60, 71
65:15–16	78		
66:1	64, 67	**Micah**	
63:9	78	5:2	71
66:3	81		
66:7	67	**Zechariah**	
66:22	169	9:9	71, 117

11:12–13	76
13:7	75

Malachi

2:10	148
3:1	105
4:1	130

Matthew

1:1	107
1:18	107
1:20	97
1:23	67, 97
2:2	97
2:6	71
2:15	97
3:3	97
3:7	96
3:9	80, 136
3:11	130
3:16	97
4:3	135, 166
4:10	167
5:6	128
5:8	139, 150
5:14	137
5:21–48	81
5:34	127
5:35	129
6:27	133, 134
8:17	72
11:9	105
11:25	126
11:27	135
12:6	138
12:17–21	106
12:27	148
12:29	167
12:31	108
13:17	141
13:38	154
13:52	137, 155
15:3	140, 144
16:16	116
19:17–18	145
21:13	127
21:5	71
21:16	143
21:18	142
22:29	131
22:37–40	78
23:2–4	145
23:34	138
23:35	163
25:21	142
26:35	168
27:9	76

Mark

1:2	102
1:24	135
1:27	81
5:22	160
11:9–11	99
16:9	102

Luke

1:2	124
1:6	98
1:8	98
1:15	99
1:17	102, 105
1:26	99
1:33	97, 99
1:46–47	99
1:68	100
1:76	100
1:78	99
2:11	101
2:20	101
2:22	102
2:29	102, 136
2:38	102
4:3	135
4:6–7	167
5:31–32	92

7:12	160	14:2	118, 169
7:26	105	14:6	91, 108
10:16	86	14:6–7	137
10:21	126	19:29	76
10:22	133, 134, 135		
11:50	163	Acts	
14:14	169	4:8	109
16:16	129	4:12	81
16:19	126	4:24	110
16:31	126	4:31	110
18:27	81, 150	4:33	110
19:8	146	5:30	110
24:26	155	5:42	110
24:47	155	7:49	64
		7:56	111
John		8:3	55
1:1–3	63, 63 n. 8	8:14	56
1:1–4	103	9:15–16	112
1:1–18	29, 32	12:8	112
1:1	107	26:15	112
1:3	39, 155		
1:6	104	Romans	
1:10–11	103	1:17	60
1:13	116	2:4–6	49
1:14	58, 80, 100, 103	3:30	100
1:15–16	100	4:3	55, 60, 132
1:18	105, 151	4:11	55
1:29	100	4:13	60
1:47	106	5	10 n. 26
1:49	106	5:14	115
1:50	138	5:19	116
2:3	105	7:6	79
2:25	98	8:15	94, 139
3:14	128	8:21	169
4:41	128	9:25	35
5:28	161	9:25–26	80
5:39–40	140	10:13	81
5:46–47	126	10:3–4	145
8:36	116	10:6–7	114
8:56	132	10:9	114
9:30	160	10:15	78
11:25	132	10:18	78
12:32	128	10:19	80

11:26	128	4:27	80
11:32	35		
11:33	35	Ephesians	
11:34	158	1:7	164
13:10	78, 144	1:10	33, 58
14:9	114	1:21	147
		2:7	131
1 Corinthians		2:13	165
1:23	114	2:15	165
2:6	87	2:17	93
2:9	170	3:21	21 n. 3
4:4	139	4:6	40, 48, 148, 155
6:20	162	4:8	77
7:31	128, 168	4:16	118, 155
8:4	95	6:12	34
8:31	168		
10:16	114	Philippians	
11:4–5	108	2:10–11	34
12:4–7	151	2:15	60, 132
12:28	105, 118	3:11	162
13:9–10	139	3:12	139
13:13	144	3:29	161
14:20	64, 81		
15	10 n. 26	Colossians	
15:13	162	1:8	61
15:25–26	169	1:18	149
15:27–28	169	1:21–22	164
15:52	161		
15:53	59, 161, 163	2 Thessalonians	
15:54	35	2:4	95
2 Corinthians		1 Timothy	
3:3	162	1:14	19
4:10	162	1:9	60
4:11	163	3:15	86, 106 n. 2
5:4	162		
		2 Timothy	
Galatians		2:23	124
3:19	9 n. 24, 165		
3:24	128	Titus	
4:4	9 n. 24, 165	3:10	90
4:6	48		
4:8–9	95		

Hebrews

1	11 n. 29
1:1–4	11 n. 29
1:1–14	11 n. 29
1:8	65
3:5	96
8:8–12	79

1 Peter

1:8	139
1:12	11, 170
2:23	149

2 Peter

3:1–2	16 n. 46

Revelation

1:5	60, 61
1:12–16	153
3:7	148
4:7	107
5:6	153
19:11–17	154
21:5–6	168
22:17	90

Baruch

3.29–4.1	82 n. 15

Bel and the Dragon

4–5	131

1 Enoch

6–8	52 n. 6

Shepherd of Hermas

Mand. 1.1	148

www.ingramcontent.com/pod-product-compliance
Lightning Source LLC
Chambersburg PA
CBHW050317120526
44592CB00014B/1949